IMAGES
of America

STERLING TOWNSHIP
1875–1968

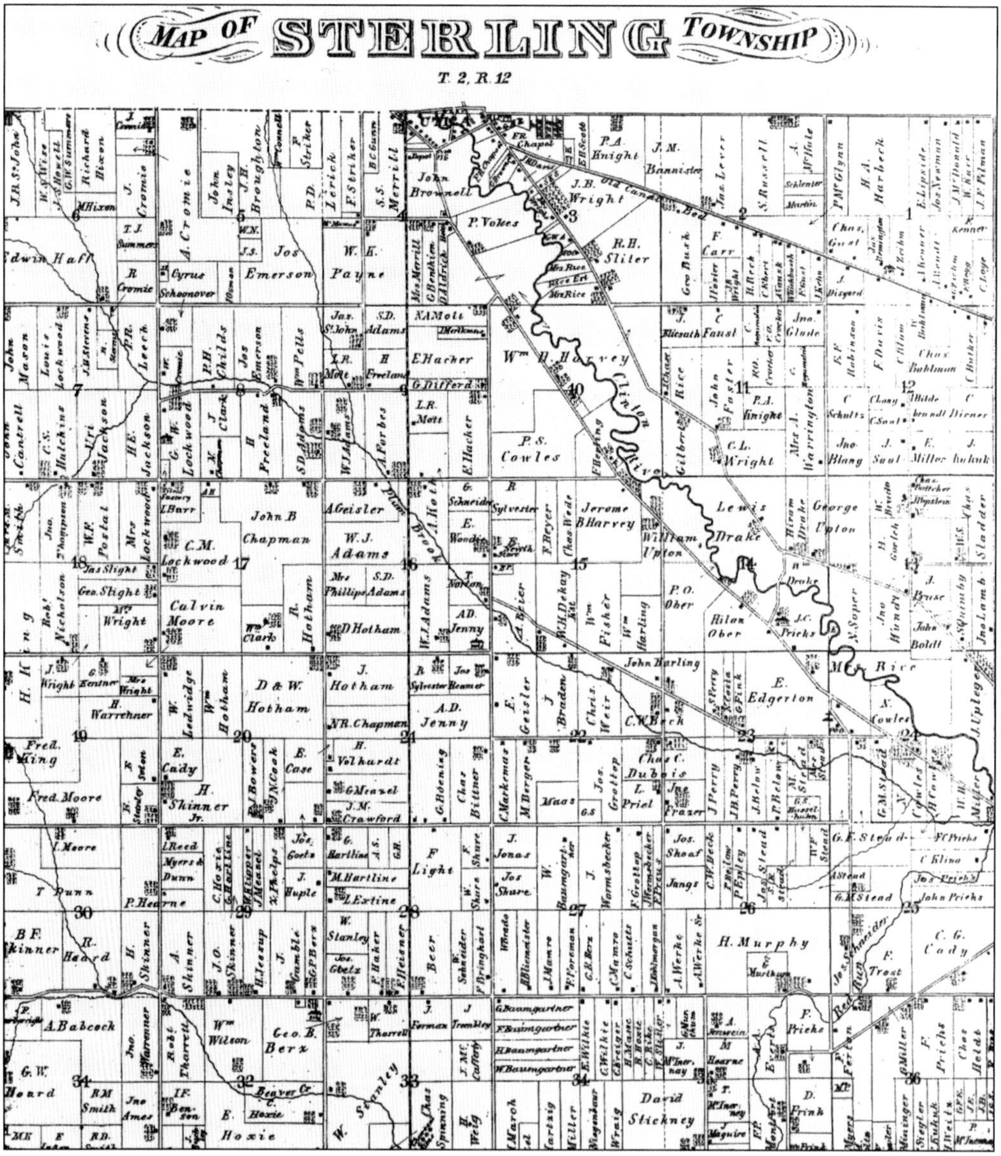

STERLING TOWNSHIP MAP, 1875. The Clinton River flows southeast, and Plumbrook Creek runs almost parallel. Almost 36 square miles are divided by seven east–west roads (referred to as "mile roads") and seven north–south roads. The Clinton River has a road running along each side of it—Utica Road on the south and Clinton River Road on the north. Canal Road, following the old Clinton Kalamazoo Canal bed, cuts across the northeast corner. At this time in township history, German farmers were beginning to edge out those from Great Britain. The village of Utica would be at the center northern boundary. The township is bordered by Shelby Township to the north, Clinton Township to the east, Warren Township to the south, and Troy Township to the west. The east–west roads start at the southern end at 14 Mile Road and what would be 20 Mile Road (also known as Hall Road, or M59). The north–south roads are, from east to west, Dequindre Road, Ryan Road, Mound Road, Van Dyke Avenue, Dodge Park Road (or Maple Lane), Schoenherr Road, and Hayes Road.

IMAGES
of America

STERLING TOWNSHIP
1875–1968

Sterling Heights Public Library and Historical Commission

ARCADIA
PUBLISHING

ISBN 978-0-7385-3975-1

Published by Arcadia Publishing
Charleston, South Carolina

Printed in the United States of America

Library of Congress Catalog Card Number: 2005931676

For all general information contact Arcadia Publishing at:
Telephone 843-853-2070
Fax 843-853-0044
E-mail sales@arcadiapublishing.com
For customer service and orders:
Toll-Free 1-888-313-2665

Visit us on the Internet at www.arcadiapublishing.com

In honor of Ruth Baker.

Contents

ACKNOWLEDGMENTS

This work consists of images from the Local History Collection of the Sterling Heights Public Library, including donations from residents, photographs taken by employees of Sterling Township and the City of Sterling Heights, and a collection of photographs from the "morgue" of the defunct Utica Sentinel. We would like to recognize the generosity of residents Eleanor Ahrens, the Backus family, Helen Cope Beuthin, Jim Boehmer, Barney Calka, Barbara Faust Counsell, Marjorie Upton DeFrancis, Wally Doebler, the Fulk family, Jeanette Glawe, Rose Bower Hacker, Lawrence Haff, Irene Holzhauer Hoffman, Elmer Measel, Eddie Nowalski, Evelyn Vogler Nowalski, Edward Ochylski Jr., Merle Drake Peters, the Ernest Pruehs family, Cheryl Wilbrett Snay, Lois Fischer Stone, Kristen Trimakas, John Urquart, and particularly Duane Kleino, Ferry Schoonover, F. James Dunlop, and Jerry Sieja for their generous donations of photographs, time, research, and support.

Thanks also to my coworkers and to the staff at the Sterling Heights Public Library, particularly Carol Lingeman and Joe Vitale, whose patience and assistance are unmatched.

The collection of the Sterling Heights Public Library, particularly their oral history interviews and access to the Ancestry Plus database, made this project much easier and more enjoyable.

Special thanks to my family, Chuck, Allison, and Lauren, for putting up with my research addictions and to Ruth Baker, local history expert and retired librarian, who years ago gave me a solid start in my research on the area and whose interests and enthusiasms I share.

—Debra Vercellone

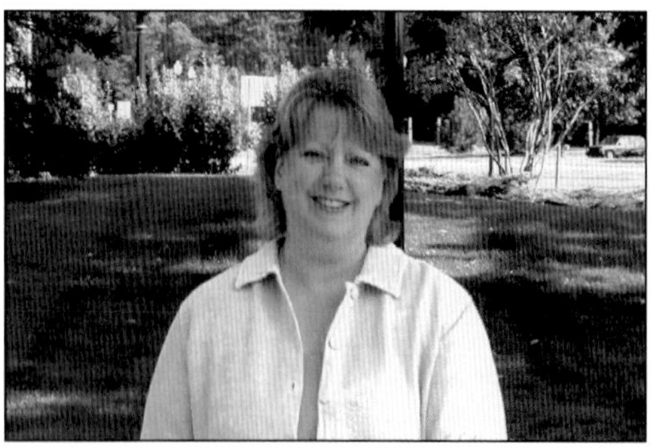

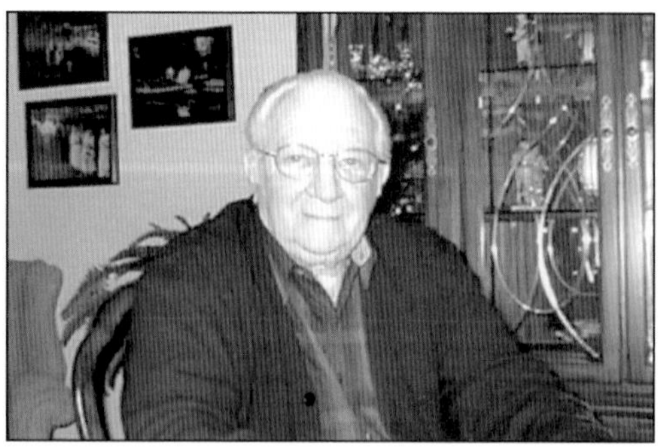

THE AUTHORS. For this volume, Debra Vercellone wrote the captions on behalf of the Sterling Heights Public Library. Wallace Doebler wrote the introduction on behalf of the Sterling Heights Historical Commission.

INTRODUCTION

A picture is worth a thousand words, and so depicting our city in pictures is one of the best ways to tell the story of Sterling Township, now our city of Sterling Heights, Michigan.

Our rural township, located 18 miles northeast of downtown Detroit, was blessed with black sandy loam soil with many streams, canals, and rivers to drain the land during the spring and fall for growing bountiful crops. The farmers grew wheat, oats, and hay for their animals. They had horses for tending the fields, as well as cows for milk and meat. They also had hogs and poultry to provide additional meat for their tables. Of course, they had large family gardens with acres of potatoes as a cash crop. Later, in the 1930s and 1940s, rhubarb and cabbage also became cash crops. Macomb County was known as the "rhubarb capital of the world."

Many English, Scottish, and Irish families from New England and especially New York settled here in the 1830s following the completion of the Erie Canal in 1825. By the later 1800s, the majority of immigrant peoples were of German descent. During the early 1900s, Belgians came into the area, replacing general farming with truck farming of fruits and vegetables. Many immigrants from Poland also established homesteads here.

The log cabins and homesteads of these farmers were soon replaced by beautiful houses and barns. After World War II, developers arrived and started to convert farms to housing projects and various corners to strip malls. The intersection of Schoenherr and Hall Roads became the site of one of Michigan's largest retail developments with the opening of Lakeside Mall in 1976, a 1.4-million-square-foot regional shopping center.

Families were very close. Church was the focal point for most of the families. The main church for Lutherans was St. Paul in Sterling Township, and for Catholics it was St. Lawrence in the village of Utica. School was not of foremost importance for the farmer. You worked the farm first, and in the fall and winter, you went to school. Most farmers applied this rule. However, some insisted their children go to school, and a few graduated from the Utica High School.

The schools consisted of one- or two-room buildings for students from the first through the eighth grade, usually taught by one teacher. In 1881, there were six schools in Sterling Township, with fewer than 40 children per school. These children walked up to one and a half miles to attend class. In 1894, the weekly salary of the teacher at Maple Grove School was $6.25.

Subdivisions grew and replaced many of the old farmsteads. By the 1960s, more than 14,000 people lived here, and demand for public services increased. The City Charter Commission was formed in 1966, and the city of Sterling Heights was incorporated in 1968 with a city manager and council form of government. The dedicated people elected to the first council were committed to work together to build a good foundation for our city. They wanted rules and regulations that were fair, and plotted the new city for growth and development. The development of the 26 parks in our city today is a good indication of their farsightedness.

This book depicts the various lifestyles of the people in our township. For older people, some of these pictures will certainly bring back memories. Younger people can now see pictures of people and things their parents or grandparents have talked about. It will be hard to believe some of the pictures, as we have changed our lifestyles and habits so much. So look them over and let your mind take you to the township way back when. Visualize living in that time, in this place.

—Wallace Doebler

Message from the Mayor of Sterling Heights

September 1, 2005

On behalf of the City Council, administration, and 127,000 residents of the City of Sterling Heights, I want to express my sincere appreciation to the Sterling Heights Public Library and the Sterling Heights Historical Commission on the occasion of the publication of this remarkable book.

Sterling Township: 1875–1968 is a priceless reference tool for residents of today and tomorrow. Photos and captions depicting life in this area over a period of 93 years showcase our community's proud people and significant accomplishments.

Noted author Robert Heinlein once said, "A generation which ignores history, has no past and no future." I applaud everyone associated with publishing this historical account of our community. Your efforts ensure that the City of Sterling Heights retains its proud past and looks forward to its bright future!

Sincerely,

Mayor Richard J. Notte

City Council: Mayor Pro Tem Joseph V. Romano, Councilman Richard L. Bracci, Councilwoman Deanna Koski, Councilman Steve Rice, Councilwoman Maria G. Schmidt, and Councilwoman Barbara A. Ziarko.

One

FAMILIES

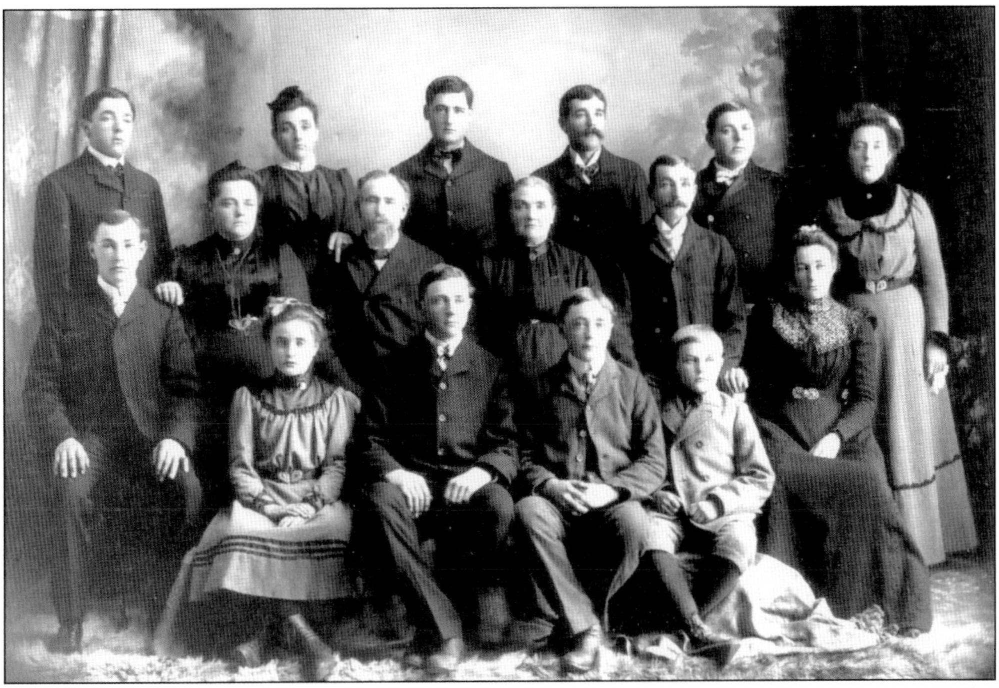

THE CHRISTOPHER AND PAULINA WEIER FAMILY. The Weier family was well known in the township for their large family, their knowledge of farming, and their civic mindedness. They farmed their 230 acres of land. The family home, built in 1872, is still standing on Plumbrook Road, just north of where 17 Mile Road crosses today. This portrait, taken around 1902, includes the entire family. Christopher Weier and his wife, Paulina Reifter Weier, are surrounded by their children—Paulina, Charles, Minnie, Gustav, Bertha, Julius, William, John, Martha, Albert, George, Louis, Elsa, and Otto. (Photograph courtesy of Elmer Measel.)

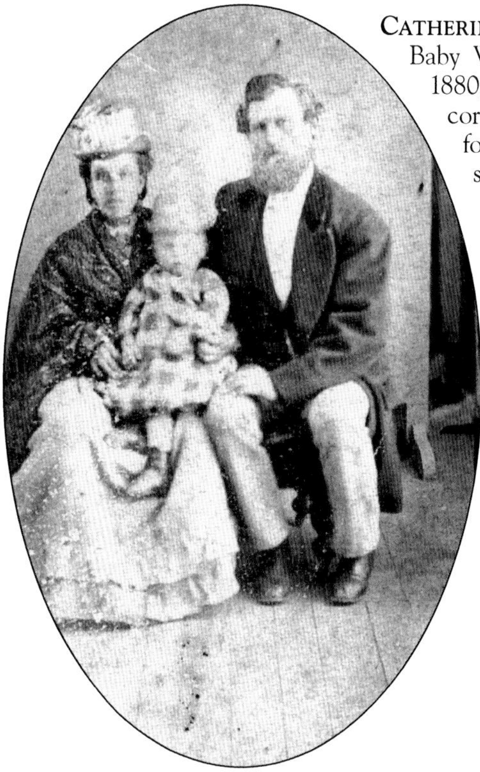

CATHERINE AND FRED HACKER WITH WILLIAM, C. 1875. Baby William is the first of the couple's 10 sons. By 1880, they were living in their family home on the corner of Mound and 16 Mile Roads with their first four sons and Fred's parents. The Hackers were successful farmers, and their family name has spread throughout Macomb County. The family home on Mound Road north of the Detroit News North Plant was demolished in 2004 to make way for commercial development.

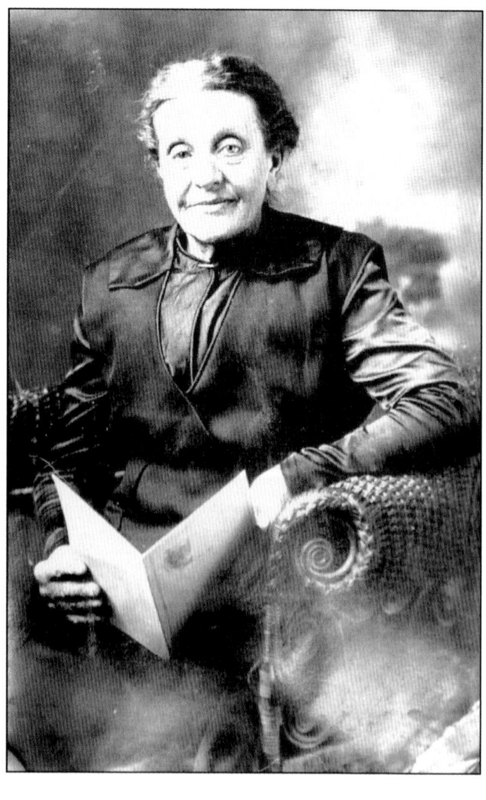

CATHERINE BAUER HACKER. This 1915 studio portrait shows the calm strength Catherine Hacker must have had to raise her sons on her own after the death of her husband, Frederick, in 1892, with the youngest less than a month old. Catherine was born in Detroit and came to Sterling Township upon her marriage. She died in 1920 at the age of 65, an admired woman. (Photograph courtesy of Rose Bower Hacker.)

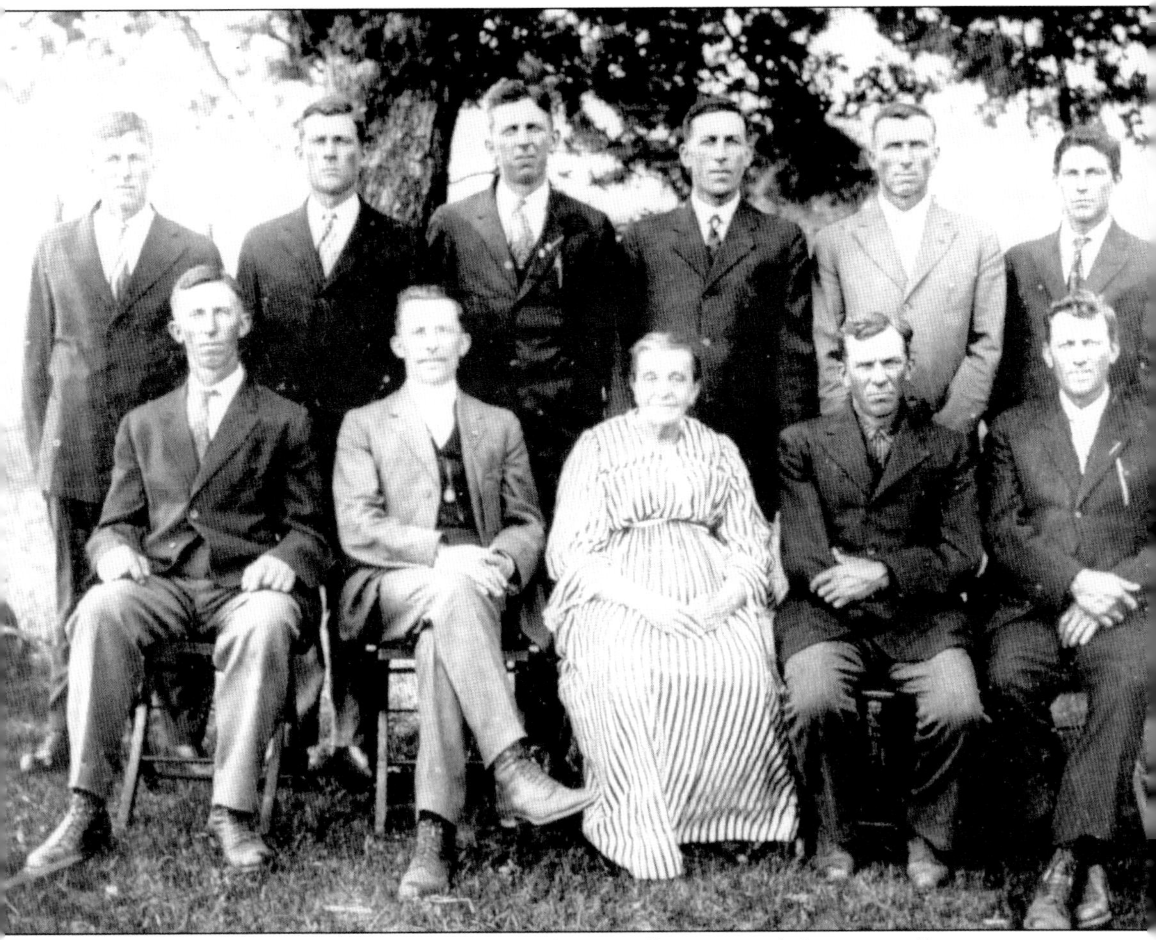

MOTHER AND SONS. In 1918, Catherine Hacker proudly poses with her sons, all grown into fine men. Pictured from left to right are (first row) Emil (farmer), William (Mount Clemens postmaster), Catherine, Albert (farmer and thresher man, lost a hand in a corn husker), and Otto (farmer); (second row) Christian (farmer with a small sawmill on 16 Mile Road), George (farmer), Charles (delivered mail out of the Utica Post Office for 30 years), Louis (Detroit police officer), Fred (tile contractor and farmer), and Benjamin (the youngest, 19 days old when his father died). According to an obituary in the *Utica Sentinel*, the sons used a variety of spellings of their family name, including Hacker, Haecker, Hecker. They were raised in a home at the northeast corner of 16 Mile and Mound Roads, which was demolished in 2005 to make way for a bank. Most of the sons stayed in Sterling Township, although a few spread out to Warren, Detroit, Mount Clemens, and Utica. (Photograph courtesy of Rose Bower Hacker.)

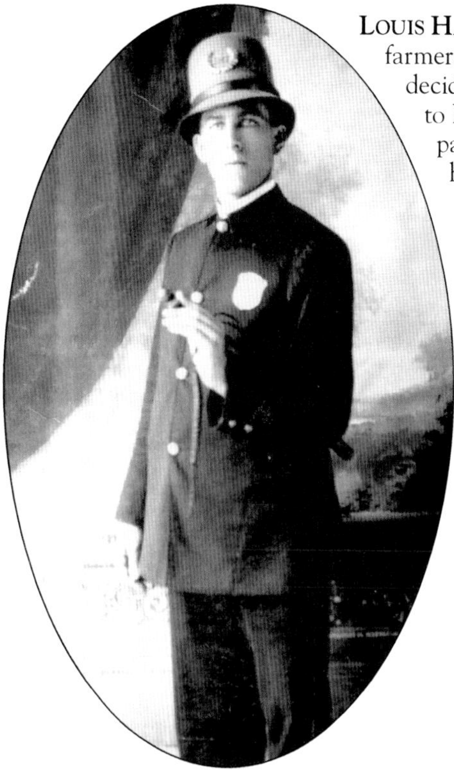

LOUIS HACKER. The fifth of the 10 sons of Sterling Township farmers Fred and Catherine Hacker, Louis must have decided to strike out on his own, leave the farm, and go to Detroit. The 1910 census shows him as a 28-year-old patrolman for the police department in Detroit, where he lived with his wife, Louise, and son Arthur, who was born a few years later. This portrait of Louis, looking quite dapper in his uniform, was probably taken about this time. (Photograph courtesy of Rose Bower Hacker.)

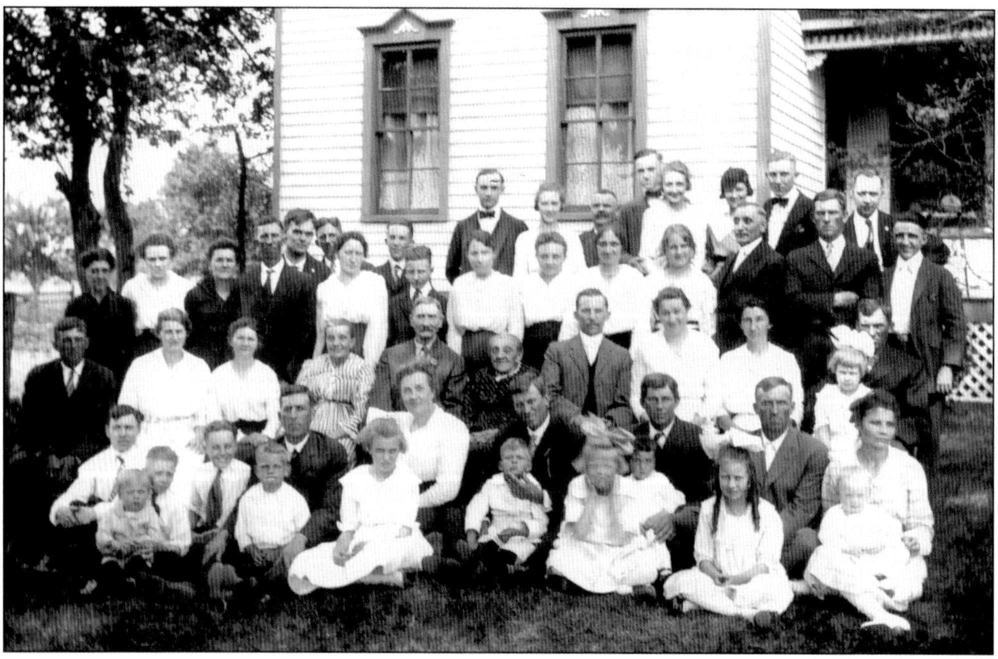

HACKER FAMILY REUNION. Widowed matriarch Catherine Hacker (striped dress) is seated in the center of this large group of family members gathered at Catherine's home on the northeast corner of Mound and 16 Mile Roads in 1918. Included in the group are her 10 adult sons and their wives and children. (Photograph courtesy of Rose Bower Hacker.)

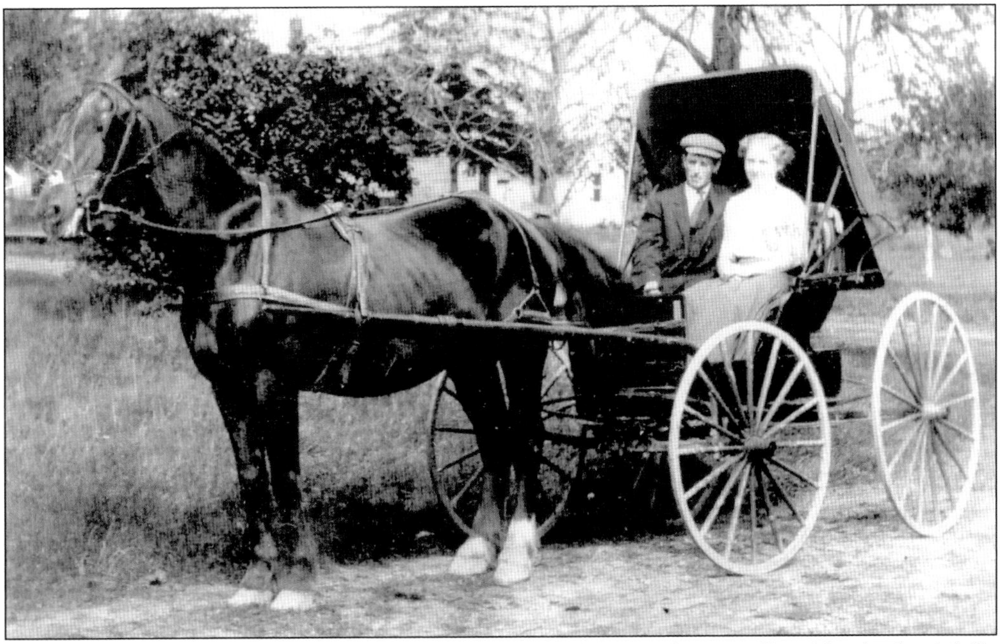

OUT FOR A RIDE. Pictured about the time of their wedding, Edwin Haff and his bride, Adella Behrendt, go for a buggy ride in 1913. The couple lived with Edwin's widowed father, Lorenzo, on the Haff farm on Dequindre Road, where they raised their five children—Vera, Gladys, Lawrence, Violet, and Ilene. The Haffs were "general farmers," and Lawrence represents the fifth generation of Haffs on that farm. (Photograph courtesy of Lawrence Haff.)

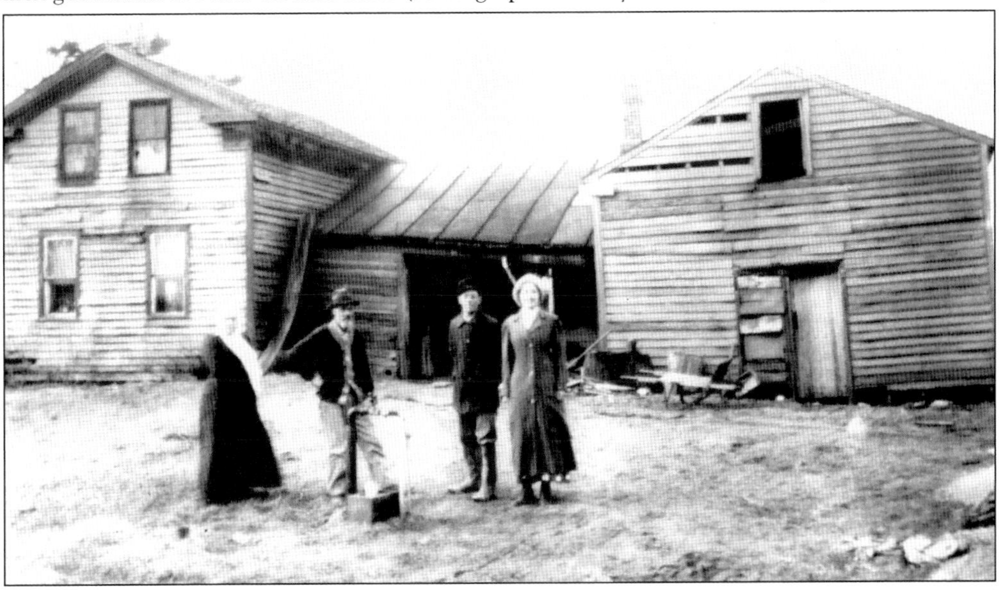

THE HAFF FAMILY. In this March 1913 photograph, Edwin and Adella Haff (right), married for four days, pose with Edwin's widowed father, Lorenzo Haff, and Lorenzo's sister Phoebe Haff Johnson. The house behind them was awaiting partial demolition so that the left wing could be remodeled. Lorenzo's grandfather Jacob Haff bought the property in 1839. The farm is located on Dequindre Road, south of Hall Road. The remodeled version of this house still stands, owned by Edwin and Adella's son Lawrence Haff. (Photograph courtesy of Lawrence Haff.)

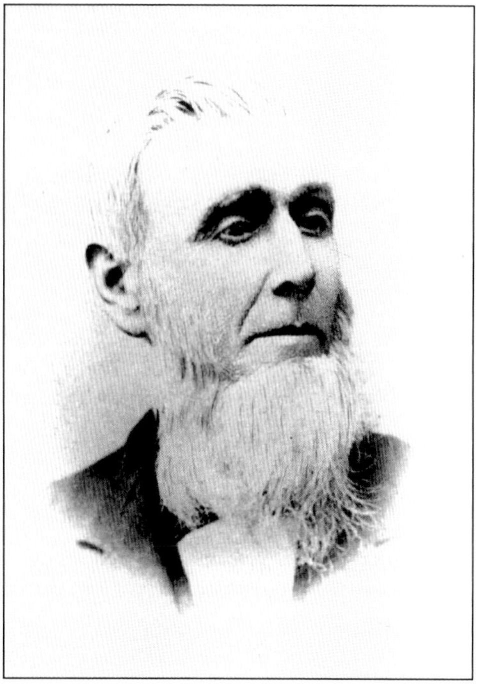

CYRUS S. SCHOONOVER. Sterling Township pioneer Cyrus S. Schoonover is pictured in a portrait taken around 1870 by the Novess Studio in Mount Clemens. Born in New York, he came to Sterling Township in 1847 with his first wife and their children—Phoebe, James, Lorenzo, and Mary. They settled on the northeast corner of 19 Mile and Ryan Roads. After the death of his wife, he married Elizabeth Donittey Wood, a widow from the area with five children. He and Elizabeth had three more children together, John, Cyrus A., and Fred. She brought to the marriage a farm south of 19 Mile Road on Ryan Road, which stayed in the family for three more generations. (Photograph courtesy of Ferry G. Schoonover.)

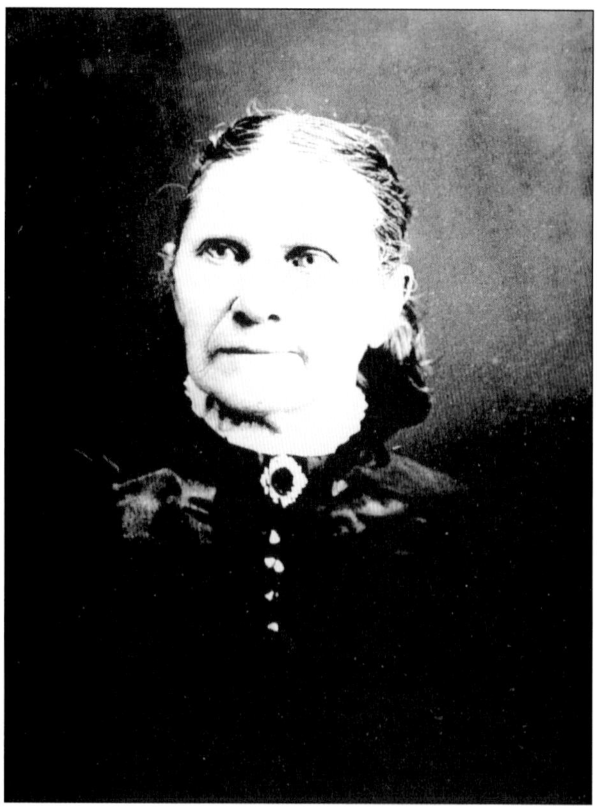

ELIZABETH DONITTEY WOOD SCHOONOVER. Elizabeth was the second wife of Cyrus S. Schoonover, marrying him in 1852 after the death of her first husband, John A. Wood. The 1850 census shows her with John and six children—Ann, Sarah, Silas, William, Margaret, and Catherine. Her marriage to Cyrus Schoonover produced three children—John, Cyrus A., and Fred. Elizabeth lived to be 87 years old. (Photograph courtesy of Ferry G. Schoonover.)

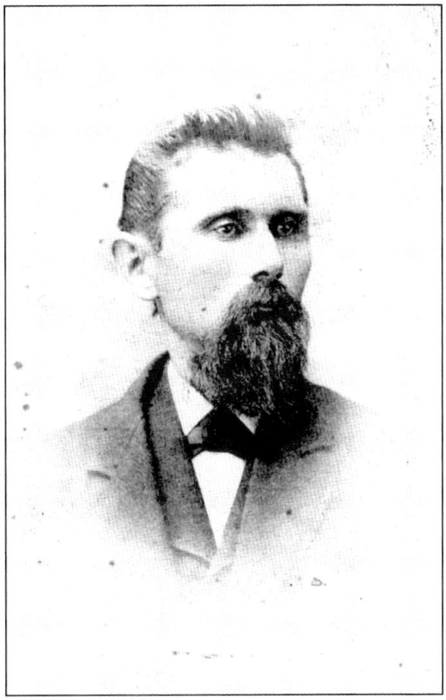

LORENZO SCHOONOVER. Lorenzo, son of Cyrus S. Schoonover and Cyrus's first wife, Mary, left the family farm on Ryan Road and 19 Mile Road in 1863 to follow his brother James and volunteer to fight in the Civil War. Lorenzo was with the 8th Michigan Cavalry and was taken prisoner in Georgia in August 1864. He spent about three months in the infamous Andersonville prisoner of war camp, returning home to his wife and child in 1865. His family continued to grow after his return, but they lost him again upon his death at the age of 34. This *c.* 1880 portrait was taken by the H. M. Kittle studio in Pontiac, Michigan. (Photograph courtesy of Ferry G. Schoonover.)

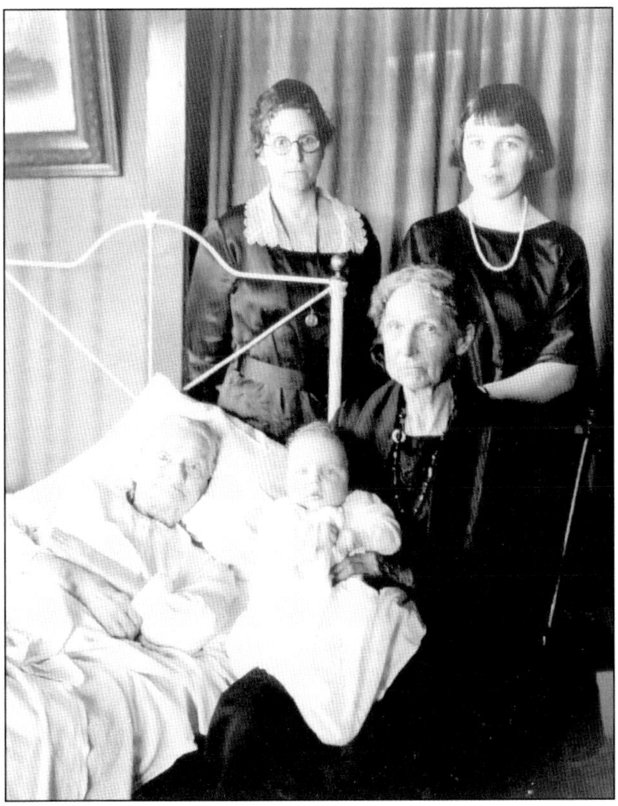

GENERATIONS. The family of Eliza Lovell (in bed) was able to gather and get this portrait taken during the last year of her life, around 1923. Included are her daughter Lydia Jane Lovell Schoonover (seated), Lydia Jane's daughter Lima Schoonover King (standing left), Lima's daughter Blanche King Hackett (standing right), and Blanche's baby David Hackett. The Schoonover family was from the 19 Mile and Ryan Roads area, spreading over into Troy. (Photograph courtesy of Ferry G. Schoonover.)

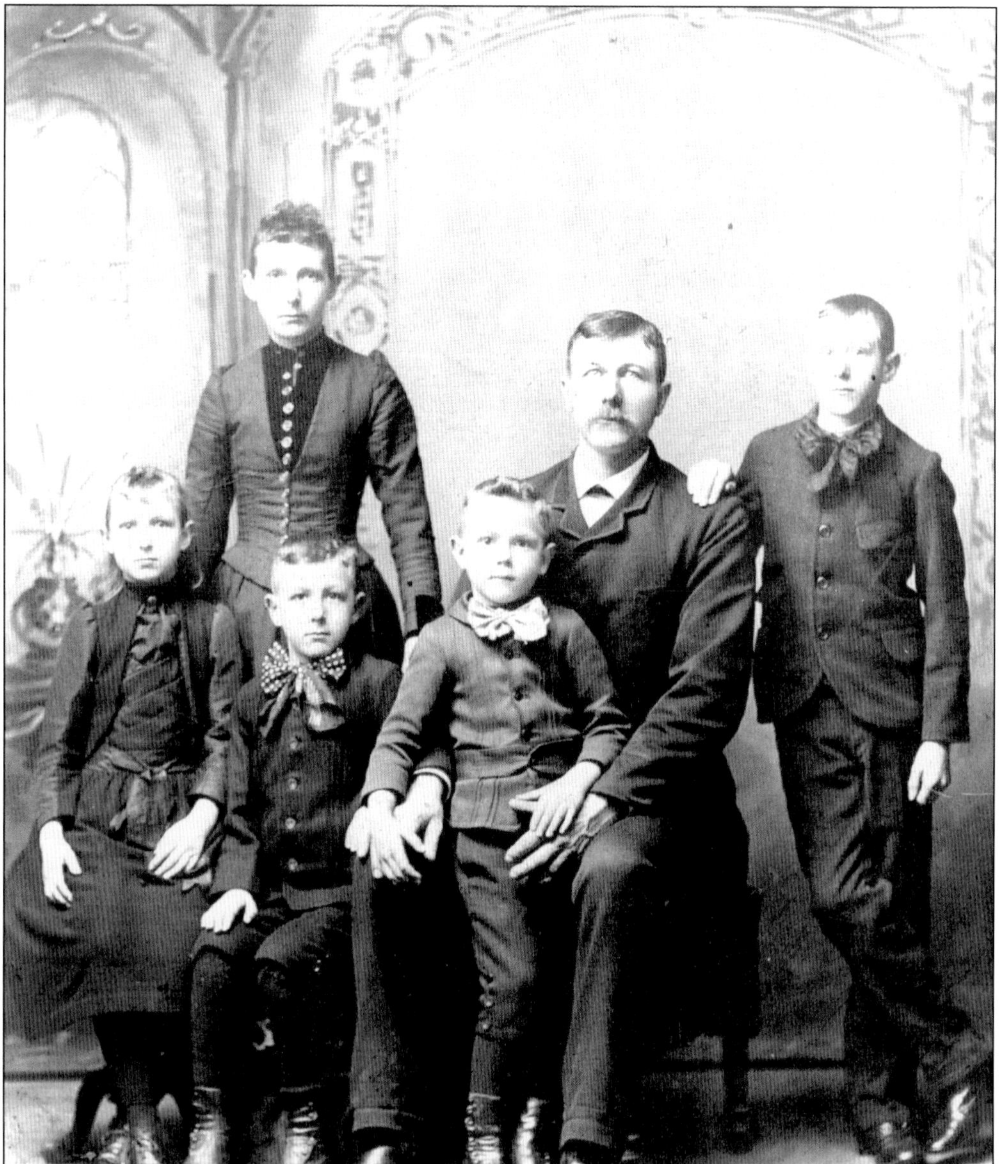

THE CYRUS AND LYDIA SCHOONOVER FAMILY. Pictured in a portrait taken *c.* 1891 by the Novess Studio in Mount Clemens is the family of Cyrus Alfred Schoonover and his wife, Lydia Jane Lovell Schoonover. The children are, from left to right, Lima (King), Carl E., Clyde, and Ira Frank. Tragedy struck the young family in the summer of 1900, when lightning struck their barn while family members were milking cows inside. Cyrus was killed instantly, and son Carl and a neighbor were also struck. Two barns, their contents (hay and wheat), and their older home all burned. The family continued bravely on, living on their Ryan Road farm for two more generations. Son Frank later became township treasurer. Cyrus was the son of Sterling Township pioneers Cyrus S. and Elizabeth Schoonover. (Photograph courtesy of Ferry G. Schoonover.)

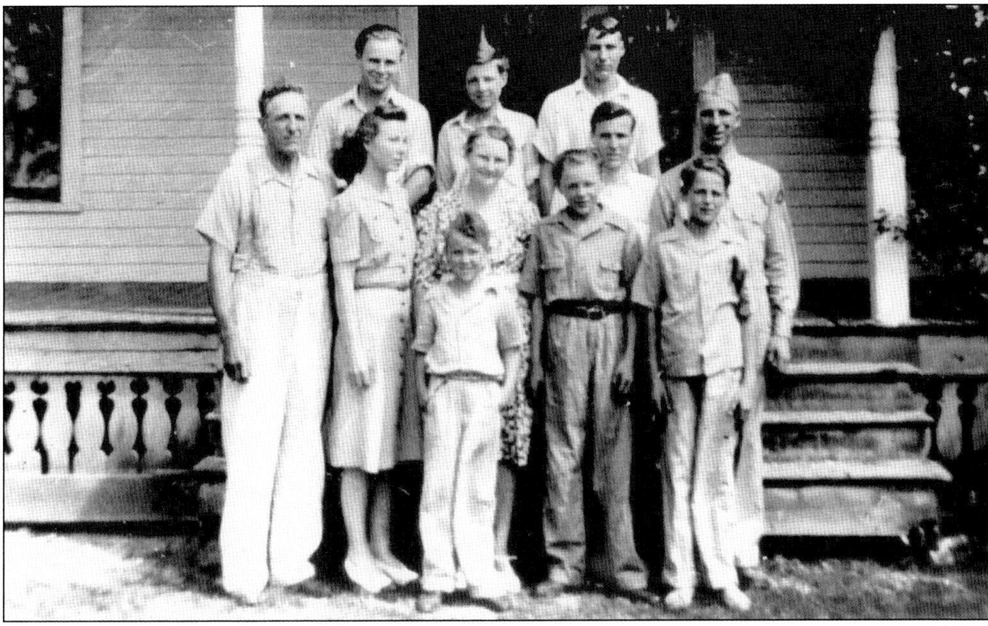

The Carl and Hilda Schoonover Family. The Schoonover generations continue with the family of Carl E. Schoonover and his wife, Hilda Houghton Schoonover. They and their nine children stand in front of the family home, built in 1900 on Ryan Road south of 19 Mile Road. Pictured in 1941 are, from left to right, the following: (first row) Alger and twins Wilbert and Gilbert; (second row) Carl E. (father), Beatrice, Hilda (mother), Alfred, and Carl; (third row) Ferry, William, and Donald. Carl (senior), the son of Cyrus A. and Lydia Jane Schoonover, served on the war board for Sterling Township, and a number of his sons served in the armed forces during World War II. (Photograph courtesy of Ferry G. Schoonover.)

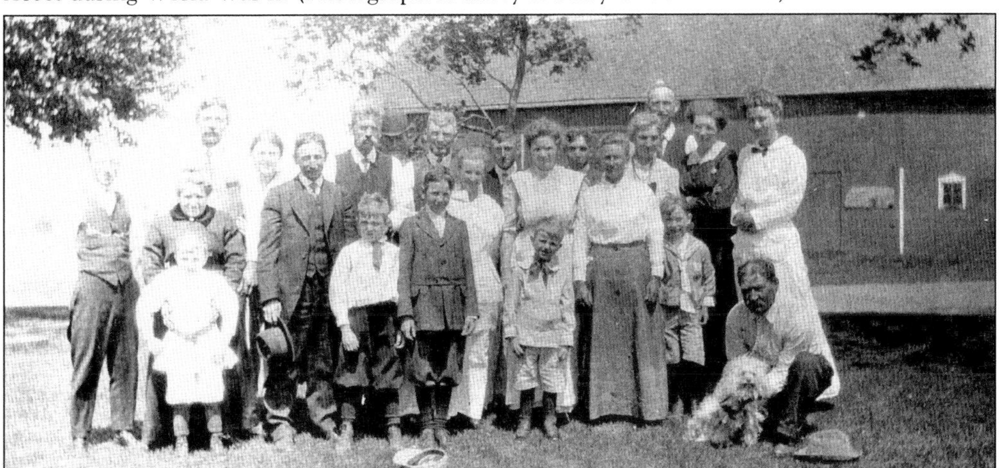

Gratopp Family Reunion. Tossing their hats on the lawn, the Gratopp family and a family dog pose on a sunny day around 1920. The couple second from the left may be Christopher and Katherine Gratopp. Former neighbors had described them as "great people, very smart about farming. Christopher was a great, big man, 6'6", with a handlebar mustache." His wife, standing in front, was a "lovely darling little lady, not 5 feet tall." The family farm, on Plumbrook Road (or Goose Road, as it was called back then) and 17 Mile Road, still stands. (Photograph courtesy of Lois Fischer Stone.)

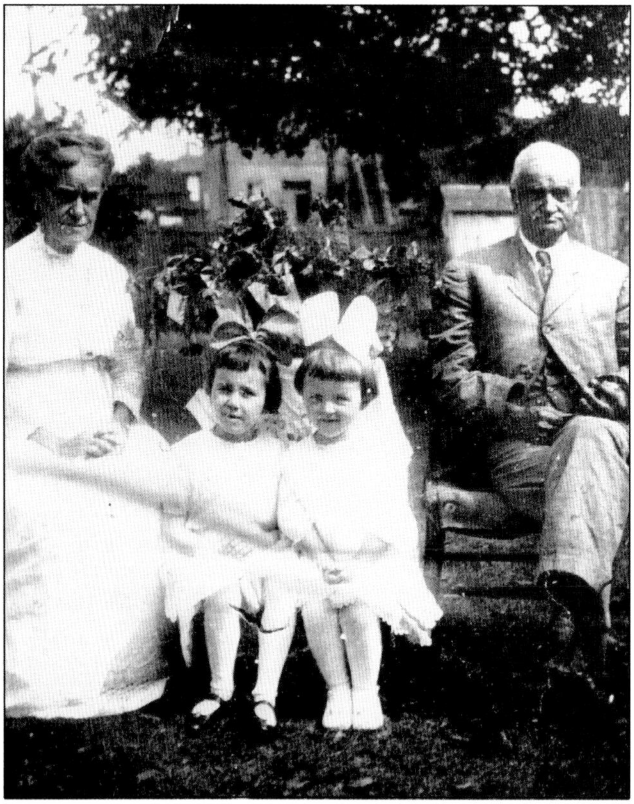

SARAH AND WILLIAM UPTON WITH GIRLS. William Upton came from a successful farming family from the area, having been born in England and moving to Sterling Township in 1845 as a young child. He became even more prosperous due to his success at farming and business, and built the grandest home in the township, known as the Upton House, in 1866. In this c. 1920 photograph, William Upton sits with his wife, Sarah Aldrich Upton, great-granddaughter Marjorie Upton Sayre (DeFrancis), left, and another little girl. Little Marjorie is the daughter of his grandaughter Sarah. The Uptons were probably living at their later home in Rochester at the time of this photograph. (Photograph courtesy of Marjorie Upton DeFrancis.)

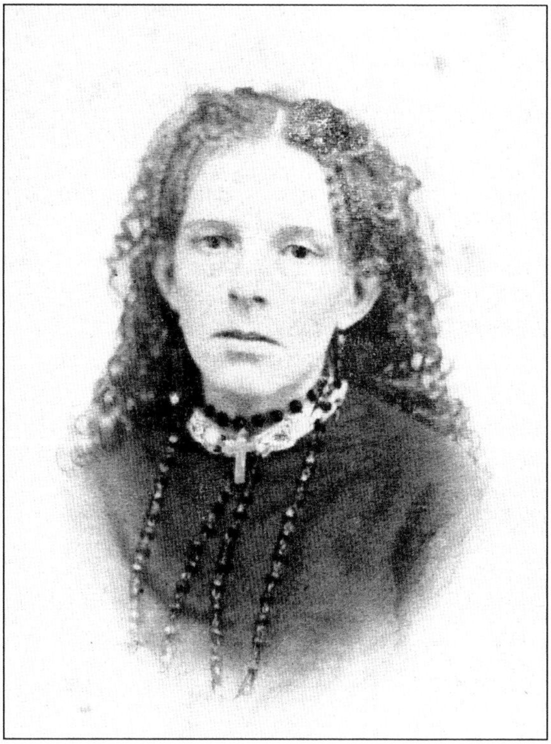

RENA UPTON. Young Rena Upton, the only daughter of prominent farmer William Upton and his wife, Sarah, died when she was only 11 years old from an illness related to her spine. She may have already been ill when this portrait was taken around 1879, not long before her death. Back in the earlier days of photography, portraits were often taken of the sick, even of the dead, if no portrait already existed. The family lived in the grand Upton House, on the corner of Utica Road and Dodge Park Road. (Photograph courtesy of Marjorie Upton DeFrancis.)

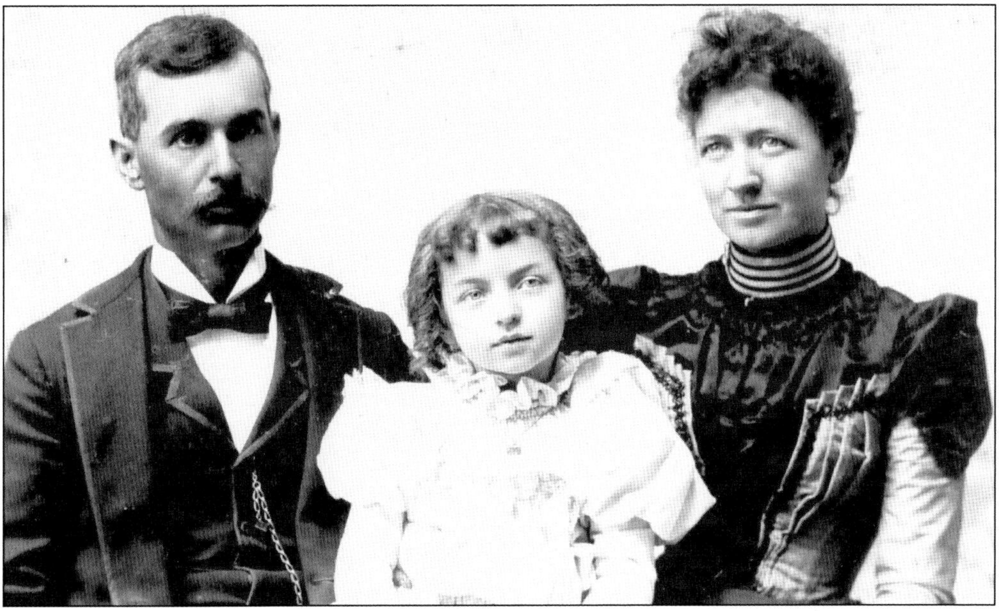

The Frank Upton Family. Frank Upton was the second son of prosperous farmer William Upton. Frank was born and raised in the Upton House, which still graces the corner of Utica and Dodge Park Roads. This *c.* 1898 portrait shows him and his wife, Alice Fox Upton, and their only child, Sarah Jeanette Upton. By 1910, the family was living in Washington Township, where Frank and Alice lived out the rest of their lives. Daughter Sarah lived only to the age of 38, but her childhood likeness is immortalized in a statue currently in front of the Upton House, depicting her and her grandmother, Sarah Aldrich Upton, doing needlework. (Photograph courtesy of Marjorie Upton DeFrancis.)

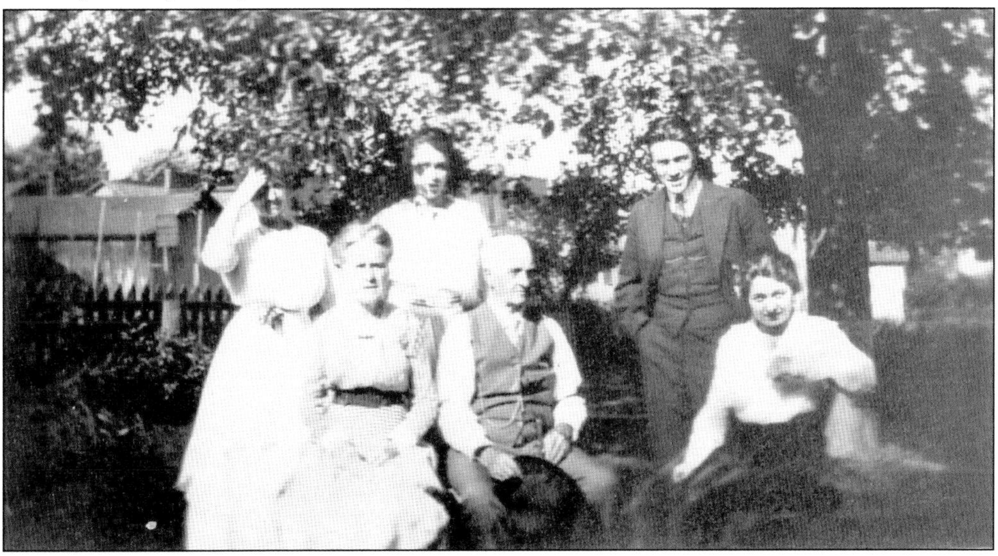

Summer Gathering. The William and Sarah Upton family is shown on a summer afternoon around 1915. The couple lived in Rochester, Michigan, at this time. From left to right are the following: (first row) Sarah Jeanette Upton, William Upton, and granddaughter Sarah Upton Sayre; (second row) daughter-in-law Alice Fox Upton, unidentified, and Oren Sayre. (Photograph courtesy of Marjorie Upton Sayre DeFrancis.)

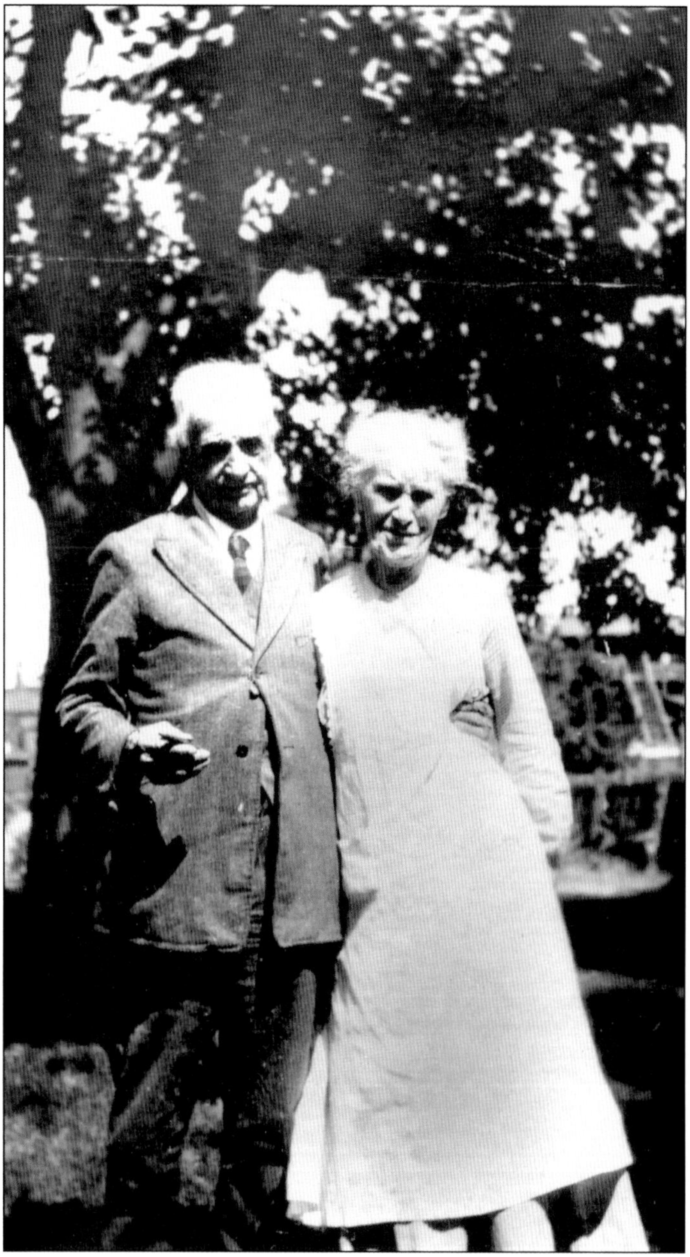

William and Sarah Upton. William and Sarah "Nettie" Upton are pictured here in their later years around 1915. By this time, the Uptons were probably living in Rochester, Michigan. After moving from the Upton House on Dodge Park Road to live in Utica in 1891, William ran a clothing and dry goods store in Utica called Upton and St. John. The store was located on the corner of Cass and Main Streets. He and his partner were also dealers in Shropshire sheep. The business was sold in 1897, and William became a general manager of a branch of the Salvation Army. The disastrous Utica fire of 1904 put him in a coma for a week after he fell from the roof of his commercial building he was trying to protect. He survived, but the building did not. The Uptons moved to Rochester not long after, and William died in 1923. Sarah lived until 1925. (Photograph courtesy of Marjorie Upton Sayre DeFrancis.)

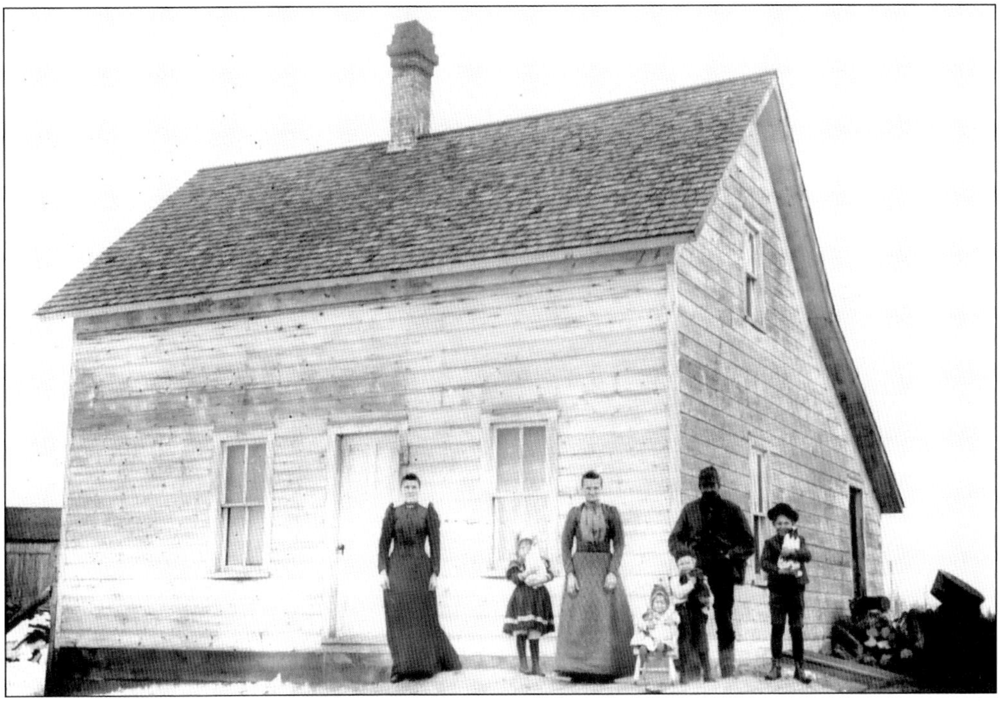

THE MAROTZ FAMILY. The Marotz homestead stood on Clinton River Road south of 19 Mile Road. This house was replaced by another one farther back off the road in 1915. Wood from this original house was used to build the garage for the newer home. The family in this view from around 1901 includes, from left to right, aunt Lena Fischer, Tillie, Wilhelmina Fischer Marotz (mother), Lillian, August Jr., August Sr. (father), and Otto. Various animals are shown in the arms of the children. Siblings Tillie, Lena, and Otto never married and continued to live out the rest of their long lives on this farm, selling corn and other vegetables they grew to appreciative suburbanites, even into the 1980s.

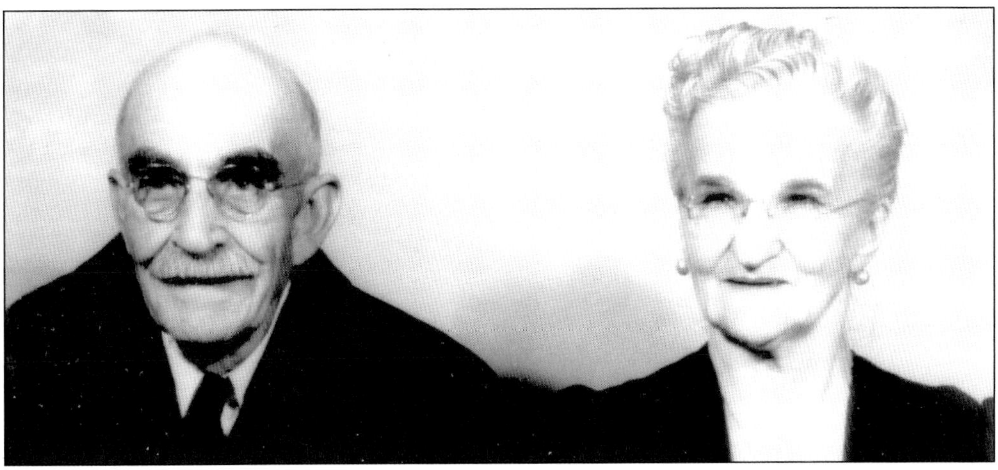

AUGUST AND WILHELMINA MAROTZ. Young August came to America as a teenager from Prussia, otherwise known as Germany, in 1883. He married Wilhelmina Fischer in 1890 and moved to a farm on Clinton River Road south of 19 Mile Road, neighboring his brother's farm. August and "Minnie," pictured here around 1945, raised five children there while doing general farming.

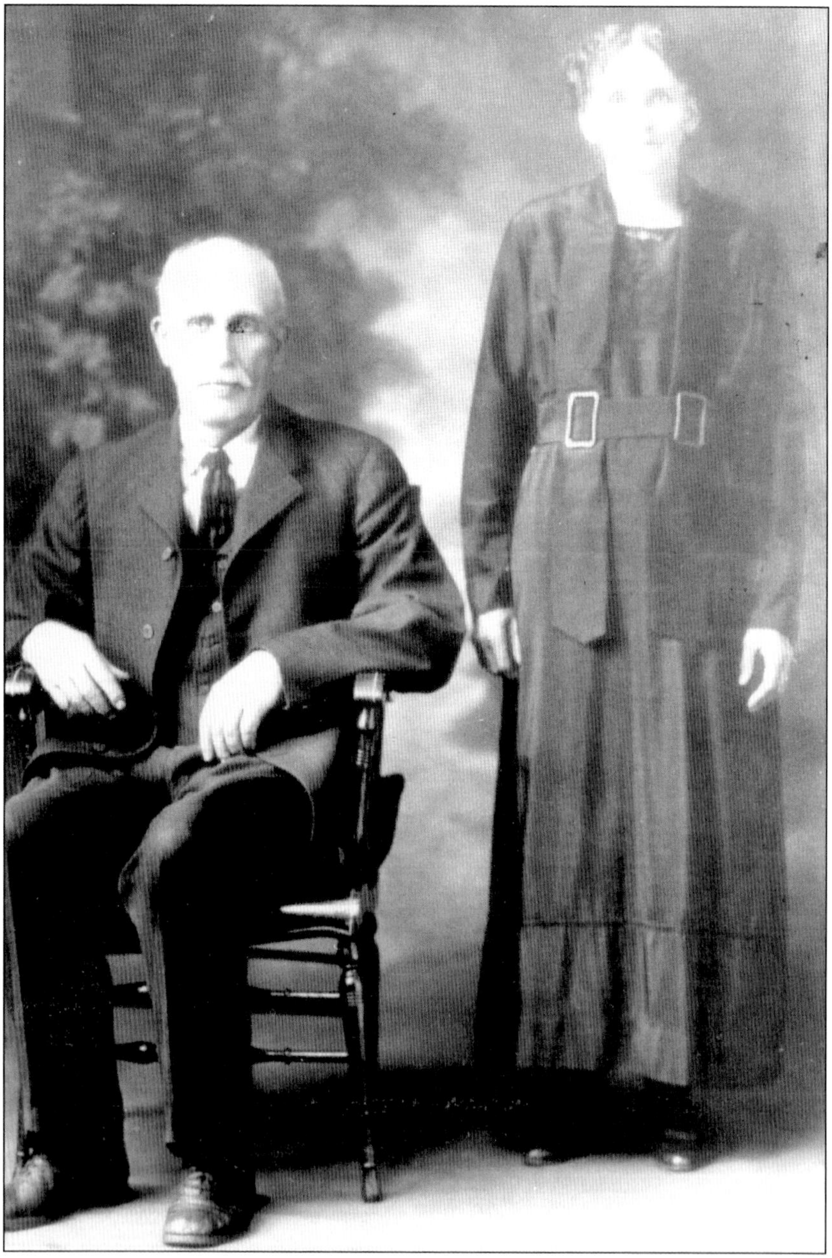

FRED AND AUGUSTA HELDT. Fred was the son of Charles and Anna Heldt, early pioneers who came from Germany and who had a farm on 15 Mile Road west of Hayes since at least the 1870s. Pictured around 1915 are Fred and his wife, Augusta Wade Heldt. They lived on that same Heldt farm on 15 Mile Road most of their lives and raised eight children there—William, John, Albert, Louis, Amanda, Rudolph, Minnie, and Paulina. In their later years, they lived in the home known as the William Upton House on Dodge Park Road with some of their younger children. The Heldts lived and farmed there from 1913 to 1927. Fred conveyed part of the property across the road to the State of Michigan in 1922 to create Dodge Park. The park became wildly popular with people from the Detroit area, as there were few other state parks within driving distance, and today it is part of the city park system.

LOUIS HELDT. The fourth son of Fred and Augusta Heldt, Louis is shown seated at an organ around 1915. His parents lived in the Upton House at the time, so this may be one of the few interior views of the elegant home if he was indeed living with them at the time. Louis married a woman named Martha and had children Edna, Bernice, Elmer, and Howard. He lived in Detroit for the rest of his life.

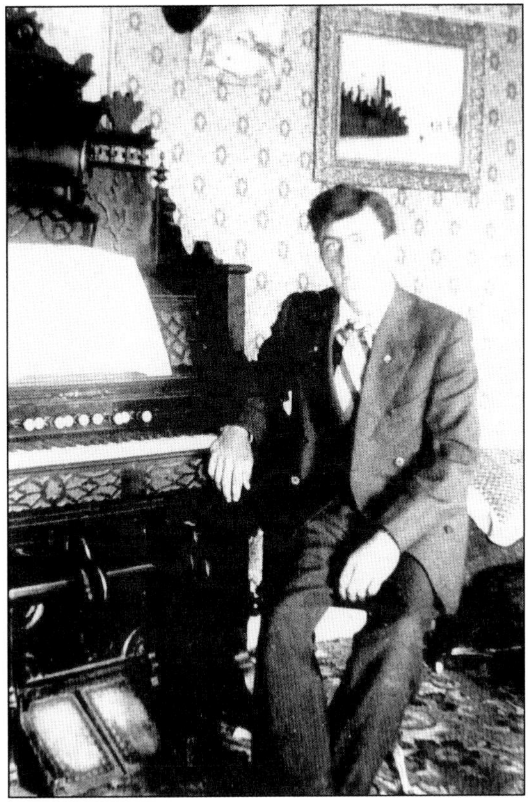

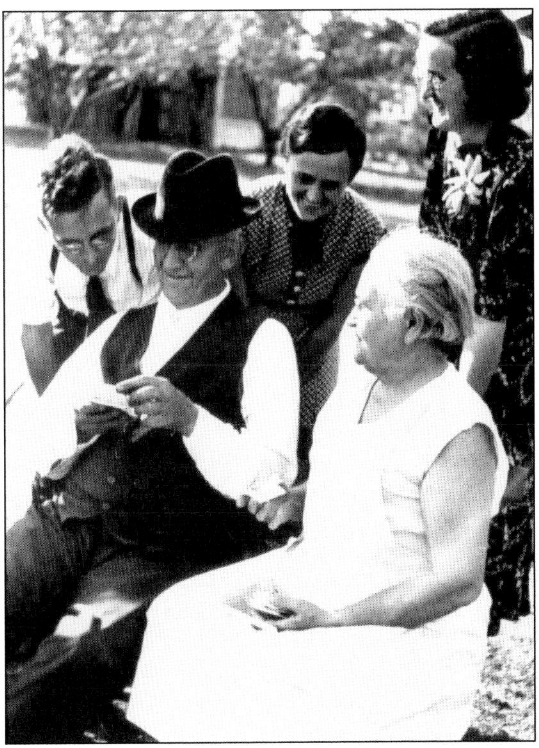

THE HOLZHAUER FAMILY. The Holzhauer family enjoys a summer day by looking through photographs. The family home was on Utica Road, west of Kleino Road, where they grew flowers and bulbs to sell in Mount Clemens and from their roadside stand. Pictured in this c. 1940 photograph are, from left to right, the following: (seated) Fred Holzhauer and his wife, Anna; (standing) son Carl, daughter Irene, and Carl's wife, Edith. (Photograph courtesy of Irene Holzhauer Hoffman.)

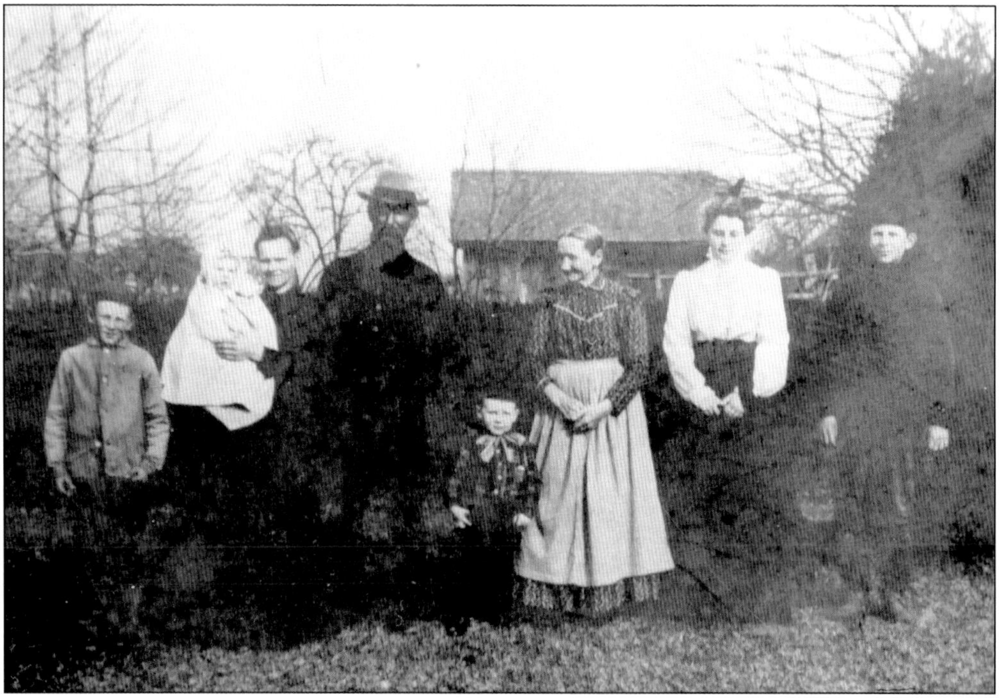

THE CHARLES AND LOUISE AHRENS FAMILY. The Ahrens farm, located on Clinton River Road just west of Hayes Road, provided the backdrop for this photograph, taken around 1905. The family includes, from left to right, Carl, infant Meta (being held by her mother, Louise Arft Ahrens), Charles Ahrens, Albert, Mary Arft, Martha, and Otto. Mary Arft was the mother of Louise. It was common for elderly parents, especially when widowed, to move in with their children. (Photograph courtesy of Armin "Duane" Kleino.)

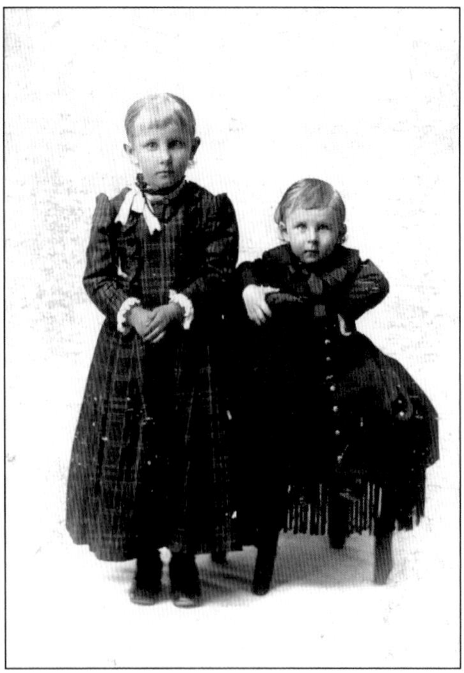

MARTHA AND OTTO. The two oldest children of Charles and Louise Ahrens of Clinton River Road are captured in this *c.* 1892 portrait, taken by the Novess Studio in Mount Clemens. Martha Ahrens (Sieger) and her little brother Otto look very cute and sit still very nicely. (Photograph courtesy of Eleanor Ahrens.)

AHRENS FAMILY PORTRAIT. The Novess Studio in Mount Clemens was the photographer for this *c.* 1900 portrait of Charles and Louise Ahrens (seated) and family. The children are, from left to right, Otto, his younger brother Carl, and their older sister Martha. Children Albert and Meta were yet to be born. (Photograph courtesy of Armin "Duane" Kleino.)

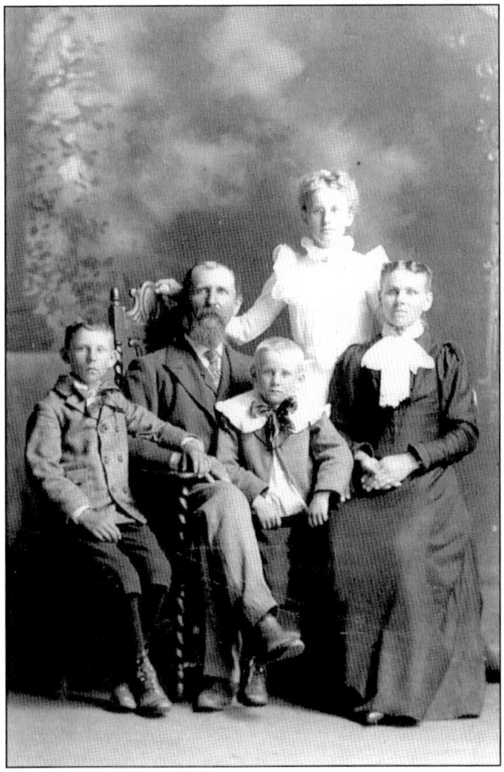

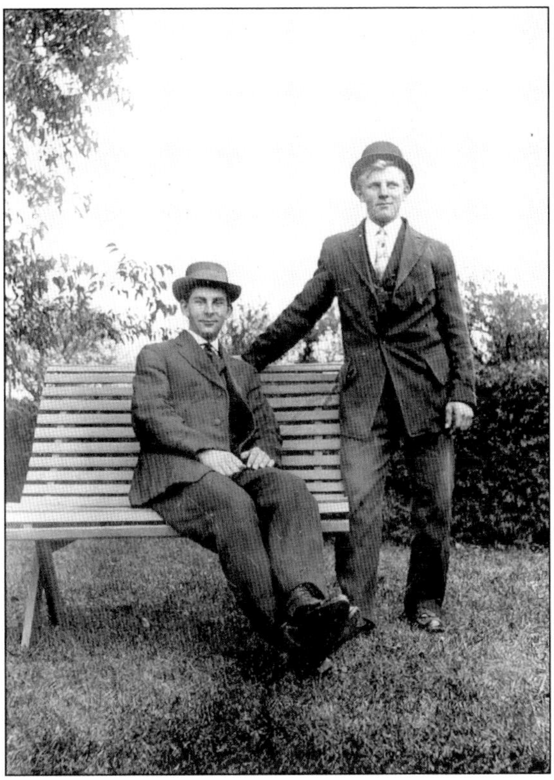

BROTHERS. Otto Ahrens (seated) and his younger brother Carl (standing) pose for this casual *c.* 1910 portrait. For a time, during his earlier teen years, Otto worked as a live-in servant for his uncle Frederick Ahrens in the Upton House, which the uncle and his family owned and lived in from approximately 1891 to 1913, following the Uptons. Otto and Carl were the second- and third-born children of Charles and Louise Ahrens of Clinton River Road. (Photograph courtesy of Armin "Duane" Kleino.)

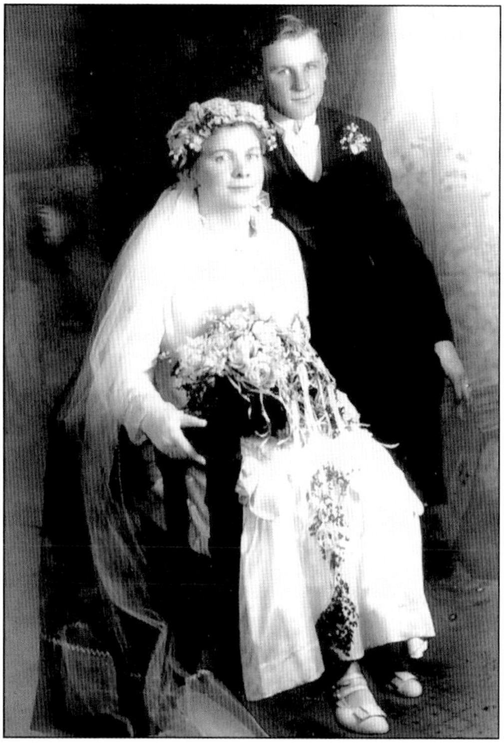

Foerster-Ahrens Wedding. Looking very handsome in their wedding finery, Ella Foerster, of Warren, and Carl Ahrens, of Sterling Township, pose around 1915. Ella was the daughter of John and Barbara Foerster, and Carl was the son of Charles and Louise Ahrens. The couple became the parents of Veola Ahrens. (Photograph courtesy of Armin "Duane" Kleino.)

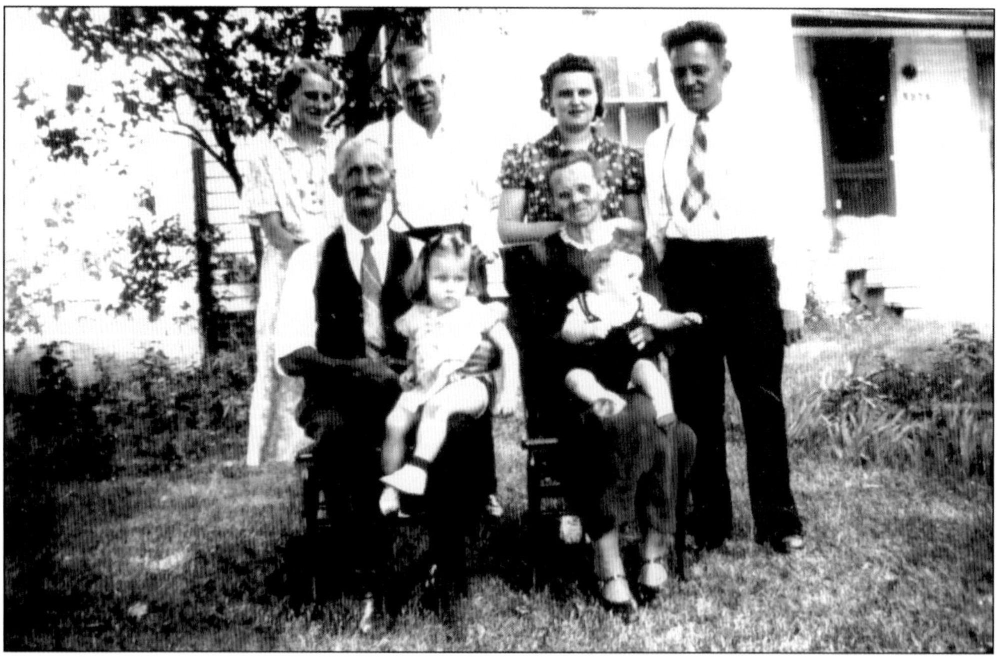

Four Generations, Ahrens-Kleino. Proud great-grandparents Charles and Louise Ahrens hold their great-grandchildren Audrey and Duane in this 1938 photograph. Behind them are, from left to right, their daughter Martha Ahrens Sieger, her husband Arthur Sieger, the Siegers' daughter Hulda Sieger Kleino, and her husband Melvin Kleino. Hulda and Melvin are the parents of the small children. (Photograph courtesy of Armin "Duane" Kleino.)

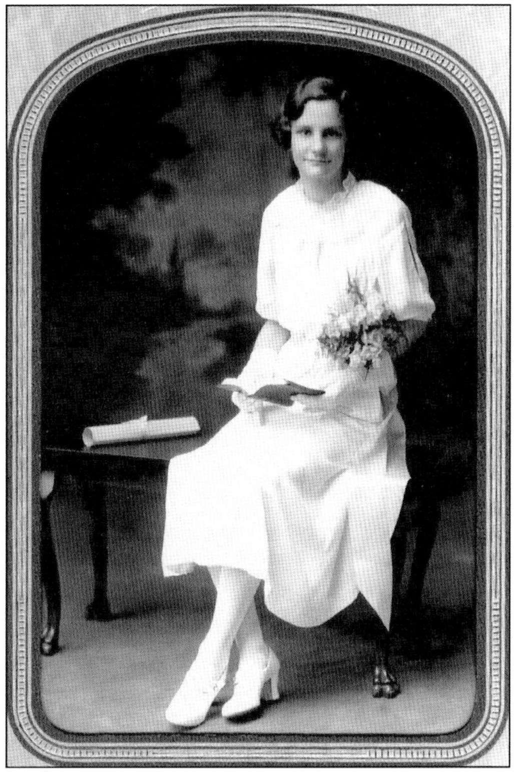

ELEANOR'S CONFIRMATION. This studio portrait by Sawn Studio of Mount Clemens commemorates young Eleanor Ahrens's confirmation at St. Paul Lutheran Church around 1936. The confirmation ceremony signaled the entrance into adulthood for young Lutherans. Eleanor and her two older sisters grew up working on the family farm. She and her sisters collected stray golf balls that landed on their property from Rammler Golf Course and used the proceeds to help pay their tuition to Utica High School. Eleanor was the daughter of Otto and Eleanor Ahrens of Clinton River Road. (Photograph courtesy of Armin "Duane" Kleino.)

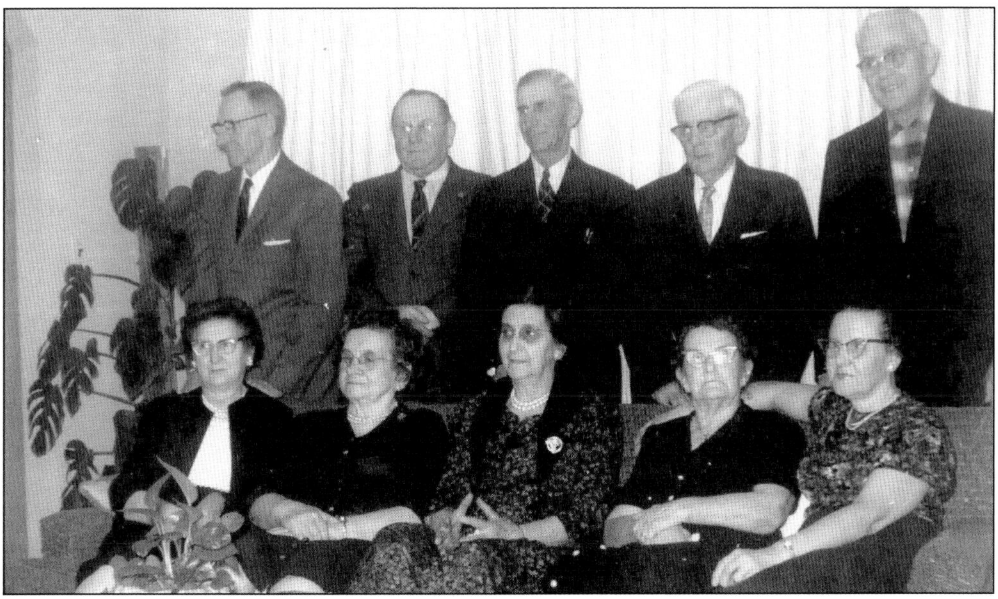

AHRENS SIBLINGS AND SPOUSES. At this *c.* 1961 gathering, the five children of Charles and Louise Ahrens of Sterling Township pose with their spouses. The husbands are standing behind their wives. From left to right are the following: (first row) Rose Lietz Ahrens, Ella Foerster Ahrens, Eleanor Zienert Ahrens, Martha Ahrens Sieger, and Meta Ahrens Schmelzer; (second row) Albert Ahrens, Carl Ahrens, Otto Ahrens, Arthur Sieger, and John Schmelzer. In 2005, Meta celebrated her 101st birthday before she passed away. (Photograph courtesy of Armin "Duane" Kleino.)

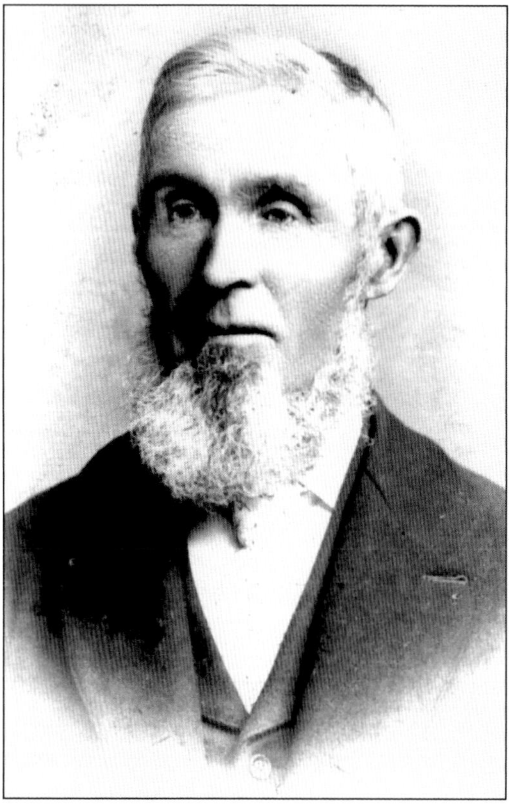

Christopher Kleino. Born in Mecklenburg, Germany, in 1831, Christopher Kleino (shown around 1890) came to America in 1862 with his new bride, Mary Harloff. The 1880 census shows that the family settled on Utica Road where the Kleino Bridge used to cross the Clinton River. The bridge, until late in the 20th century, was the only place to cross the river in the township. (Photograph courtesy of Armin "Duane" Kleino.)

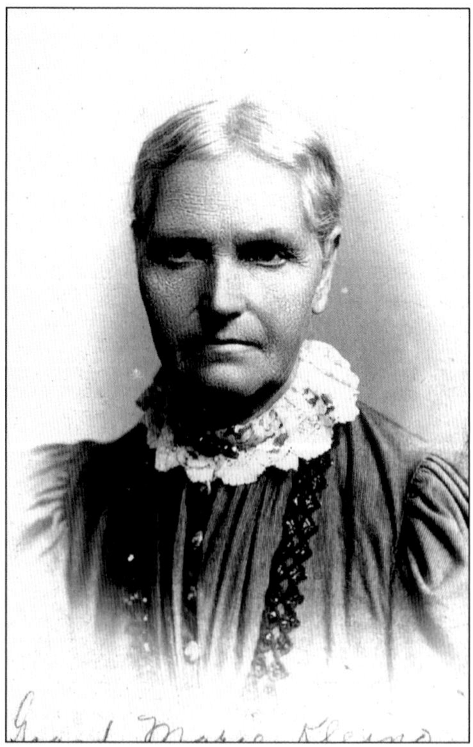

Mary Harloff Kleino. Mary Kleino, the newly married wife of Christopher Kleino, came with him from Germany to raise their family on a farm on Utica Road. Their six children were Henrietta, Louisa, Mary, Charles, Louis, and Fred. Mary is pictured here around 1890 in a portrait taken by the Novess Studio in Mount Clemens. (Photograph courtesy of Armin "Duane" Kleino.)

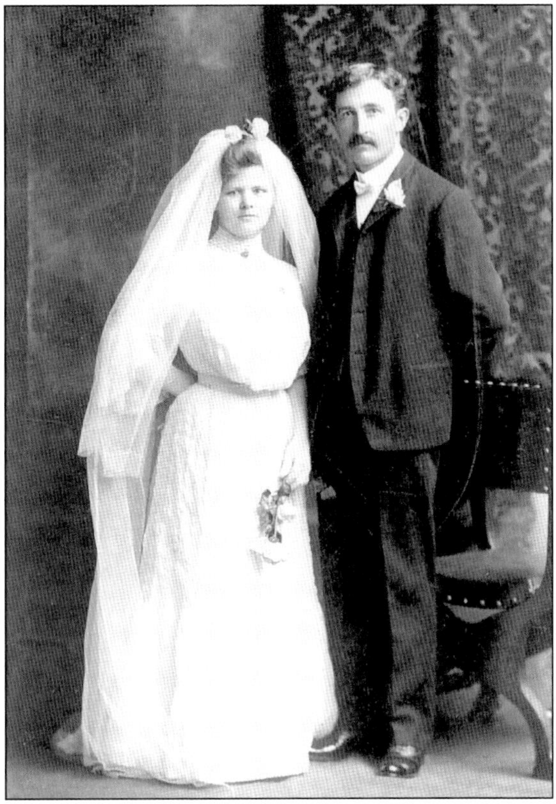

The Rewoldt-Kleino Wedding. This handsome couple poses for their wedding portrait at Huntington and Company photographers in Detroit, Michigan, around 1902. Martha Rewoldt of Waldenberg, Michigan, and Louis Kleino of Sterling Township, raised their children Elmer, Edgar, Melvin, Marion, and Norma on their Kleino Road farm. (Photograph courtesy of Armin "Duane" Kleino.)

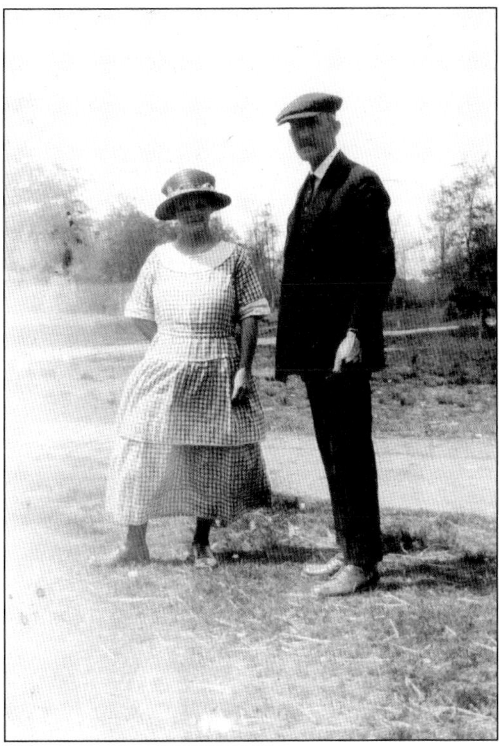

Martha and Louis Kleino Celebrate 20 Years. This photograph was taken around 1922 in honor of the 20th wedding anniversary of the couple. Louis was a prominent farmer and official of Utica and Sterling Township. He had been township clerk, health officer, and official of the Maple Grove school board for many years. He was also one of the founders of the Utica Farm Bureau. Together the couple raised five children. (Photograph courtesy of Armin "Duane" Kleino.)

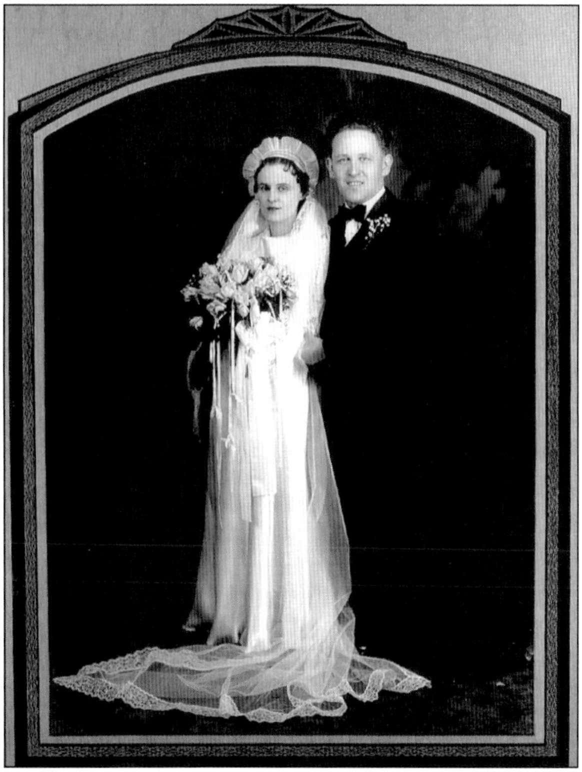

SIEGER-KLEINO WEDDING. St. John Lutheran Church in Fraser was the site of the 1935 wedding of Hulda Sieger and Melvin Kleino. Hulda was the daughter of Arthur Sieger and Martha Ahrens Sieger, and Melvin was the son of Louis Kleino and Martha Rewoldt Kleino of Sterling Township. The newlyweds resided at the Kleino farm on Kleino and Utica Roads in Sterling Township. (Photograph courtesy of Armin "Duane" Kleino.)

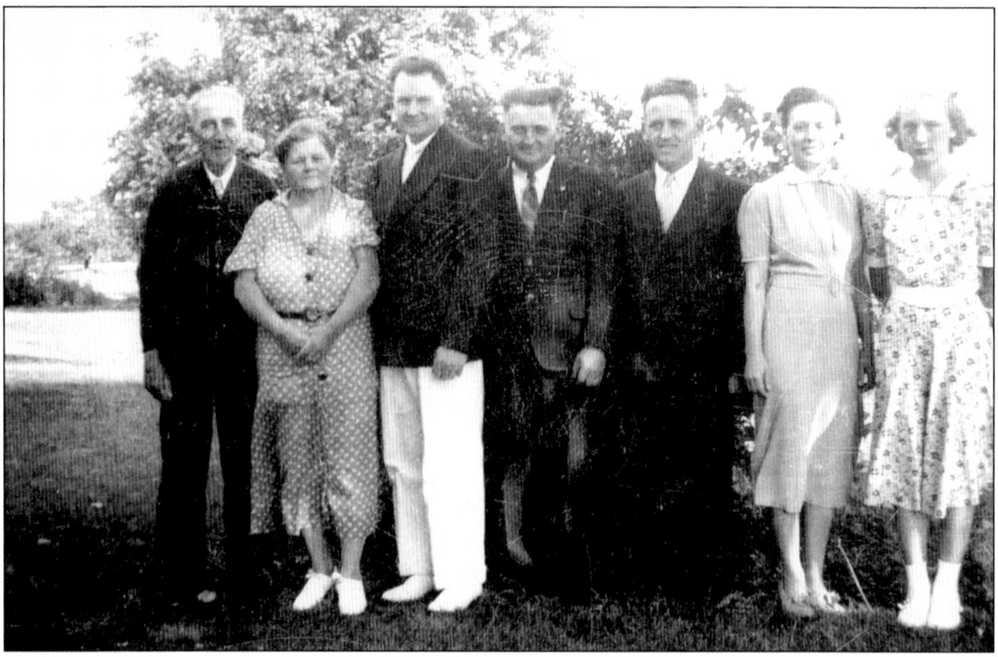

THE LOUIS AND MARTHA KLEINO FAMILY. Here Louis and Martha Kleino pose with their grown children on a summer day around 1938. Pictured from left to right are Louis Kleino, Martha Rewoldt Kleino, Elmor Kleino, Edgar Kleino, Melvin Kleino, Marion Kleino Reindel, and Norma Kleino (Schurig). (Photograph courtesy of Armin "Duane" Kleino.)

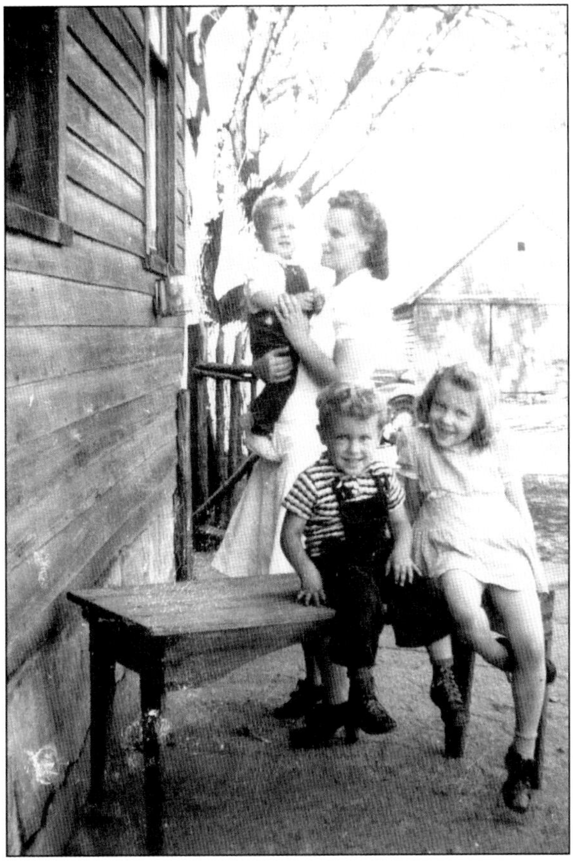

KLEINO CHILDREN WITH MOM. Hulda Sieger Kleino holds Lonnie while Duane and his big sister, Audrey, share a bench next to the Kleino home on Kleino Road in this photograph from around 1942. These children were the fourth generation of Kleinos to live on this farm. Their father was Melvin Kleino. (Photograph courtesy of Armin "Duane" Kleino.)

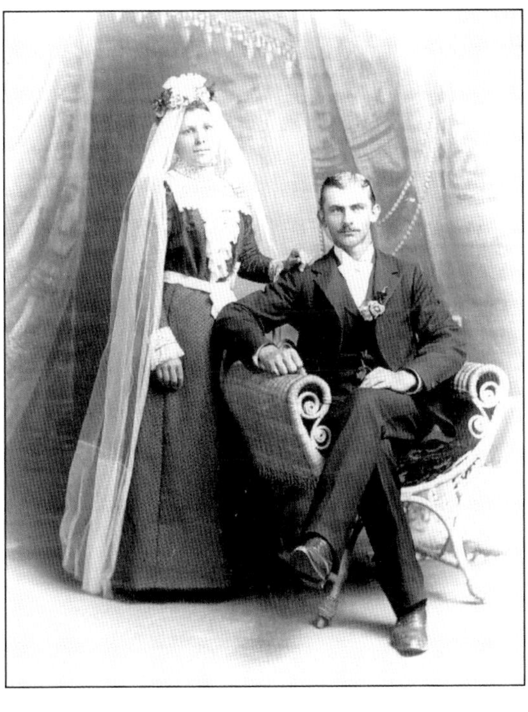

THE JOHN AND LOUISE ARFT WEDDING. John, the son of Sterling Township farmers John and Mary Arft, is shown here in a Novess Studio portrait upon his wedding to Louise in 1898. The Arft family came from Germany in 1840 and settled on Clinton River Road. After John and Louise's marriage, they lived for a few years with his parents. They then moved to Pontiac, Michigan, and raised their children Carl, Clarence, Harold, and Linda. John worked as a carpenter in the auto plants and later worked in the home-building trades. (Photograph courtesy of Armin "Duane" Kleino.)

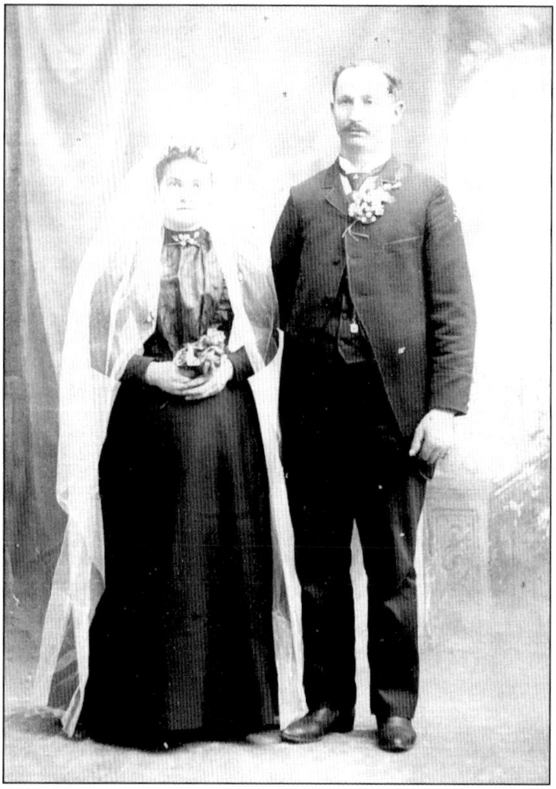

THE ARFT-SCHULDT WEDDING. Minnie Arft and Charles M. Schuldt are seen in this wedding portrait taken at the Baron Studio on Monroe Avenue in Detroit in November 1897. Charles came to America as a young boy from Prussia (Germany), and Minnie may have come from the Arft family of Warren, Michigan. The couple had a dairy farm on Clinton River Road, south of 19 Mile Road, and raised three children there. (Photograph courtesy of Armin "Duane" Kleino.)

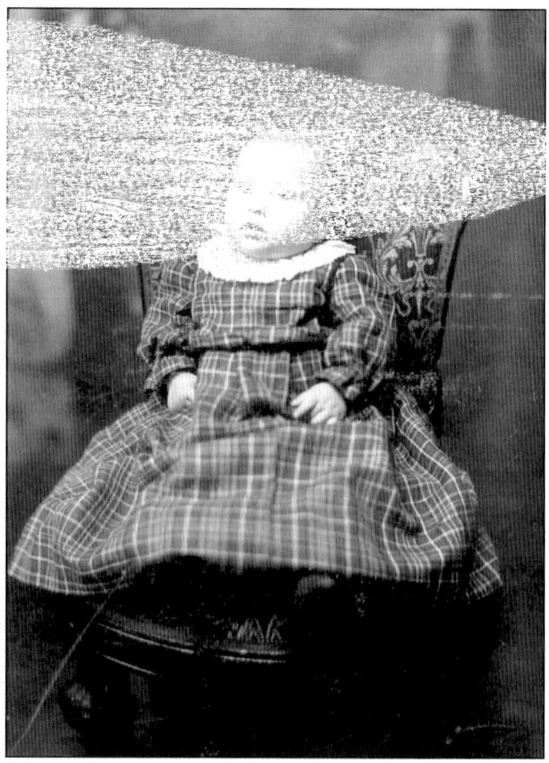

BABY ALBERT SCHULDT. Albert Schuldt was the first child of Minnie and Charles Schuldt of Clinton River Road. Here, he has his portrait taken in Rochester, Michigan by E. N. Auten, photographer, around 1899, coinciding with the short time the young family was farming in Avon Township. Young Albert wears a dress for this portrait, as was the custom at the time. Very young children, whether a boy or a girl, usually wore a dress-type garment. (Photograph courtesy of Armin "Duane" Kleino.)

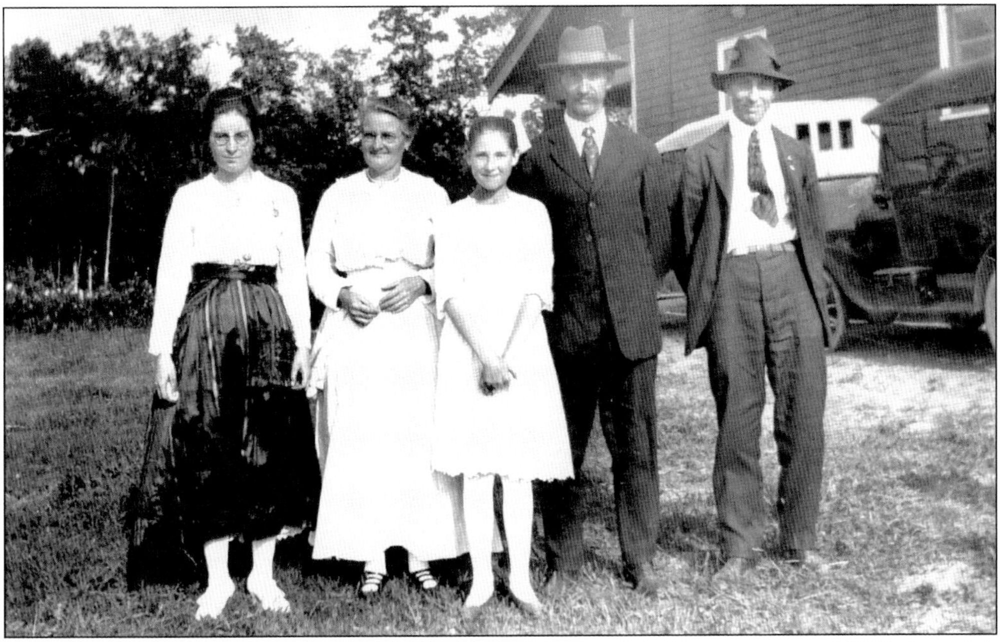

THE SCHULDT FAMILY. The family of Charles and Minnie Schuldt poses around 1920. From left to right are Meta Schuldt (Schoenberg), Minnie Arft Schuldt, Lenora Schuldt (Witt), Charles Schuldt, and Albert Schuldt. Note the early automobiles parked nearby.

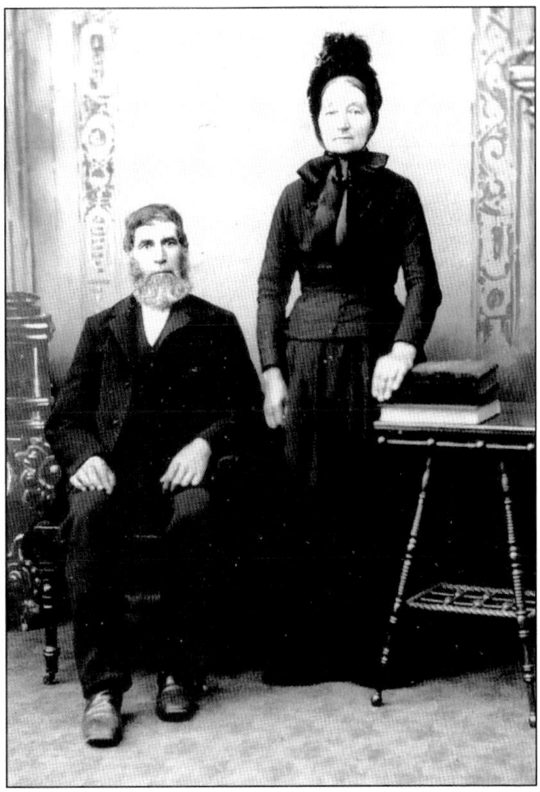

FRED AND FRIEDERICKA KARR. After Friedericka's first husband, John Doebler, died, leaving her with two small children, August and baby John, she married neighbor Fred Karr. Two more children, Bertha and Louise, had been born by 1869, when they left Germany and came to America and settled in the Schoenherr and Hall Road area of Sterling Township. By 1885, they had built a log cabin home on 19 Mile Road. This portrait of the couple was taken by the Novess Studio in Mount Clemens around 1890. (Photograph courtesy of Wallace Doebler.)

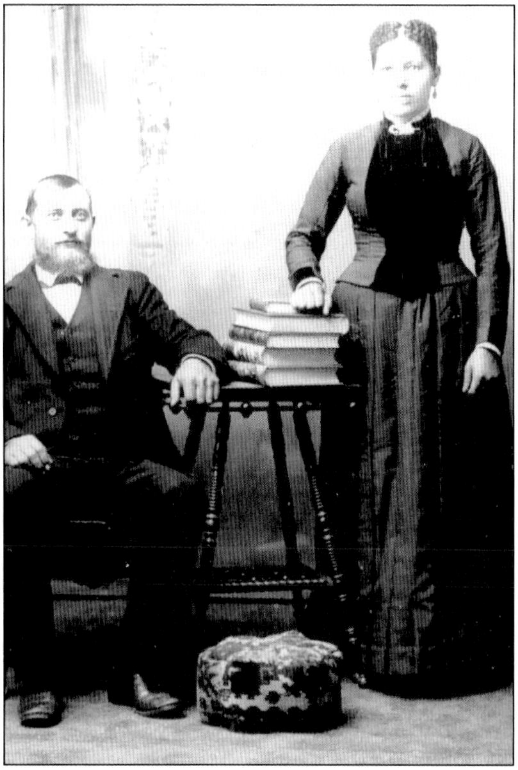

JOHN AND MARTHA DOEBLER. The Novess Studio in Mount Clemens takes the credit for yet another portrait of Sterling Township residents, this one around 1890. Pictured are John Doebler and his wife, Martha Schulz Doebler. Both born in Germany, they met in Michigan, married, and raised their family on a 40-acre Canal Road farm, later increased to almost 100 acres. Their children were Agnes, Ada, Herbert, and Reno. Sadly, baby Reno lived only a few months. The Doeblers were very successful general farmers, having a route in Detroit to sell their excess cabbage, potatoes, eggs, and chickens. (Photograph courtesy of Wallace Doebler.)

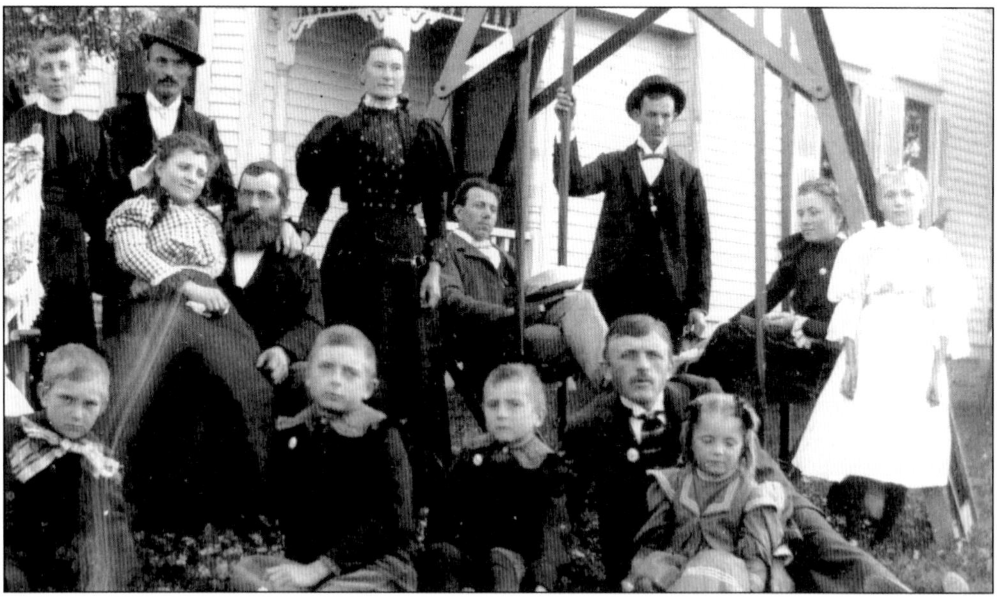

THE DOEBLER AND SCHULZ FAMILIES. A wooden swing in the front yard of the Doebler home on Canal Road provides the gathering point for this *c.* 1904 photograph of the Doebler and Schulz families. From left to right are the following: (first row) Herbert Doebler, Roland Schulz, Edgar Schulz, Arthur Schulz, and Bernice Schulz; (second row) Martha Doebler, Alma Schulz, Carl Daus, Alice Schulz, John Doebler, Fredericka Karr, unidentified, unidentified, Elda Schulz, and Anna Schulz. (Photograph courtesy of Wallace Doebler.)

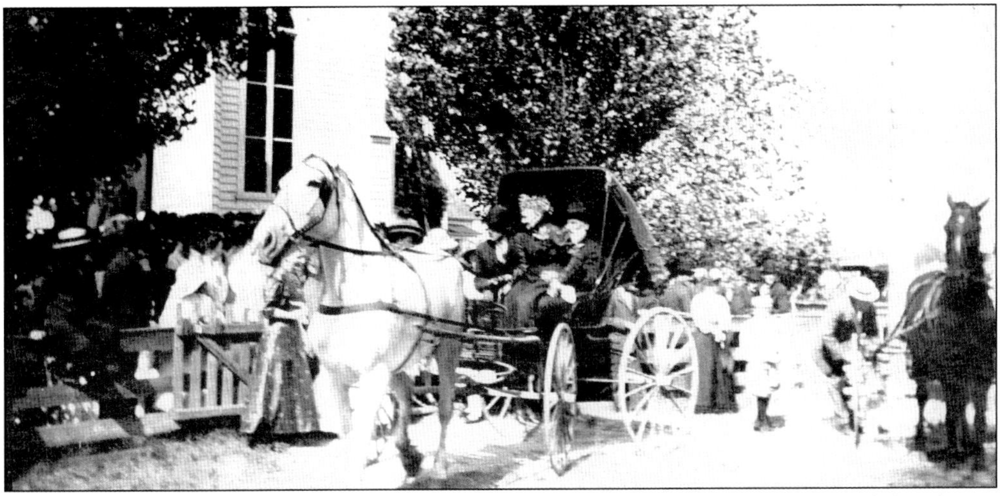

Frank and Friedricka Schulz. Ferdinand (Frank) Schulz and Friedricka (Ricky) Lehman Schulz leave St. Paul Lutheran Church in a buggy after having had a ceremony honoring their 50th wedding anniversary, a rarity for a married couple to both live that long. They were born and married in Germany and moved into a log cabin on Schoenherr Road north of Canal Road in 1879, where they raised six children. The anniversary celebration occurred in 1910, and the church was filled with family and friends. (Photograph courtesy of Wallace Doebler.)

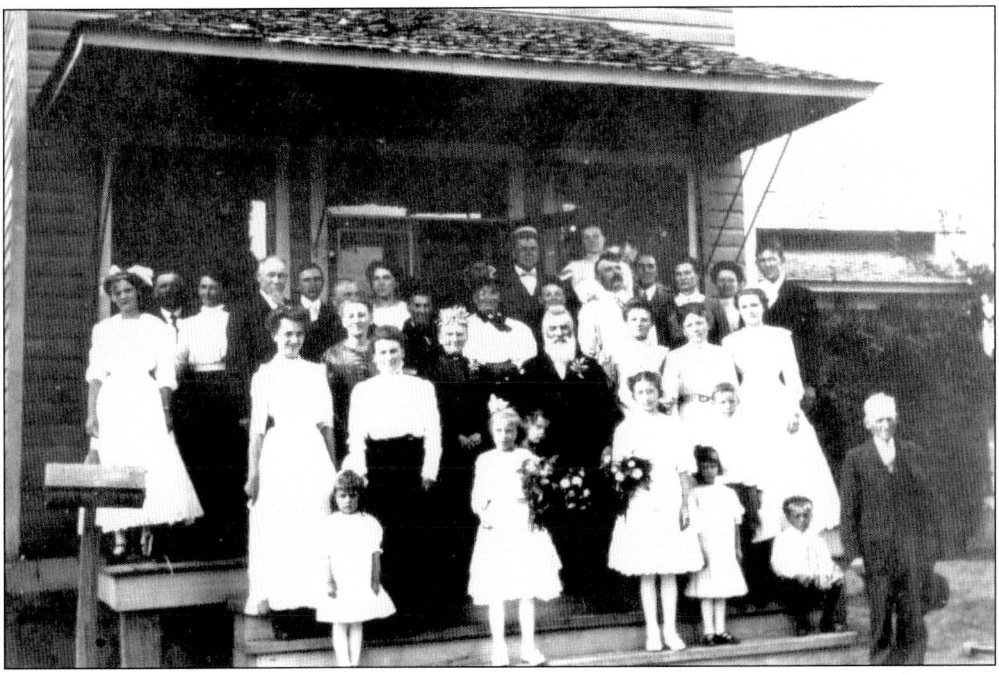

Anniversary Party. The family gathers at the Schulz home to continue the party honoring Frank and Ricky Schulz on their 50th wedding anniversary. This house, as pictured in 1910, was built in the 1880s on Canal Road east of Saal Road. The front part was a store, and the back had a blacksmith shop. Ricky, pictured wearing a wedding wreath, and Frank, with a white beard, enjoy the gathering that included a chicken dinner with all the trimmings, and a shivaree, complete with dynamite and beer. A good time was had by all. (Photograph courtesy of Wallace Doebler.)

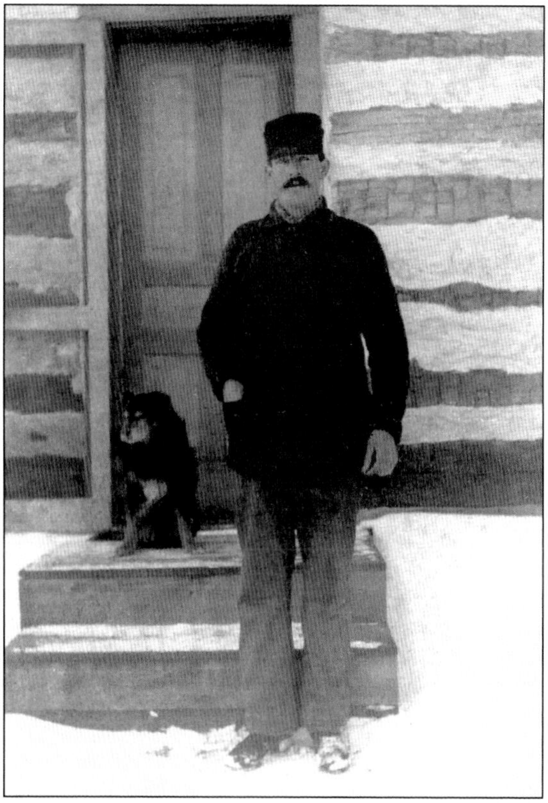

Snowy Day at the Faust Log Cabin. William W. Faust, son of Charles and Sophie Faust, poses with his dog at the front door to the family log cabin around 1900. The home, located on 19 Mile Road west of Schoenherr Road, was built in 1873 by his father, Charles Faust. The home still stands and is located in front of Browning Elementary School.

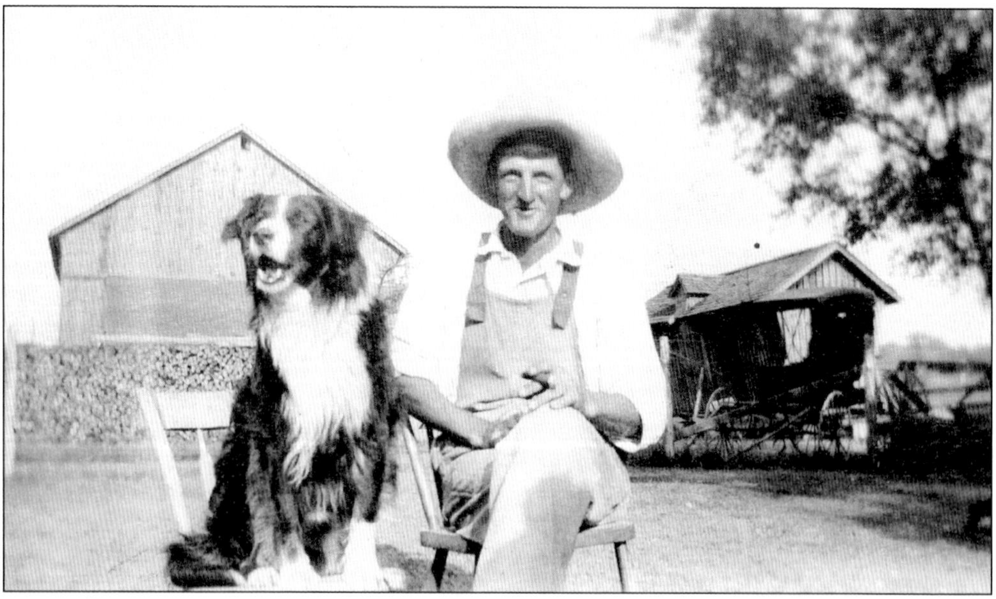

Man's Best Friend. Pictured around 1910 are Albert "Mike" Faust and his dog Shep, comfortably seated in their farmyard on 19 Mile Road east of Clinton River Road. Mike never married and lived on the farm alone for about 30 years. Notice the buggy in the background, waiting for the Saturday night trip into town, and the cigar in Mike's hand, a common accessory for German farmers. (Photograph courtesy of Barbara Faust Counsell.)

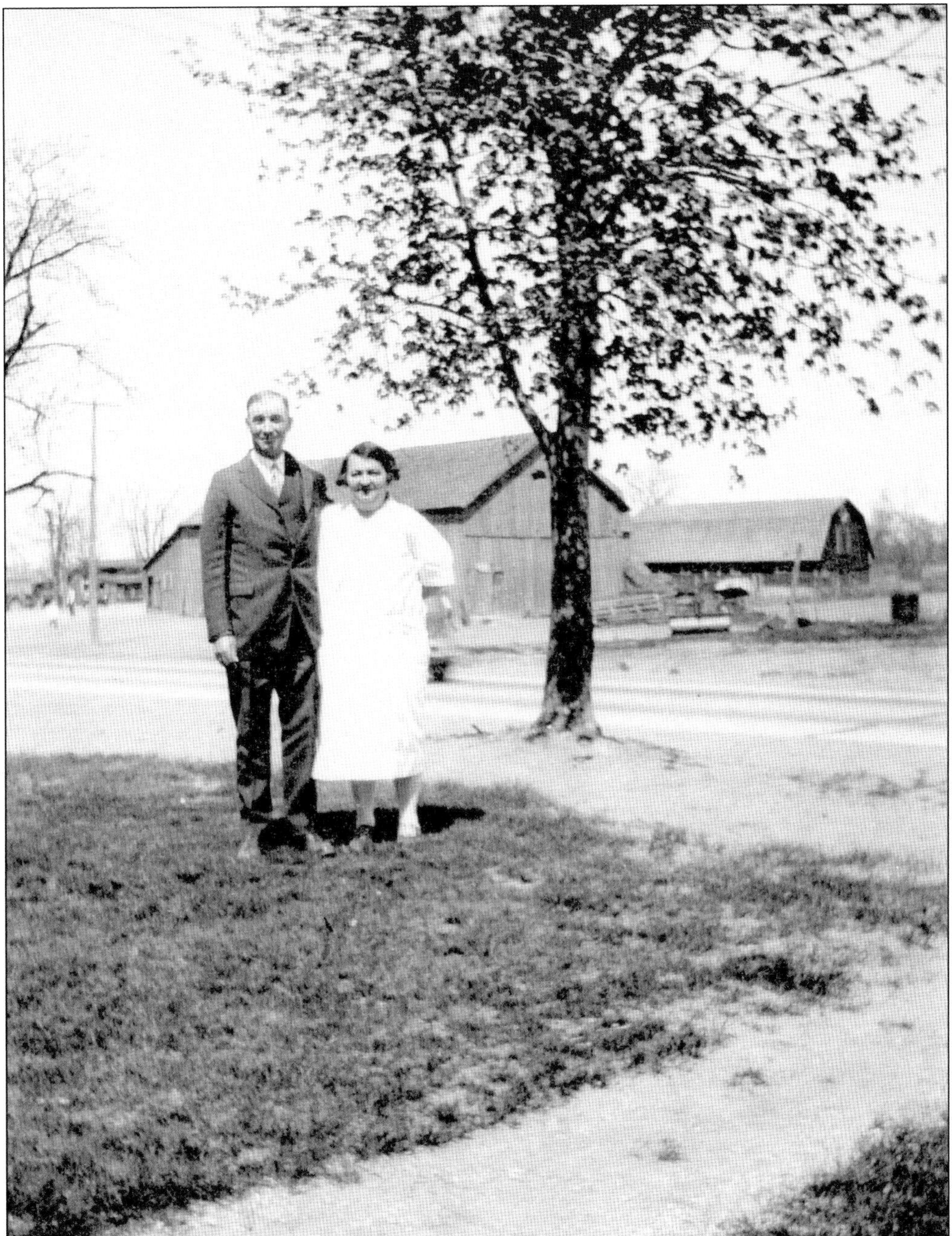

WILLIAM AND BERTHA LIEBERENZ. The Lieberenz 80-acre farm was on the southwest corner of 17 Mile Road and Van Dyke, sharing the property with the Plumbrook School, for which the family donated land. William and Bertha Beier Lieberenz had three children and did a little bit of everything. They were both very active in the community, William being township supervisor, township clerk, and an officer for the Sterling School District No. 2. He was a very "modern" farmer, attended the Detroit Business Institute, and always liked to have the newest, most modern conveniences. Their large home on Van Dyke was very up to date. In this 1927 photograph, the couple stands in their front yard, with Van Dyke Avenue behind them.

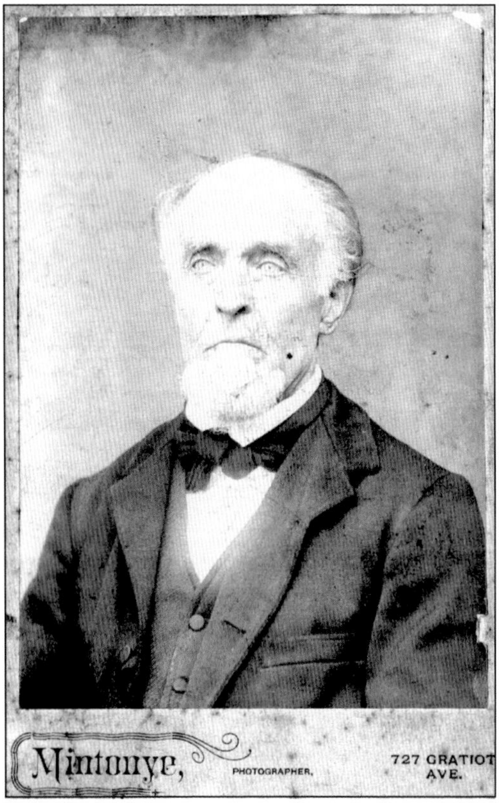

PHILLIP BOWER. Phillip Bower, his wife Catherine, and their two small sons, George and Lenhart (or Leonard), came from Prussia around 1859, living in Warren Township for a time before settling in Sterling Township on a farm on 16 Mile Road between Mound and Ryan Roads. The family built a log cabin there, and by 1875 another, more permanent home was added. That home still stands. The couple raised an additional seven children on their family farm: Frederick, Michael, Lizzie, Charles, John, Lambert, and Mary. This portrait, by a Mount Clemens photographer, was probably taken about 1880.

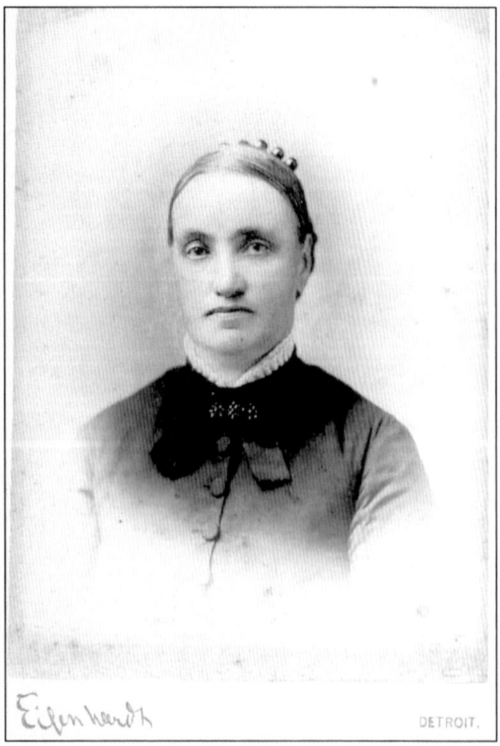

CATHERINE SCHUMMEL BOWER. Married to Phillip Bower, Catherine came with her husband from Prussia with an apparent stay in Canada for a few years before eventually settling in Sterling Township on 16 Mile Road, where they raised nine children. This *c.* 1880 portrait was taken by Eisenhardt at his Detroit studio. (Photograph courtesy of Rose Bower Hacker.)

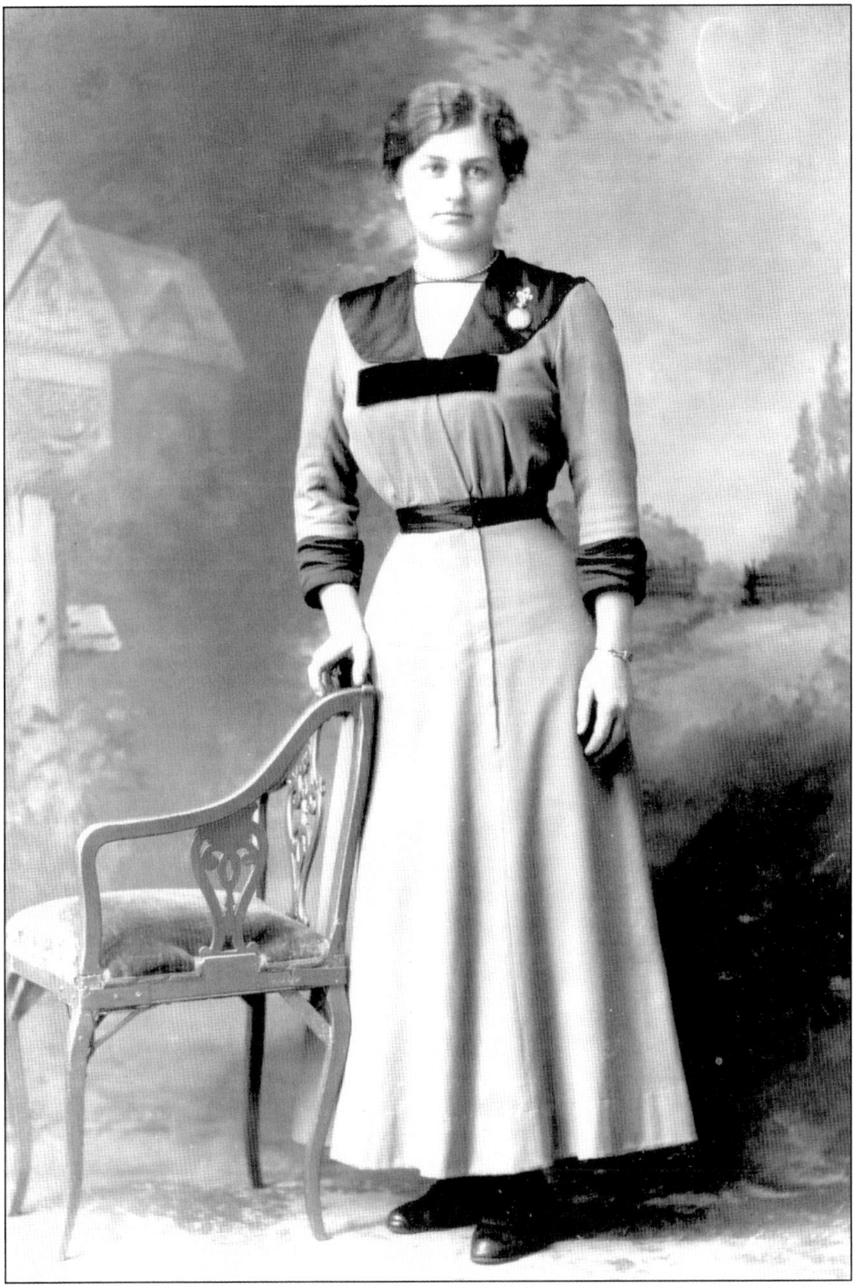

Rose Bower Hacker. Rose Hacker was born on the farm of her father, Michael Bower, on the northwest corner of 17 Mile and Mound Roads. Her mother died when she was three. Later, she attended the Plumbrook School. She met and married Christopher Hacker (the 8th of the 10 Hacker boys) and bought the 1875 house built by her grandfather, Phillip Bower, on 16 Mile Road between Mound and Ryan Roads. There she raised their three children—Marvin, Norma, and Shirley. At the age of 92, Rose became well known when the 1986 widening of 16 Mile Road threatened the old farmhouse she still lived in. She and community activists were finally able to get permission to save the house by moving it to a nearby subdivision, where it still stands today. (Photograph courtesy of Rose Bower Hacker.)

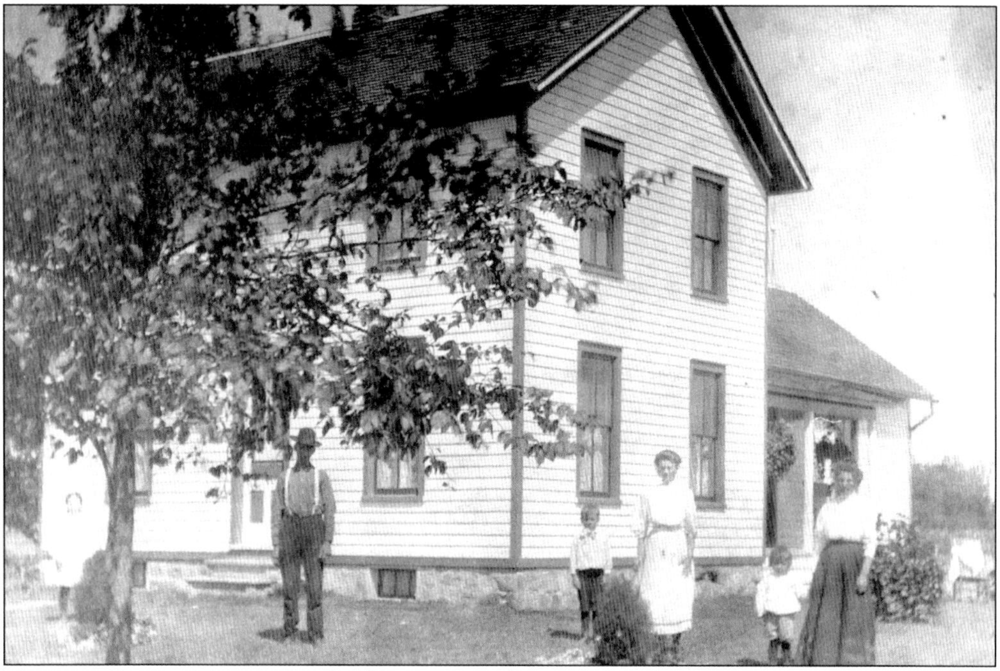

MICHAEL BOWER HOUSE. Michael Bower was the son of Phillip and Catherine Bower, whose farm was on 16 Mile Road. Michael and his first wife built this home on 17 Mile Road just west of Mound Road and were parents to Louis and Rose. Michael's wife died, and he married Catherine, with whom he had three more children—Bertha, Albert, and Edwin. Pictured around 1910 are, from left to right, Bertha, Michael, Albert, Rose, Edwin, and Catherine. (Photograph courtesy of Rose Bower Hacker.)

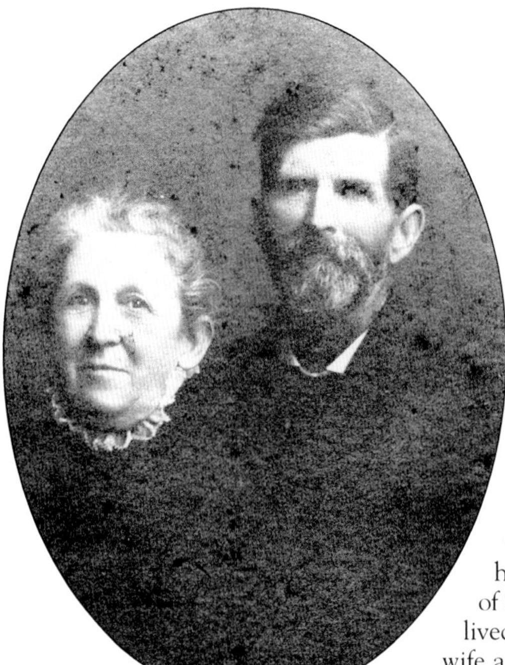

LOUISE AND WINFIELD DRAKE. Winfield Scott Drake was born in a log cabin on the Drake farm on Clinton River Road in 1849. His relatives have lived in the area since 1832. Winfield married Louisa (Louise) Stead, from another Sterling Township pioneer family, in 1874 and raised their family on the River Road near Kleino Road. This photograph of the couple was taken around 1900. Winfield held numerous township offices and was director of Sterling School No. 3 (Maple Grove). Winfield lived to be 92 years old and was buried with his wife at Edgerton Cemetery. (Photograph courtesy of Merle Drake Peters.)

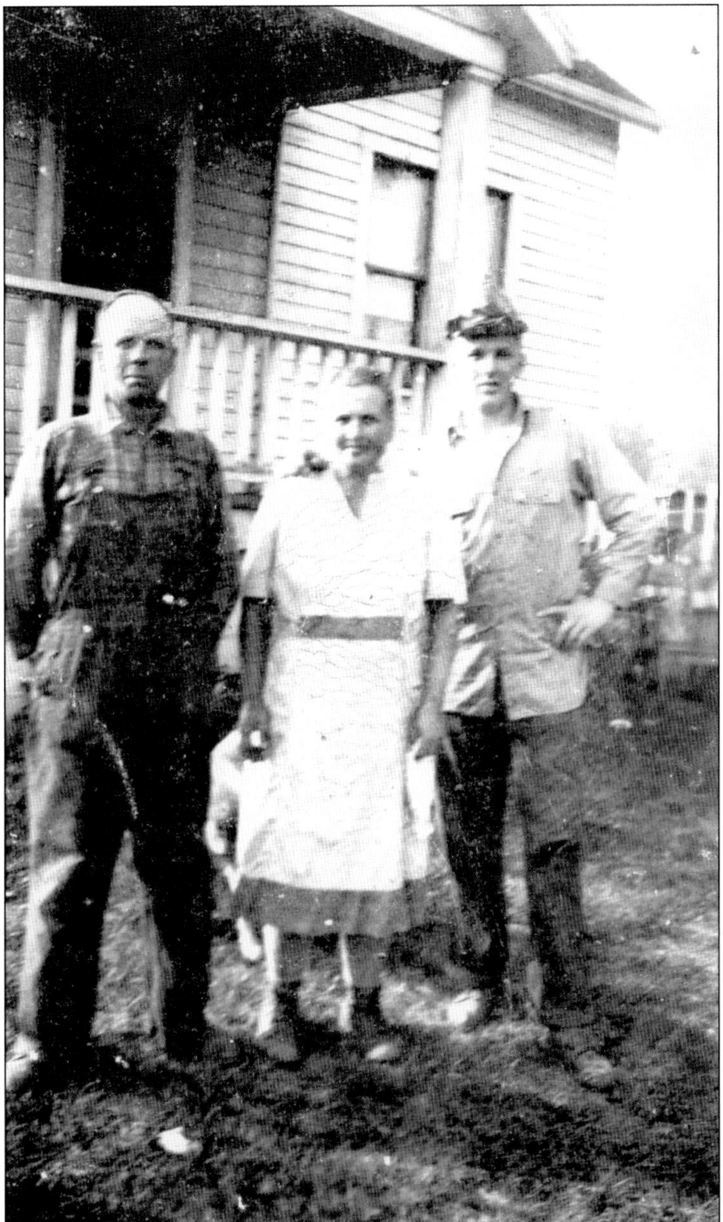

THE CALKA FAMILY. Andrew and Katherine Calka came from Poland and after some hard times eventually purchased a farm on Hayes Road in Clinton Township where St. Joseph Hospital is today. They raised five boys. Pictured c. 1944 are Andrew, Katherine, and their youngest son Bernard, or Barney. Barney and all his brothers were World War II veterans, Barney being an MP in the Philippines. Upon his return, he got married and had five children. Moving into Sterling Township, he started as a volunteer firefighter and ended up working for the department for 26 years, retiring as assistant fire chief in 1984. His lifetime volunteer efforts include creating the Michigan State Fireman's Memorial in Roscommon, Michigan, raising money for underprivileged fire departments across the nation, and work with the Sterling Heights Lions Club. (Photograph courtesy of Bernard Calka.)

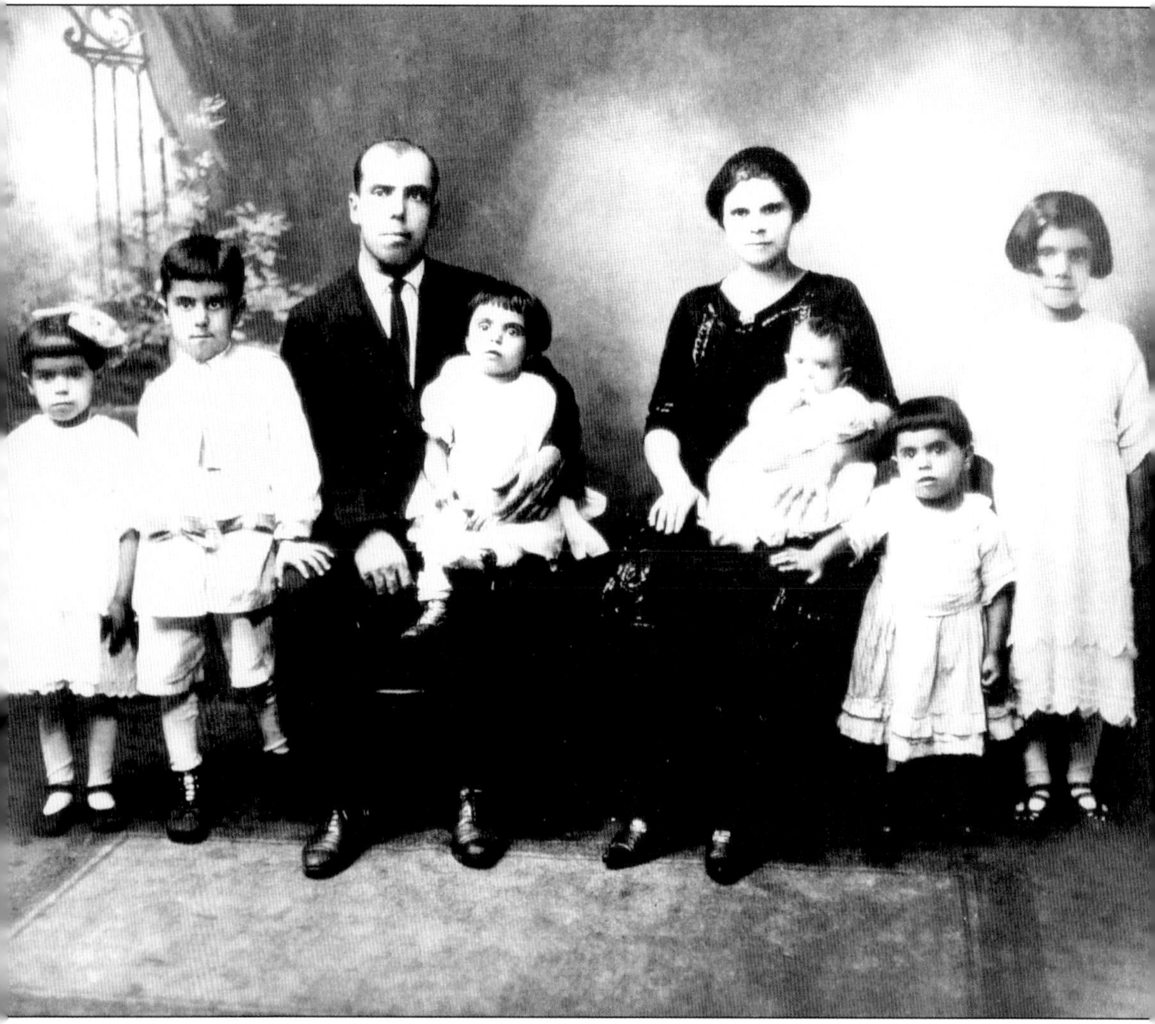

THE BACKUS FAMILY. Shown around 1922 are the beginnings of the large Emin and Eva Backus family. From left to right are Josephine, Anthony, father Emin (holding Nellie), mother Eva (holding Marie), Agnes, and Madeline. More children were born later—Joseph, Catherine, Peter, Louis, Eva, Margaret, and Paul. Emin came from Lebanon in the early 1900s, operated a business in Detroit, and came to Sterling Township around 1945. The family had a small farm on 17 Mile Road west of Van Dyke Avenue and, in the 1960s, opened a car wash that still operates today. Joe and Paul Backus were on the township's first volunteer fire department. Paul was one of the first four full-time paid men and retired years later as a captain. The Lebanese Backus family represented the first wave of Middle Eastern immigrants to contribute to the area. (Photograph courtesy of the Backus family.)

THE WILBRETT FAMILY. Pictured around 1939 are, from left to right, Wilhelmina Juengel, her daughter Albertine Juengel Wilbrett, Myrna Kage (baby granddaughter of Albertine), and proud grandfather Albert Wilbrett. Albert had been a streetcar conductor in Detroit before coming to the southwest corner of Hall Road and Schoenherr Road to farm. He died in 1945 from an accidental fall from their hayloft. (Photograph courtesy of Cheryl Wilbrett Snay.)

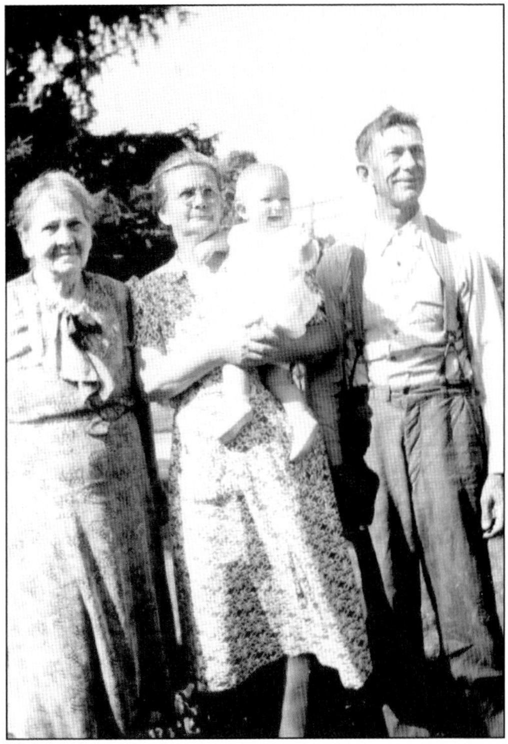

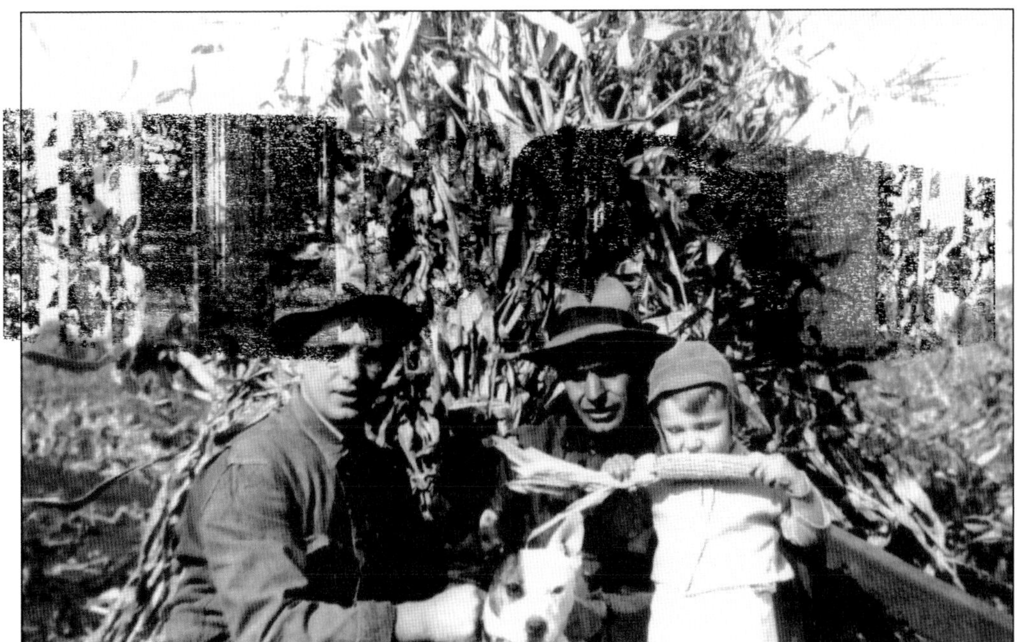

THE WILBRETT BOYS. Howard Wilbrett, his brother Arnold, Arnold's son David, and a watchful canine friend pose out in the cornfield in this 1945 photograph. The Wilbretts also grew rhubarb, strawberries, greens, tomatoes, and melons on their farm at the corner of Hall and Schoenherr Roads. The corn must have been especially tasty that year. (Photograph courtesy of Cheryl Wilbrett Snay.)

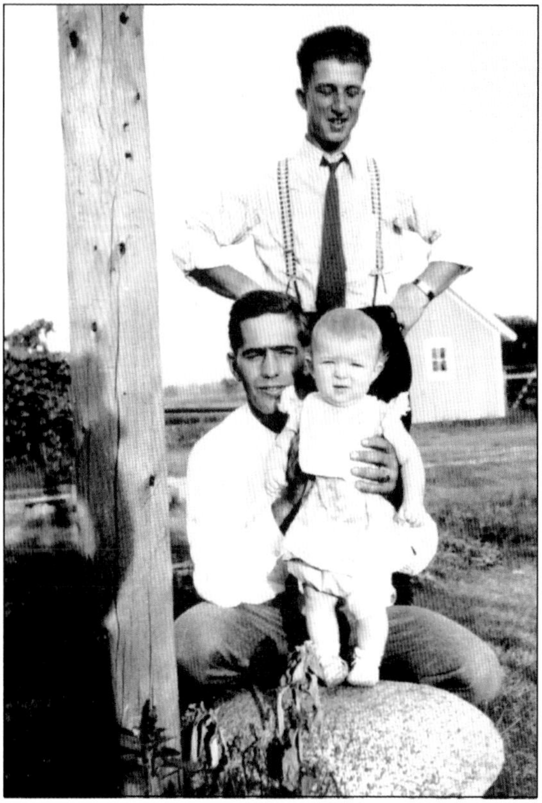

Little Myrna Kage. Baby Myrna Kage, held securely by her uncle Arnold Wilbrett, poses for this 1939 photograph. Her father, Marvin Kage, watches from behind. The Kage and Wilbrett farms were neighbors on Hall Road, west of Schoenherr Road, and their land was later developed for the Clinton Valley Mall. (Photograph courtesy of Cheryl Wilbrett Snay.)

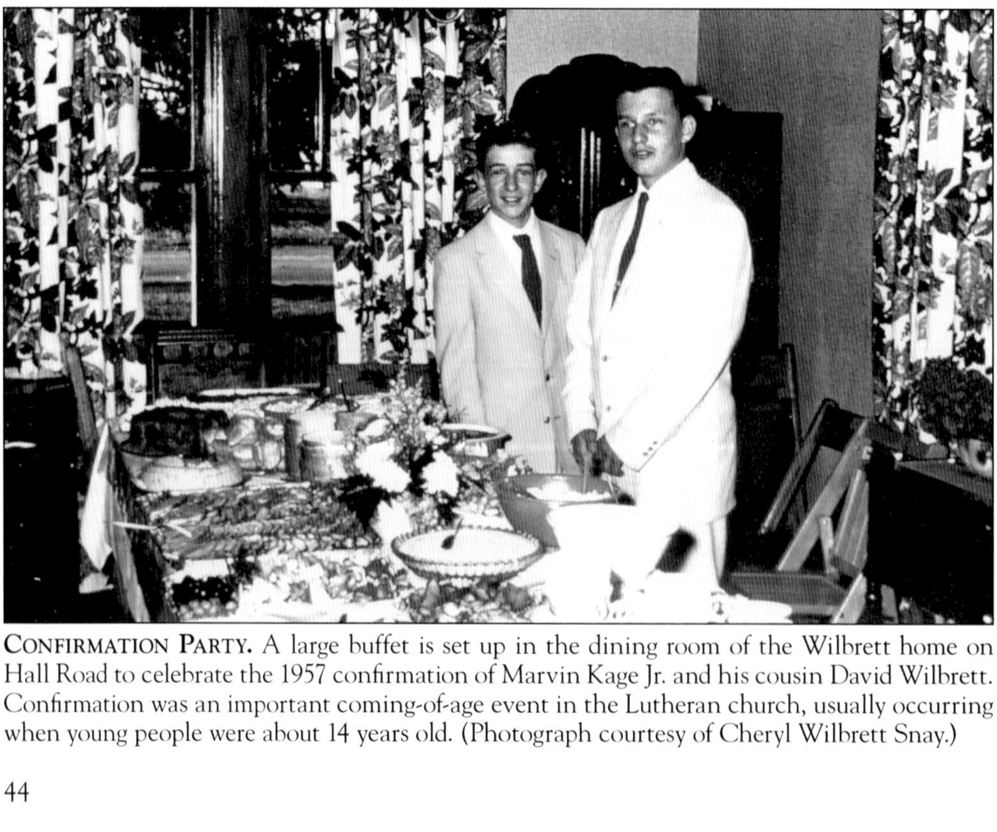

Confirmation Party. A large buffet is set up in the dining room of the Wilbrett home on Hall Road to celebrate the 1957 confirmation of Marvin Kage Jr. and his cousin David Wilbrett. Confirmation was an important coming-of-age event in the Lutheran church, usually occurring when young people were about 14 years old. (Photograph courtesy of Cheryl Wilbrett Snay.)

Two

FARMS

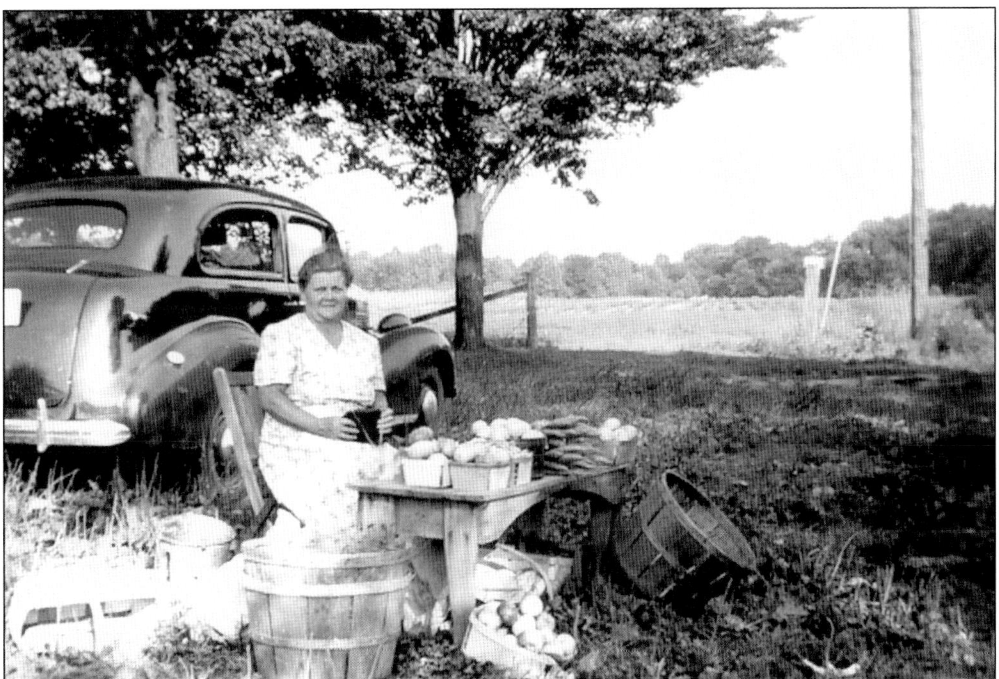

ROADSIDE STAND. Fresh apples and an assortment of vegetables are being offered for sale by Martha Kleino at her temporary stand around 1940, probably along either Kleino or Utica Roads near their farm. Beginning in the 1930s and 1940s, farmers realized money could be made by catering to the city dwellers out for a ride, who appreciated the special freshness of produce right off the farm. These little stands lined the major roads in Sterling Township until the farms got pushed away by development. Notice Martha's pocketbook on her lap, ready for business. (Photograph courtesy of Armin "Duane" Kleino.)

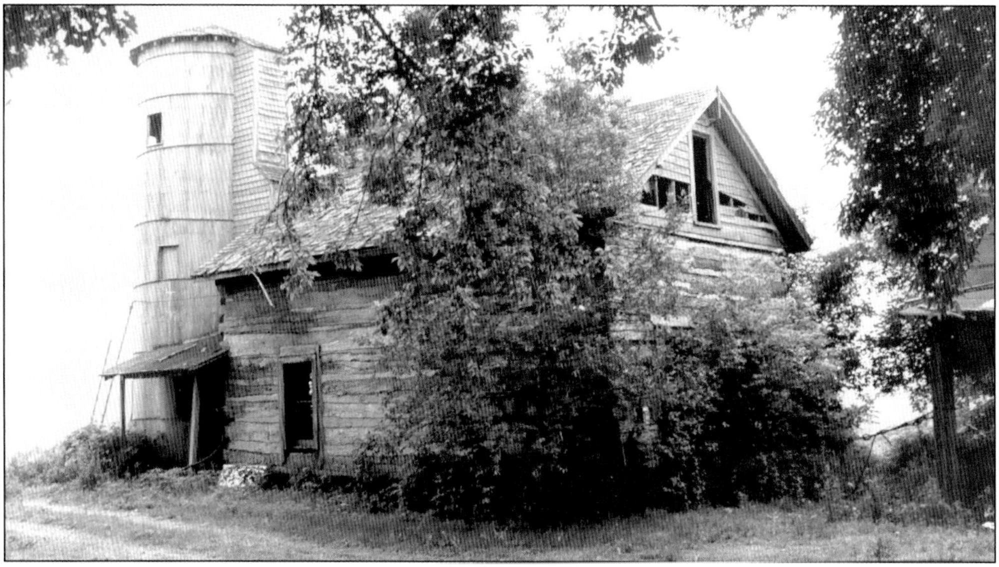

Maple Lane Log Cabin. This abandoned log home, pictured around 1970, was located on the east side of Maple Lane Road, just north of 14 Mile Road. It was believed to be one of the oldest homes still standing at the time. Not much is known for sure about the house. It may have been built around 1840 by the McInerney family. The Sterling Heights Historical Commission was formed for the purpose of trying to restore this building, but the home was burned by vandals just as efforts were beginning in 1971.

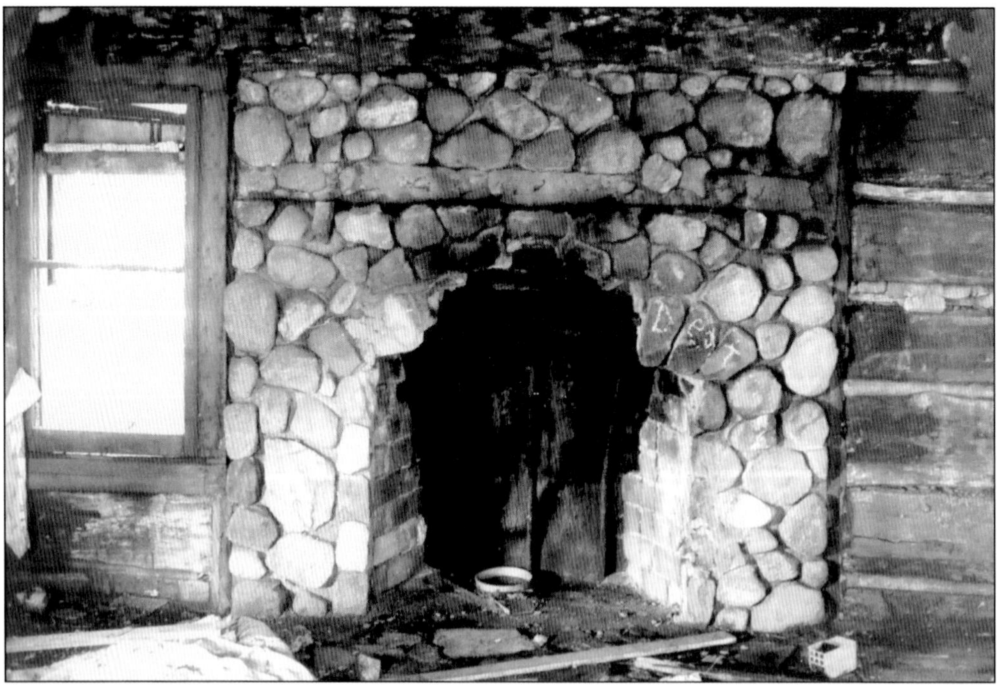

Maple Lane Fireplace. This interior view of the log cabin shows the disrepair caused by age, squatters, and vandals. Research done in the 1970s speculated the cabin may have been built by the French in the 1700s based on the style of construction, but this conclusion is unsubstantiated.

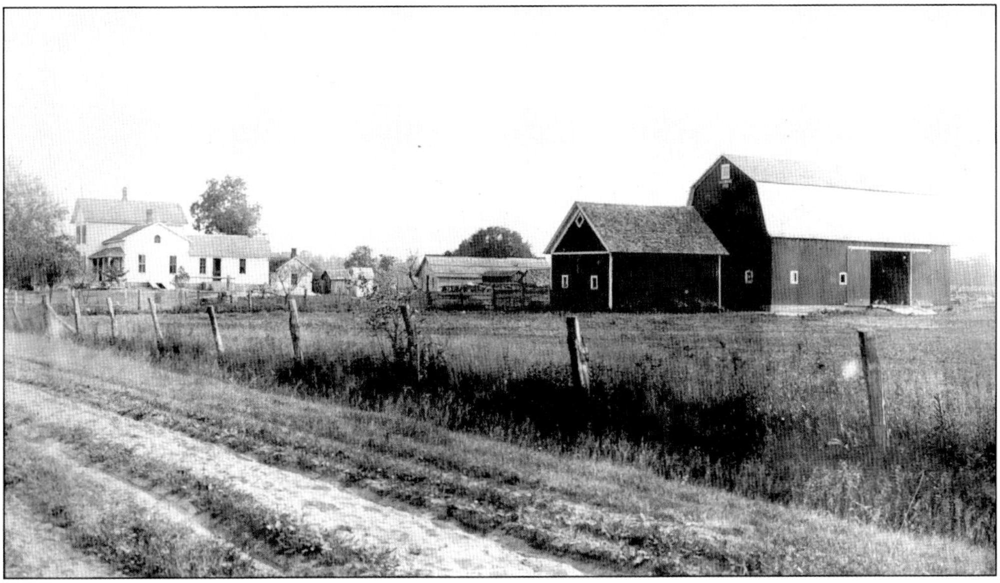

LEMBKE FARM. This 1914 view of John Lembke's centennial farm on Hayes Road between Clinton River Road and Stadler Road shows the poor condition of Hayes Road at the time, which was probably typical of most area roads. If you look closely, horse footprints can be seen in the center of the road.

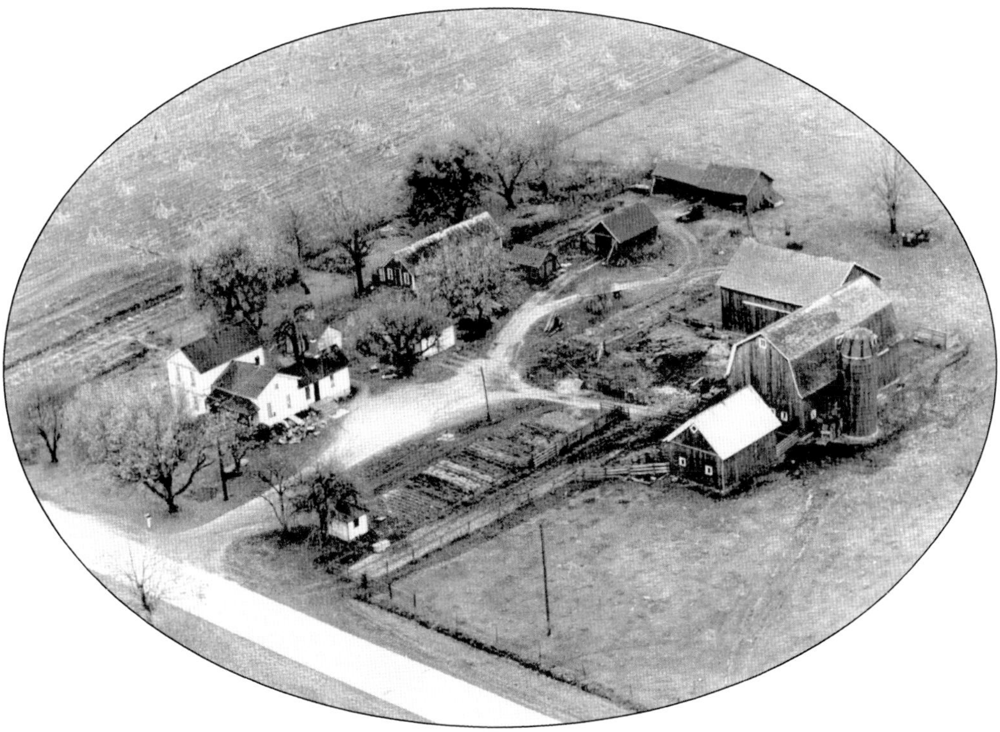

LEMBKE FARM 35 YEARS LATER. This c. 1950 view of the same location on Hayes Road shows the road paved with concrete. The aerial vantage point shows the layout of the 40-acre farm, with a small garden area in the center, the many outbuildings, and a portion of their fields showing the corn shocks from the previous year.

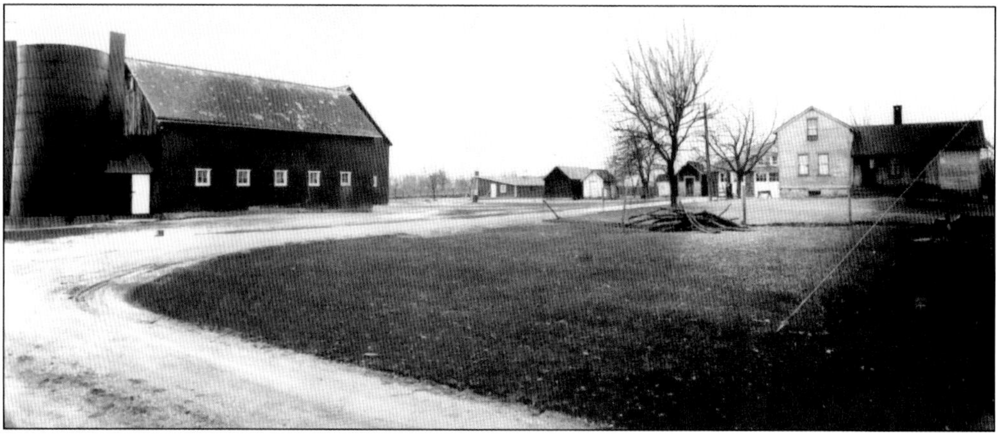

ERNEST PRUEHS FARM. Dodge Park Road was still a dirt road in 1931, as this photograph of the Pruehs dairy farm shows. The farm was on the southwest corner of Dodge Park Road and 16 Mile Road, along with additional property along the east side of Dodge Park Road. The farm had been in the family since 1873, when Ferdinand and Dora Pruehs first settled here. Ernest, their son, added a new brick house in 1939. (Photograph courtesy of the Ernest Pruehs family.)

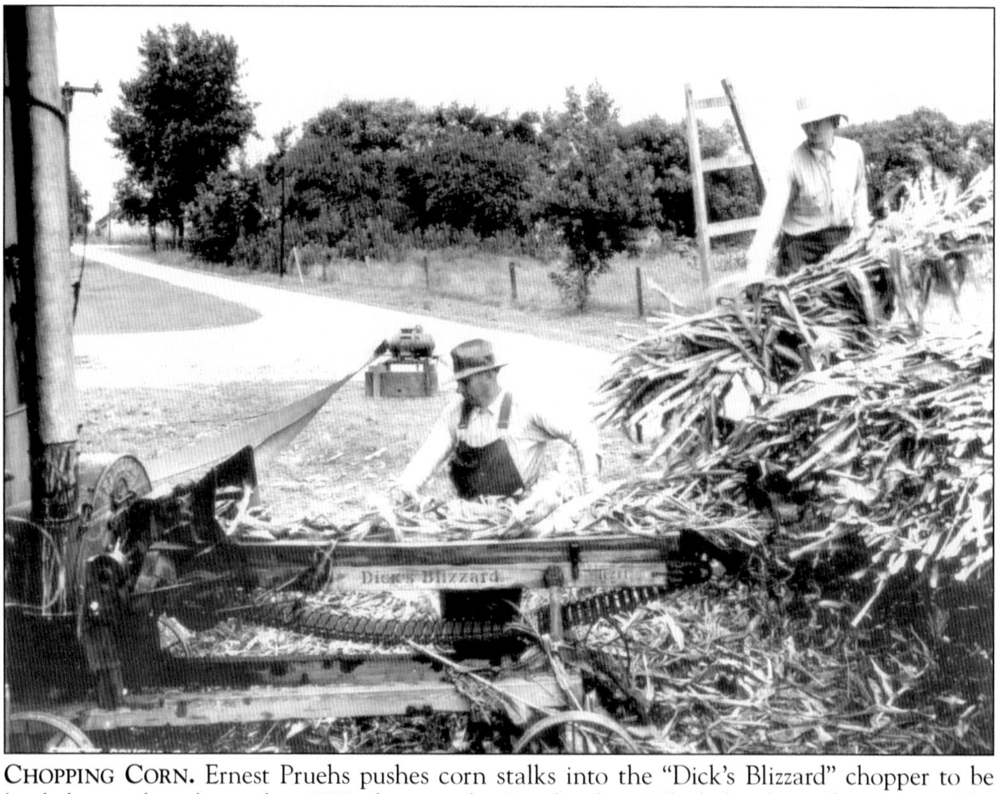

CHOPPING CORN. Ernest Pruehs pushes corn stalks into the "Dick's Blizzard" chopper to be loaded into the silo in this 1935 photograph. His daughter Ella helps from the wagon. The Pruehs dairy farm was on the southwest corner of Dodge Park Road and 16 Mile Road and was well known in the 1970s for the controversy caused by homeowners in the new subdivisions nearby who complained of the flies and odors that came along with living near cows. The farm was a centennial farm, meaning the family had owned that land for 100 years or more. They eventually sold the property and moved their farming operation farther north in the county.

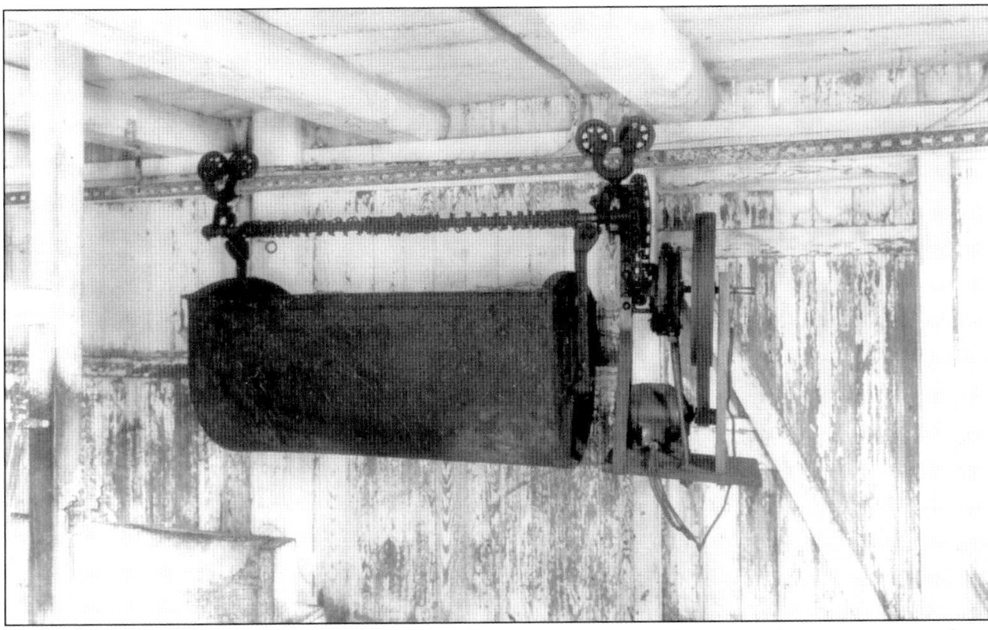

LITTER CARRIER. In 1932, this labor-saving device was mounted on a track on an interior barn wall, enabling the farmer (in this case, the Ernest Pruehs family) to shovel used litter and manure from livestock into a container, which was sent down the track and dumped in another area. Ernest Pruehs ran this one on an electric motor. (Photograph courtesy of the Ernest Pruehs family.)

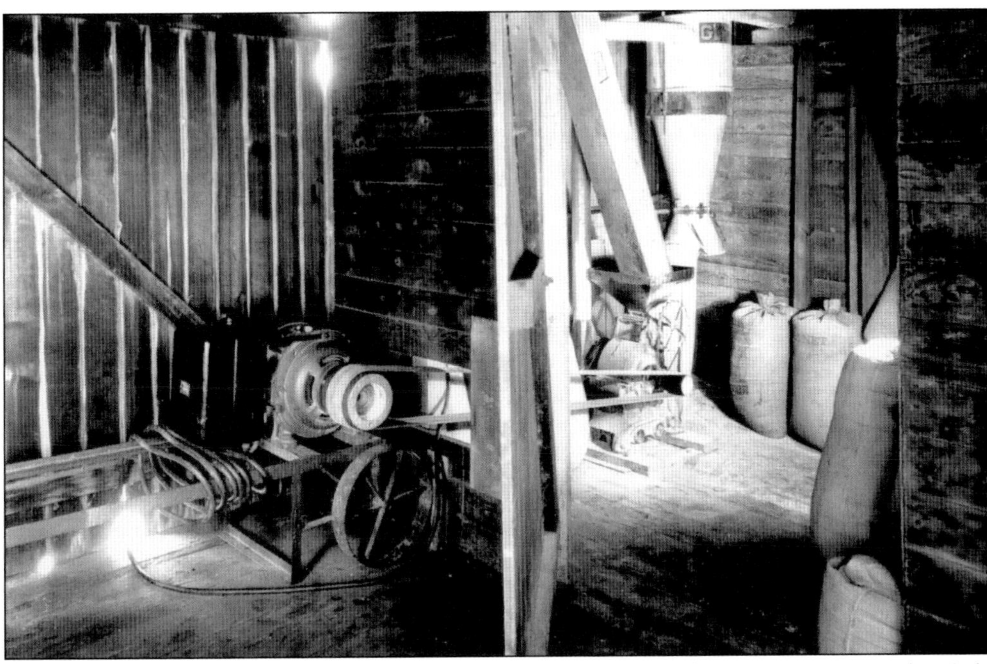

GEHL MILL. Ernest Pruehs used his seven-and-a-half-horsepower electric motor to run this Gehl grain mill, pictured in 1932. The mill is the white vertical unit on the right. His portable motor, on wheels, is at the left. The dairy farm was on Dodge Park Road at 16 Mile Road. (Photograph courtesy of the Ernest Pruehs family.)

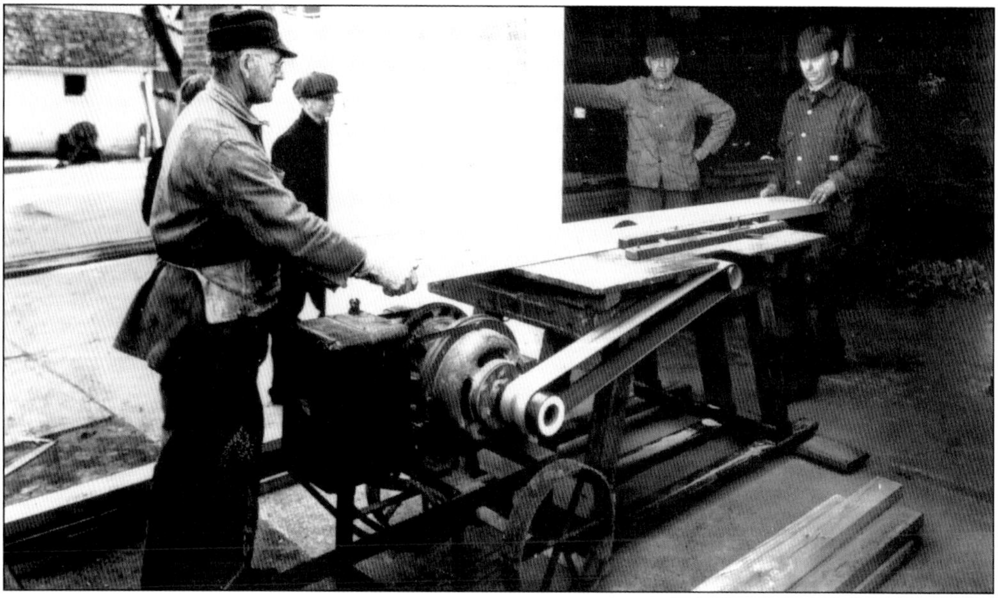

CIRCULAR SAW. The men of the Pruehs family use their electric table saw outside the garage in 1938. A portable electric motor was used to run this and other equipment on their farm. Adults pictured are brothers Ernest (left), Louis (center), and Fred. The two boys watching in the background are Ernest's sons, Victor and Norman. The farm was located on the southwest corner of Dodge Park Road and 16 Mile Road. (Photograph courtesy of the Ernest Pruehs family.)

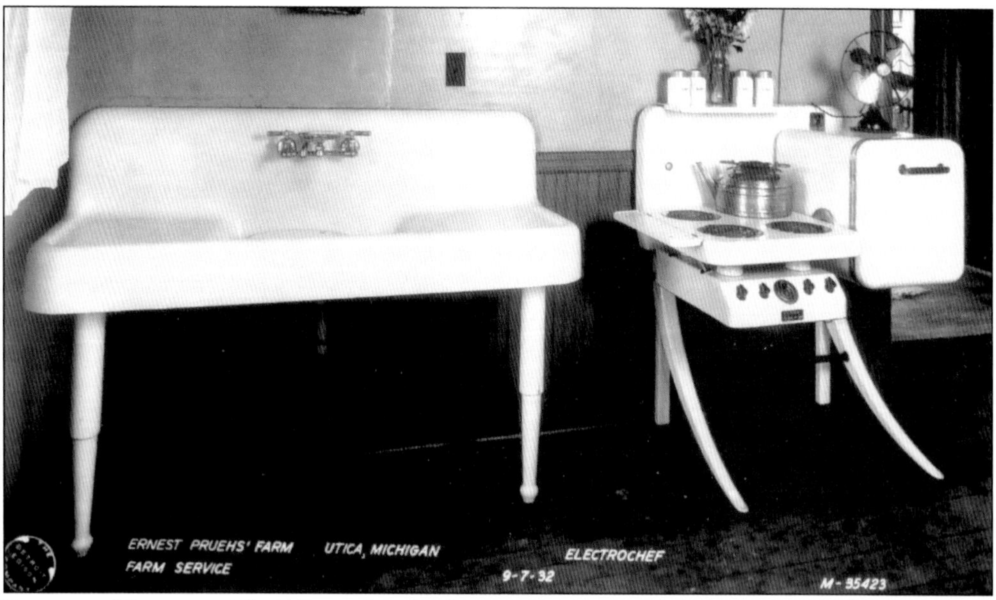

ELECTRIC KITCHEN. The Ernest Pruehs farm was an example of what could be done with electricity on the farm in 1932. Pictured is their kitchen, complete with electric lights, clock, fan, and the ultramodern Electro Chef stove and oven. The *Utica Sentinel* advertised this stove for sale at $105 installed, so it was not something the average farm family had. Electric lines were just becoming available (installation at the farmer's expense), and a selling point for electricity in the home was how clean it was compared to other methods. (Photograph courtesy of the Ernest Pruehs family.)

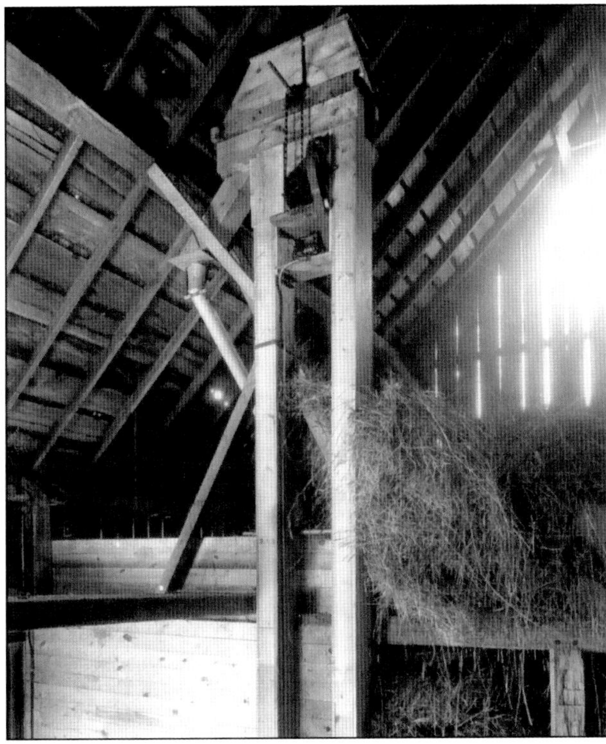

GRAIN ELEVATOR. This motorized bucket-type grain elevator, pictured in 1932, was used at the Ernest Pruehs farm on Dodge Park Road. Such elevators were used to move oats and other small grains into overhead storage areas. Most of the Pruehs family's farm conveniences operated on electricity. (Photograph courtesy of the Ernest Pruehs family.)

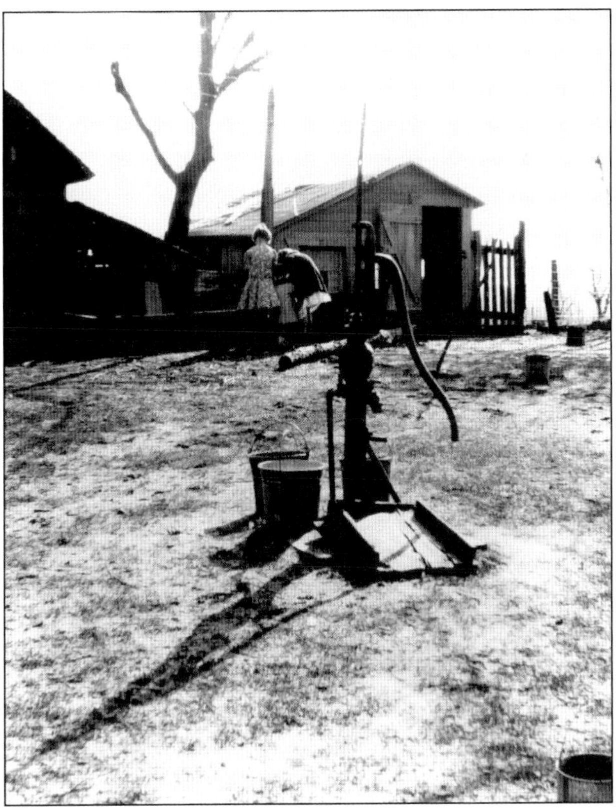

THE OLD PUMP. The water pump was an important part of life for the farmers before "city water" started becoming available in the 1960s, and even then they usually had to pay extra to be hooked up. Families depended on their wells and cisterns for their household needs and for farming operations, such as washing off produce to sell and watering their livestock. This pump, seen around 1930, was on the Ahrens farm on Clinton River Road. (Photograph courtesy of Eleanor Ahrens.)

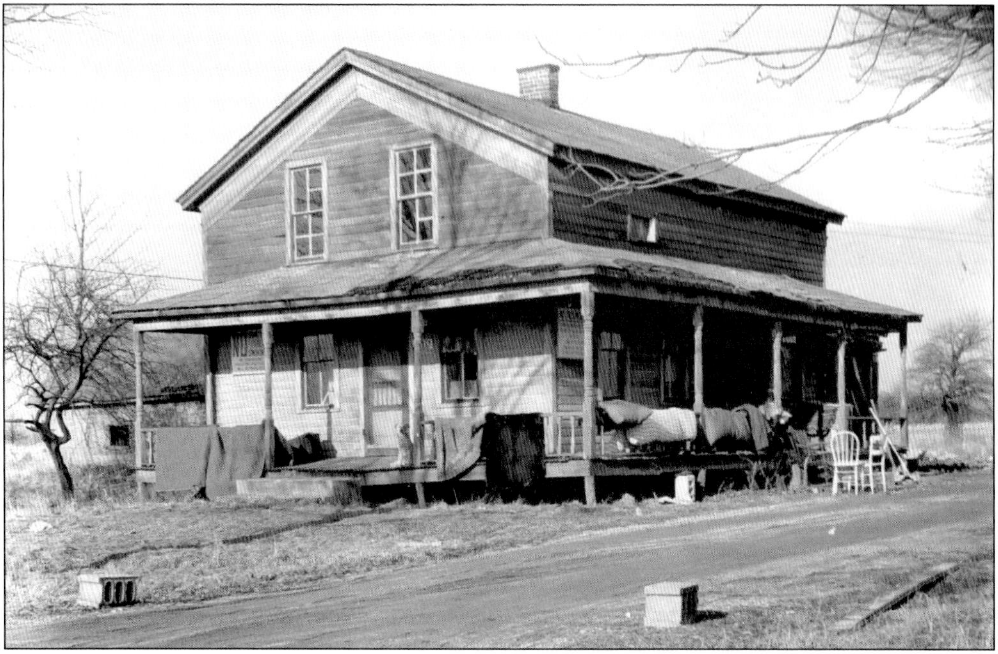

MOVING DAY. The Trimakas family moved into this weathered farmhouse in March 1952 and found chickens living on the second floor. The family dog, Maury, sits on the front porch along with quilts set to air out. The family rented the farm, located on Dequindre Road near current Fox Hill Drive, from Robert and Dora Hesse of Warren in order to work the 100-acre Christmas tree farm. The Trimakas family fixed this home up nicely and lived here until the subdivisions came in 1969. (Photograph courtesy of Kristen Trimakas.)

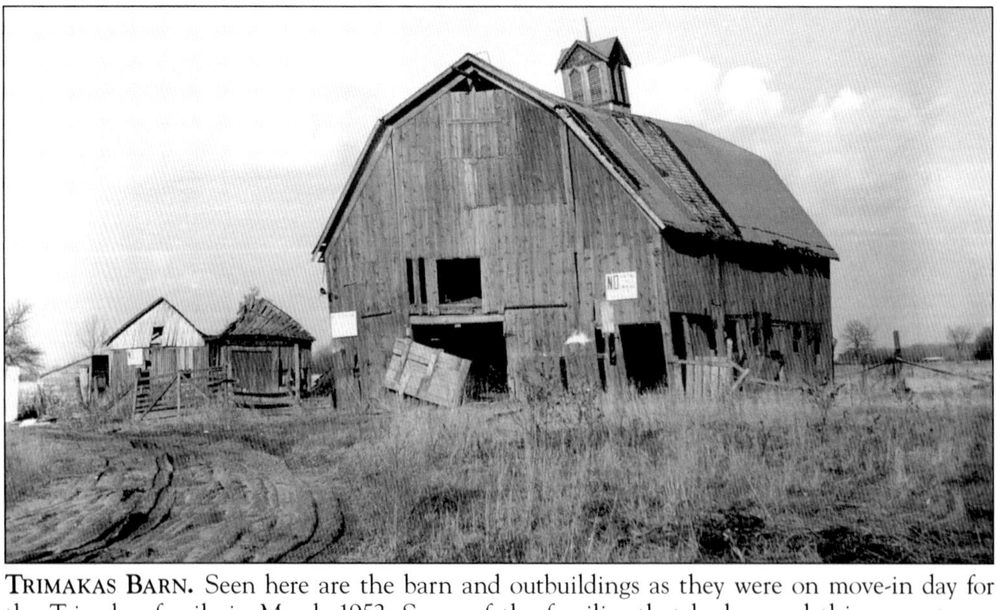

TRIMAKAS BARN. Seen here are the barn and outbuildings as they were on move-in day for the Trimakas family in March 1952. Some of the families that had owned this property on Dequindre Road north of 16 Mile Road over the years include King, Fernald, Curtis, and Hesse. At one point, it was a 160-acre farm. This barn, with its detailed cupola, must have been quite a handsome structure at one time. (Photograph courtesy of Kristen Trimakas.)

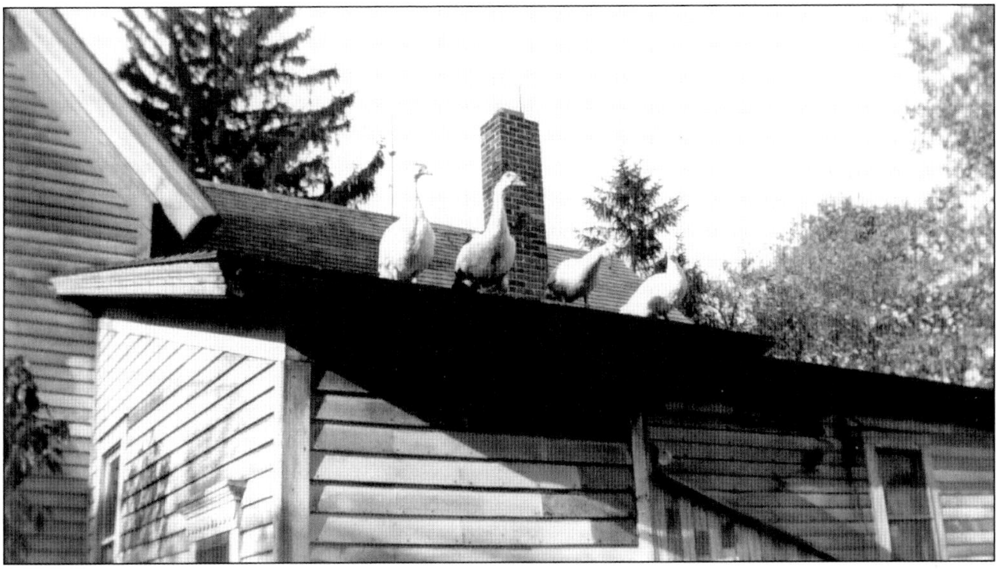

MUSCOVY DUCKS. These four Muscovy ducks have found a good vantage point, or maybe a safe haven, on the roof of the Ahrens house on Clinton River Road in this *c.* 1935 photograph. Muscovy ducks were popular on farms, as they were easy to take care of and good to eat. Some were kept as pets. (Photograph courtesy of Eleanor Ahrens.)

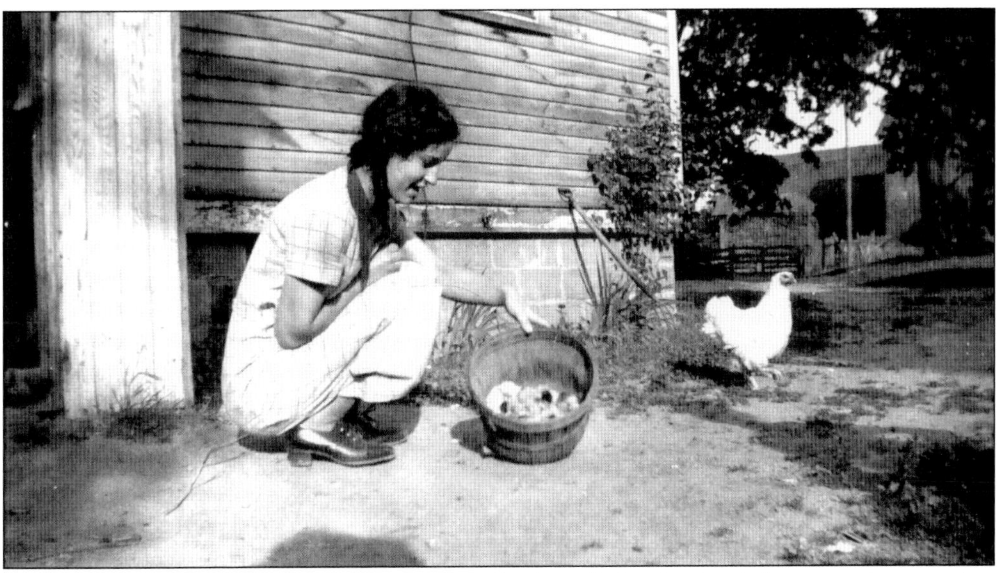

RUTH AHRENS. Young Ruth Ahrens displays a bushel of baby chicks while mother hen watches nearby in this 1938 photograph. Ruth was the daughter of Otto and Eleanor Ahrens, whose family dairy farm was on Clinton River Road just west of Hayes Road. Ruth later married and became Ruth Sochowski. She was the church organist at St. Paul Lutheran Church for 45 years. (Photograph courtesy of Eleanor Ahrens.)

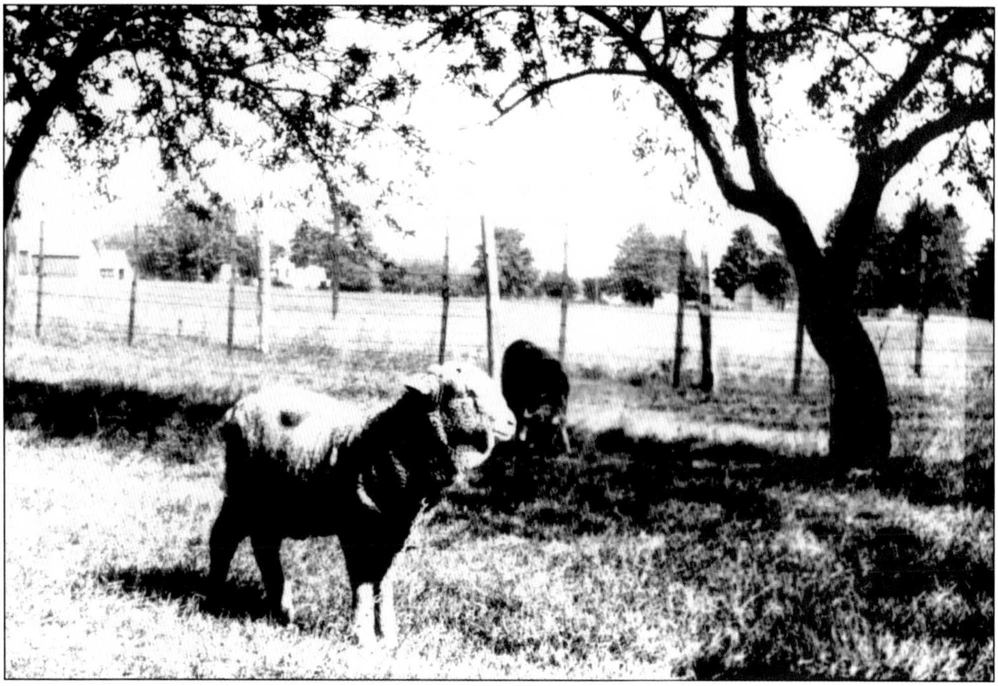

Holzhauer Farm. These two sheep, nibbling grass on a summer day around 1920, belonged to the Holzhauer family on Utica Road. The family also had chickens, goats, and a horse. The sheep were only kept as pets. The family did not do full-scale farming but used their property first as a summer home and then grew flowers commercially. (Photograph courtesy of Irene Holzhauer Hoffman.)

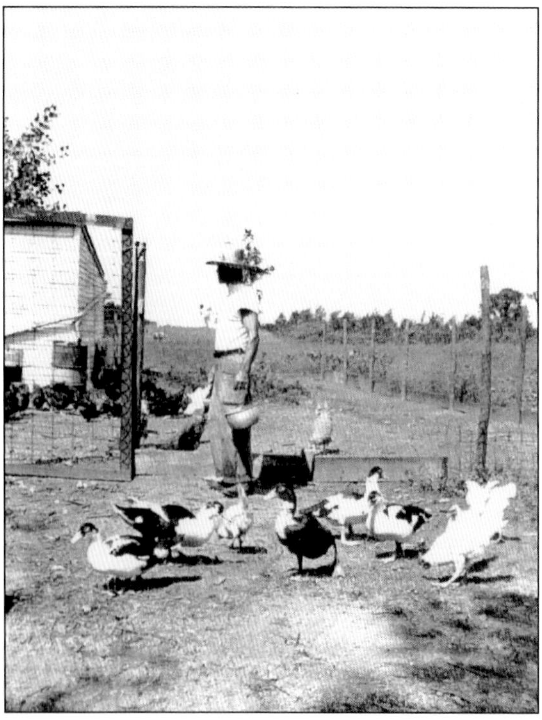

Backus Farm. Now the site of the Backus Car Wash, the Backus farm was on 17 Mile Road just west of Van Dyke Avenue. In this 1940s view, Emin Backus feeds the ducks and chickens. (Photograph courtesy of the Backus family.)

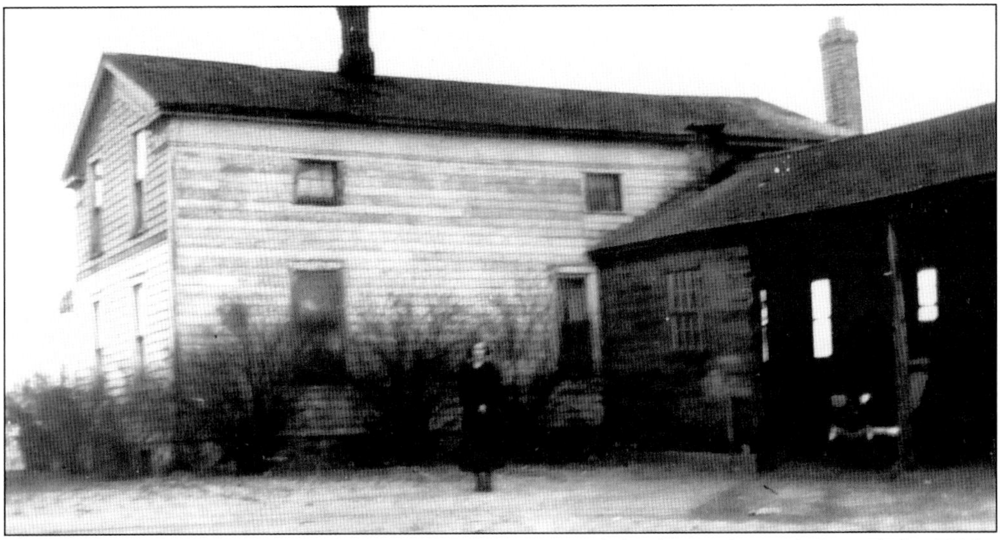

Bert Fox House. Herbert Fox or his descendants owned this house from 1919 until the 1980s, though he was not the builder. Built around 1850, it is one of the oldest homes still standing in the city. Now located on Utica Road south of 18 Mile Road, the house (according to Fox family tradition) was moved from the neighboring Upton property at Utica and Dodge Park Roads early in the house's existence, perhaps having served as the William Upton home prior to the construction of their larger home (the Upton House), built in 1867. This *c.* 1930 photograph shows a woman who may be Eugenia Fox, Bert's wife.

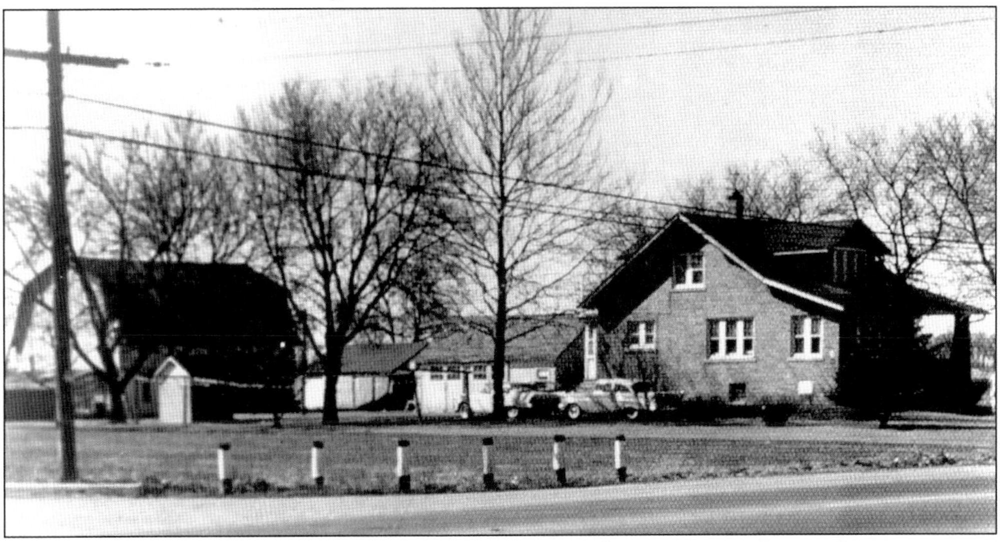

Albert Landerschier Farm. This farm, as seen around 1960, was on the northwest corner of Van Dyke and 18 Mile Roads where the Ford plant is today. The Landerschier family came from Germany in 1888, settling first in Shelby Township and then moving south to Sterling Township, where they eventually owned a number of farms along Van Dyke Avenue and along Mound Road. They were general farmers but switched to truck gardening later, selling to wholesalers at Eastern Market in Detroit. Albert Landerschier, son of Carl and Lena, lived at the pictured farm with his wife, Vernie, and children Norman, Iva, and Wilma. Their families, while living in Sterling Township, had been very active with Trinity Lutheran Church in Utica and also held various positions with local banks.

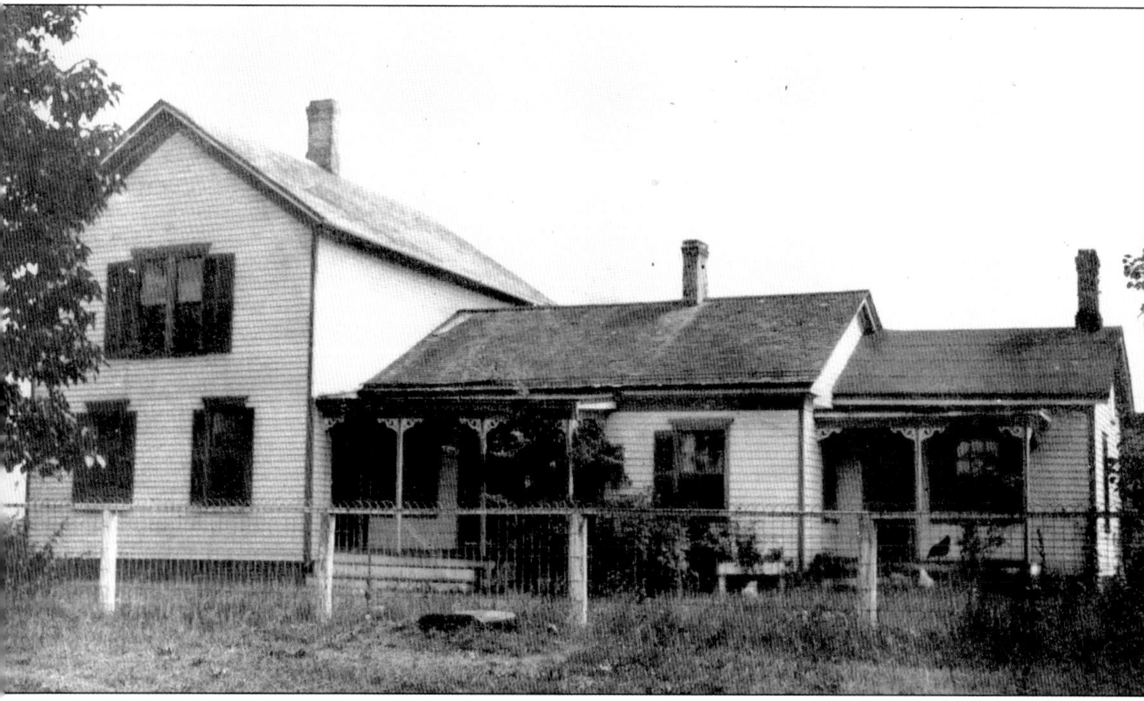

JOHN B. WRIGHT HOUSE. Ralph Wright came from New York in the 1830s and first cleared this land. John B. Wright later lived on this 60-acre dairy farm (pictured around 1910), on Clinton River Road just south of the village of Utica with his wife, Catherine, and children Dean, Cora, John, and Maude (who died in infancy). He was a racehorse enthusiast who had an oval track built on his property to run his prized horse. Son Dean owned the farm later, and then John J. Wright owned it in the 1950s. At some point, the one-story east wing was removed and made into a second house. John J. Wright was township clerk for 30 years, and his son remembers board meetings held at home with beer, sandwiches, and euchre after official business was done.

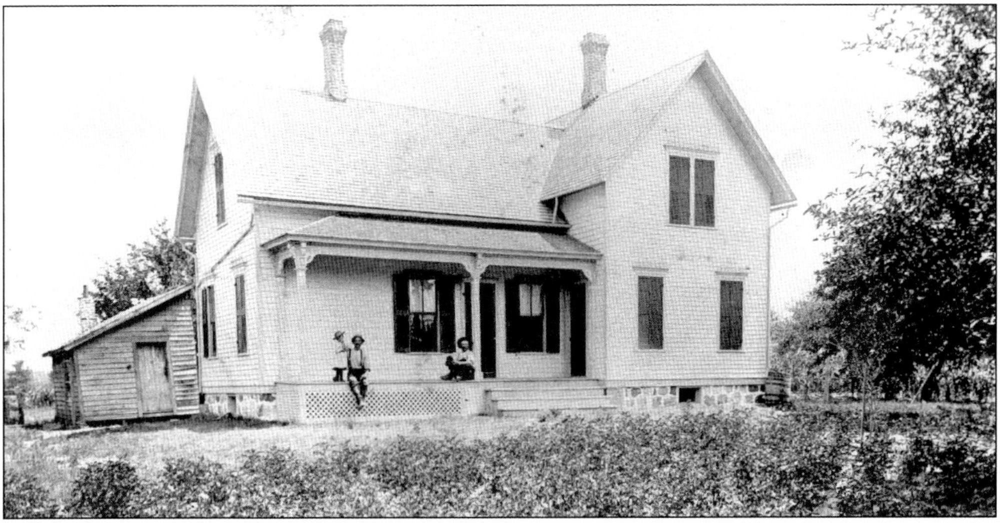

AHRENS HOMESTEAD. Charles and Louise Ahrens married in 1885 and bought this farm on the south side of Clinton River Road, just west of Hayes Road. This *c.* 1889 photograph shows the home, still looking crisp and new, with Charles relaxing on the front porch with his daughter Martha, the first of five children. The other person leaning on the post is unidentified. The farm, which stayed in the family for two more generations, was about 75 acres and reached back a half-mile to the Clinton River. It appears as if crops may have been grown on the land in front of the house. (Photograph courtesy of Eleanor Ahrens.)

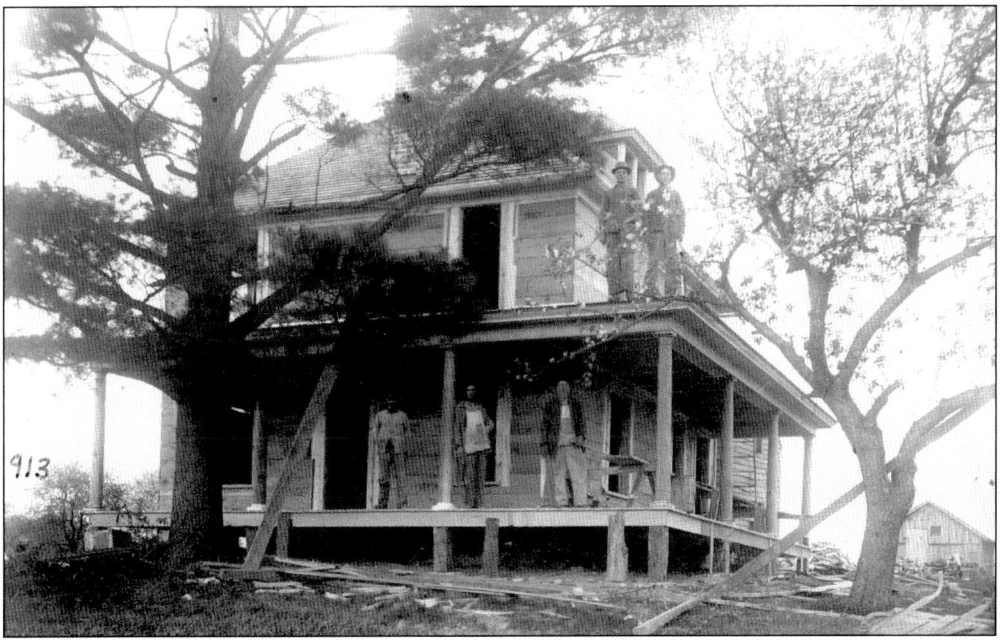

THIS OLD HOUSE. It is summer 1913, and Lorenzo Haff and his son Edwin remodel the family homestead on Dequindre Road south of Hall Road. One of the original wings of the home had been demolished a few months earlier, and the remaining portion of the home underwent massive redesign. The group on the porch includes, left to right, Lorenzo Haff, Fred Becket, and Fred Dahlman. Standing up on the roof are Ruben Moore and Edwin Haff. The house, near Troy Beaumont Hospital today, still stands. (Photograph courtesy of Lawrence Haff.)

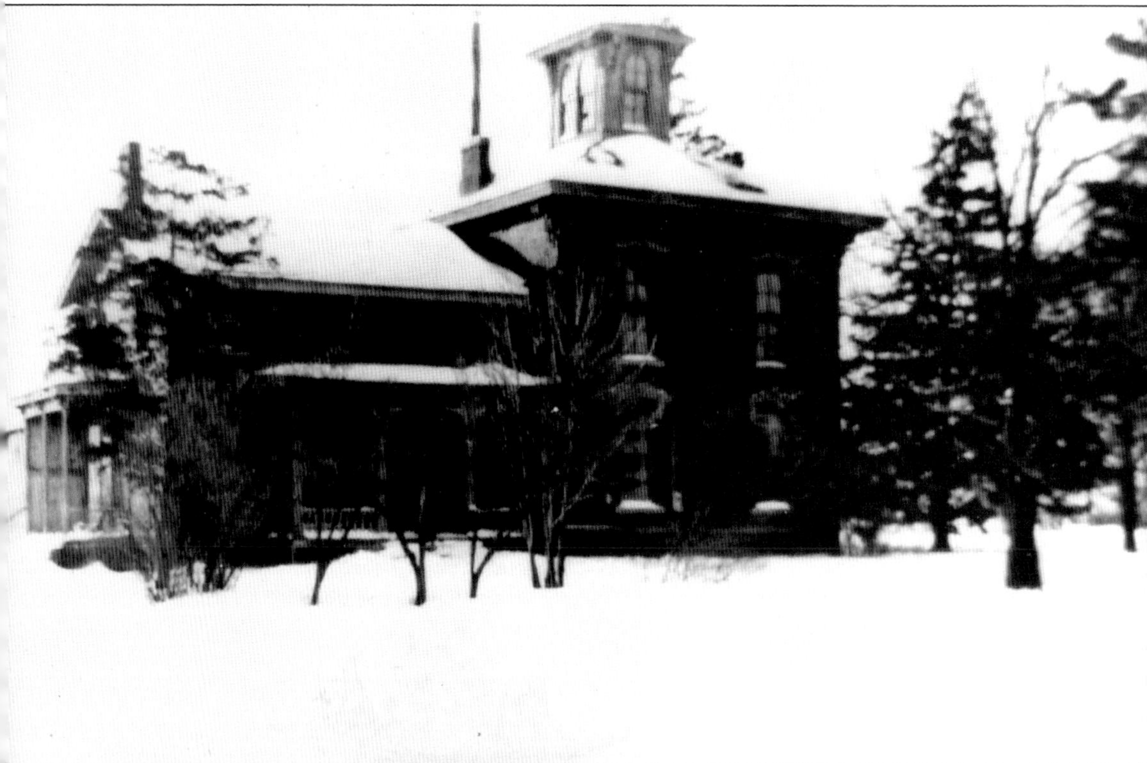

THE UPTON HOUSE. The William Upton home, pictured around 1930, is located on the corner of Utica and Dodge Park Roads. Built for young William Upton and his wife, Sarah Jeanette Aldrich Upton, in 1866 and 1867 of brick and materials imported from England, it was the jewel of the area and the center of Upton's large prosperous farming, fishing, and business operations. The Italianate home was originally red brick, with the cupola and porches as added details. By the 1960s, the cupola and other details had been removed and the brick painted white. Restoration in the 1980s returned the home close to its original exterior look. The Uptons and their children lived here until 1891, when they moved to Utica. The Frederick Ahrens family was the next occupant, and they sold to Fred Heldt in 1913. The Heldts lived there until 1927, when they sold to Stella Boylan, who may have been the owner at the time of this photograph. Up until 1964, a number of owners and renters had lived here. That year, the Macomb Child Guidance Center bought the building to be used for their operation. Later, the City of Sterling Heights bought it, using it as the offices for the parks and recreation department and finally returning it to the look of a 19th-century home and using it for meetings and displays. Its current beauty and state historical marker on the lawn make it the centerpiece of the municipal complex that grew around it.

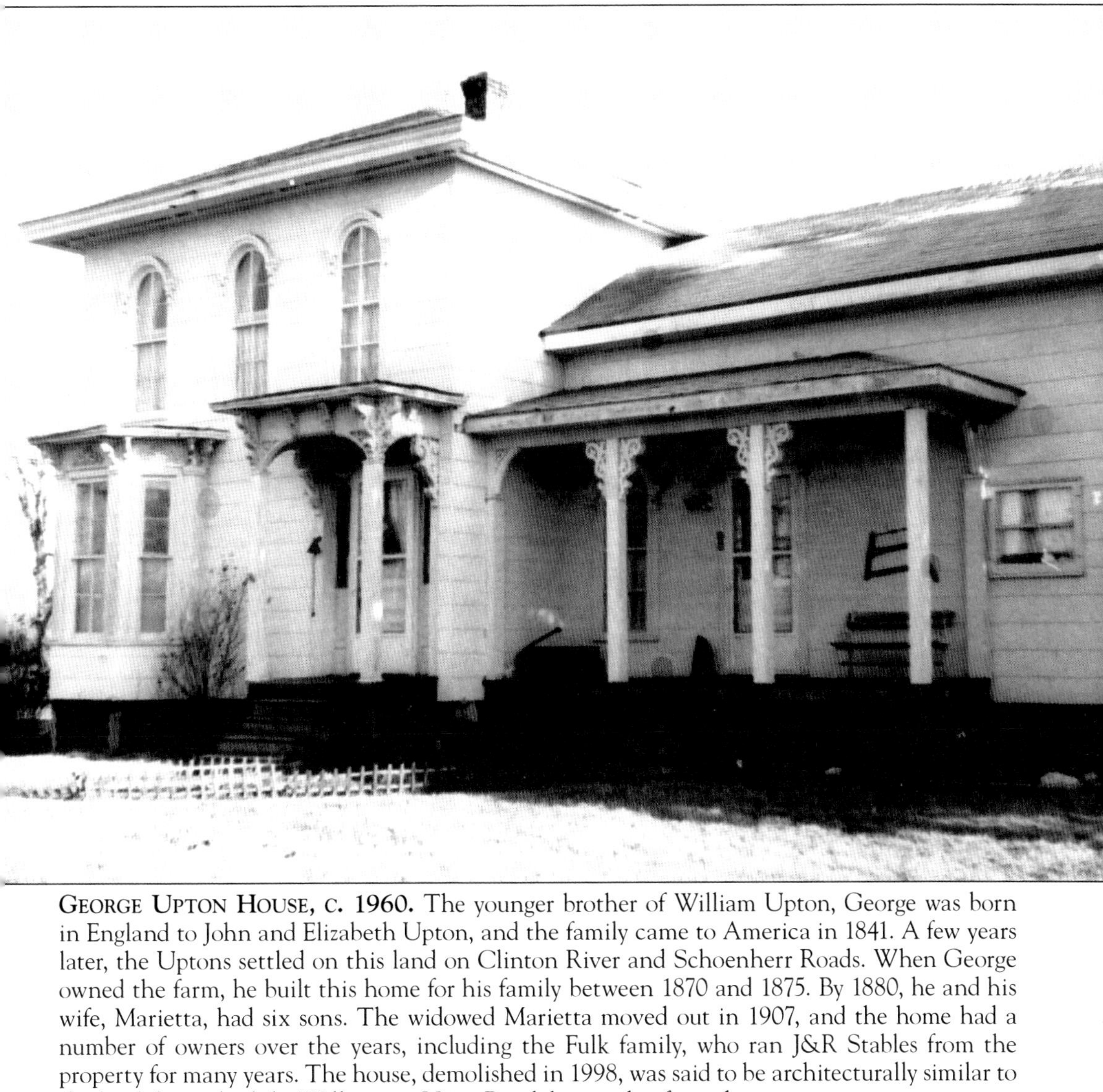

GEORGE UPTON HOUSE, C. 1960. The younger brother of William Upton, George was born in England to John and Elizabeth Upton, and the family came to America in 1841. A few years later, the Uptons settled on this land on Clinton River and Schoenherr Roads. When George owned the farm, he built this home for his family between 1870 and 1875. By 1880, he and his wife, Marietta, had six sons. The widowed Marietta moved out in 1907, and the home had a number of owners over the years, including the Fulk family, who ran J&R Stables from the property for many years. The house, demolished in 1998, was said to be architecturally similar to the brick home built by William on Utica Road, but made of wood.

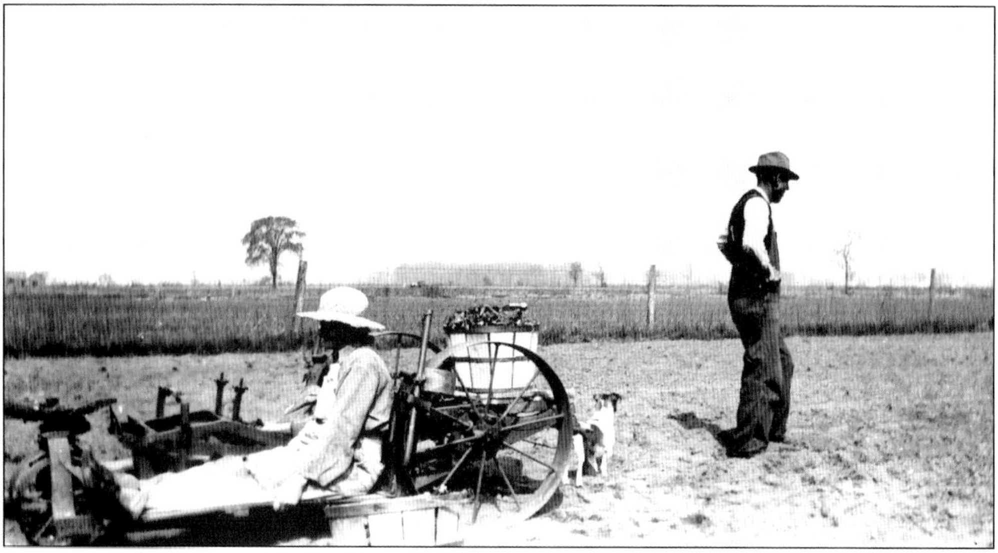

Ada and Bill Glawe. Ada Doebler and Bill Glawe met in Detroit, where Bill was a barber, and married in 1910, moving back to her grandparents' farm on Schoenherr Road north of Canal Road. They became general farmers but grew strawberries and rhubarb as cash crops. The Utica and Sterling Township area was known as the hothouse rhubarb capital of the United States because most of the nation's crop was grown not far from Hall Road. Ada is on the planting machine with Bill behind, planting young rhubarb shoots around 1930. Plants were left in the fields for two years. They were then dug up in the fall, and the root clumps were left to freeze, waiting for the next step. (Photograph courtesy of Jeanette Glawe.)

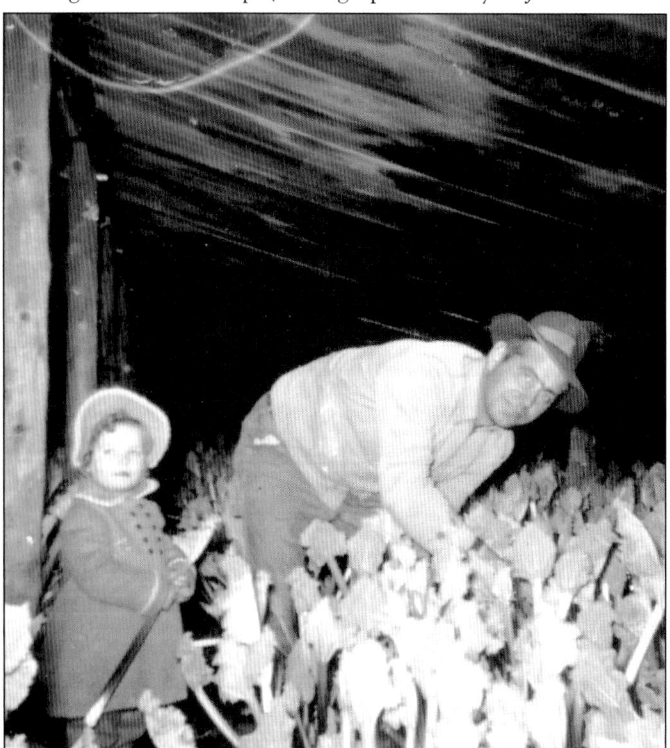

Rhubarb Shed. Pictured around 1955 is Arnold Wilbrett and his daughter Cheryl in his shed, or root house, on the family farm on the southwest corner of Hall and Schoenherr Roads. The very long sheds had concrete outer walls and removable pitched roofs that were applied for the winter. The frozen 50-pound root balls were arranged in beds in the sheds during the winter. After six weeks in the stove-heated shed, the forced shoots were ready to pick. Hothouse rhubarb was more delicate than field grown, pink and tender. Picking was backbreaking work, as the sheds were barely tall enough to stand in. (Photograph courtesy of Cheryl Wilbrett Snay.)

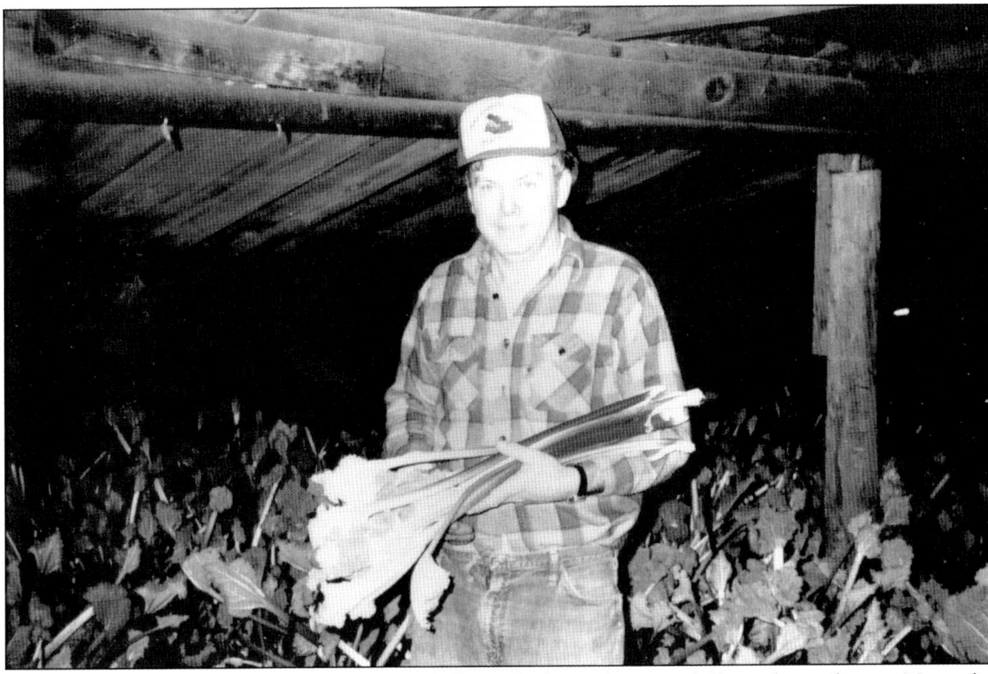

HARVESTING RHUBARB. Workers moved through the aisles, carefully picking shoots. Next the shoots were brought to a basement or barn to be sorted, graded, and packed into long cardboard cartons. Then they were cased and shipped to major cities. Rhubarb was a profitable crop, a table delicacy in the earlier days when fresh fruit in the winter and spring was rare. Even though it was actually a vegetable, it was used as a fruit in pies and other recipes. Pictured is Lawrence DeHondt holding harvested rhubarb in 1985, at the end of rhubarb cultivation in the area due to residential and commercial development.

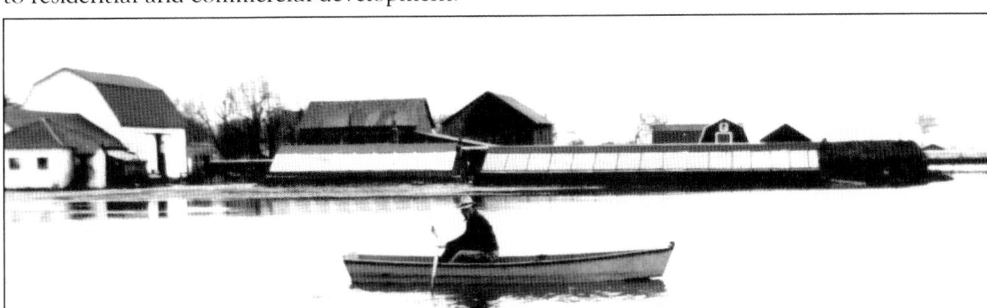

FLOODED CARROT FIELD. Remi Van den Brouck rows across his flooded carrot field in the 1940s. The cause is not known, whether it was heavy rains, melting snow, or a swollen stream, but severe flooding occurred a number of times in the Hall Road area. This farm, with its long rhubarb shed in the background, was near where the Lakeside Mall J.C. Penney is today. Area farmers have said that the soil in the Hall Road area was the best for farming in the area, and they really hated to see it covered up by mall parking lots. The Flower Barn Nursery is all that remains of the farm today.

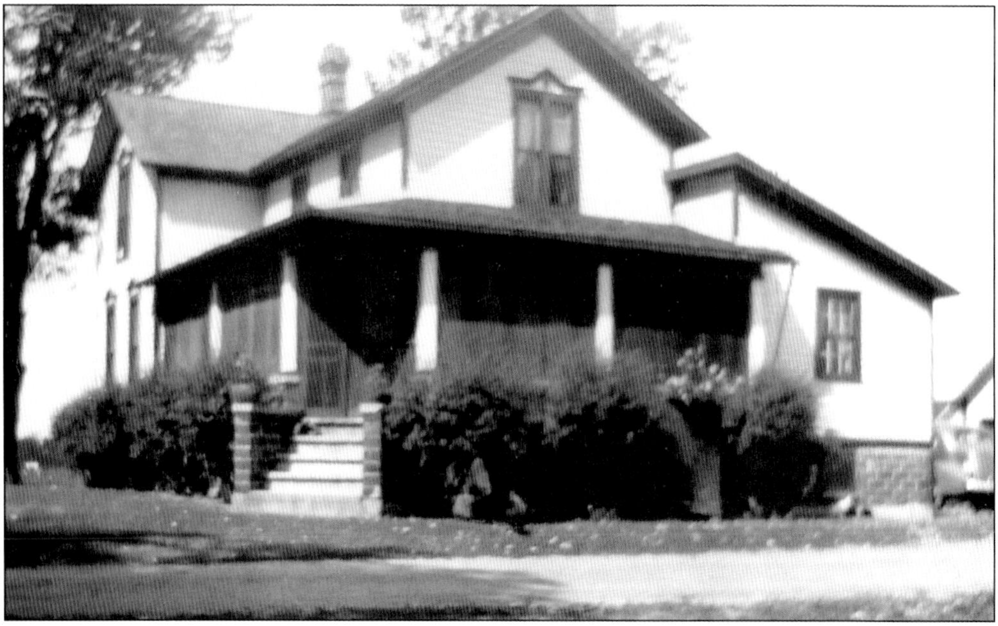

Bower-Hacker House. Pictured as it looked in 1939, the home that Phillip and Catherine Bower built in 1875 incorporates the kitchen from the original 1863 log cabin. Located on 16 Mile Road halfway between Mound and Ryan Roads, it was the center of a controversy during the 1980s when the two-lane road was scheduled to be widened to a six-lane divided highway, and the house was in the way. This caused many emotional newspaper stories about Bower's 92-year-old granddaughter, Rose Bower Hacker, the owner, and her plight. The home was eventually turned and moved onto Colgate Court, a nearby street, and the Hackers moved to Armada. (Photograph courtesy of Rose Bower Hacker.)

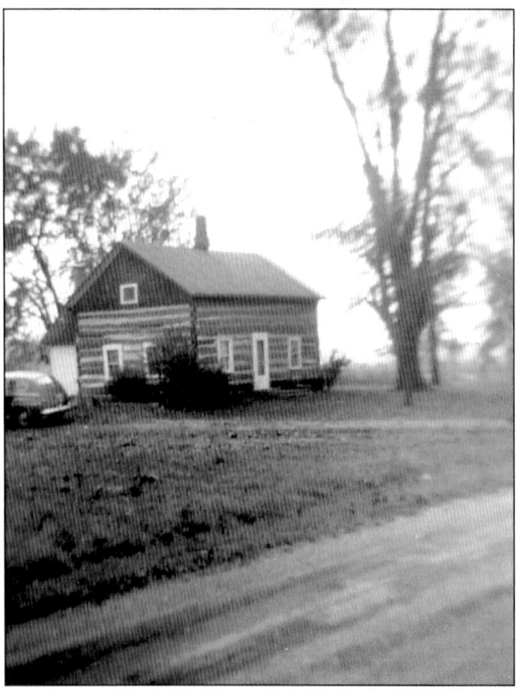

Faust Log Cabin. This 1945 view of the Faust home shows 19 Mile Road unpaved and a few of the many large walnut trees that once graced the yard. The log cabin was built in 1873 with the kitchen addition put on the back in the early 1940s. Charles Faust built the cabin, and the property remained in his family until the 1960s. The cabin is still there today near Browning Elementary School, looking very much the same. (Photograph courtesy of Barbara Faust Counsell.)

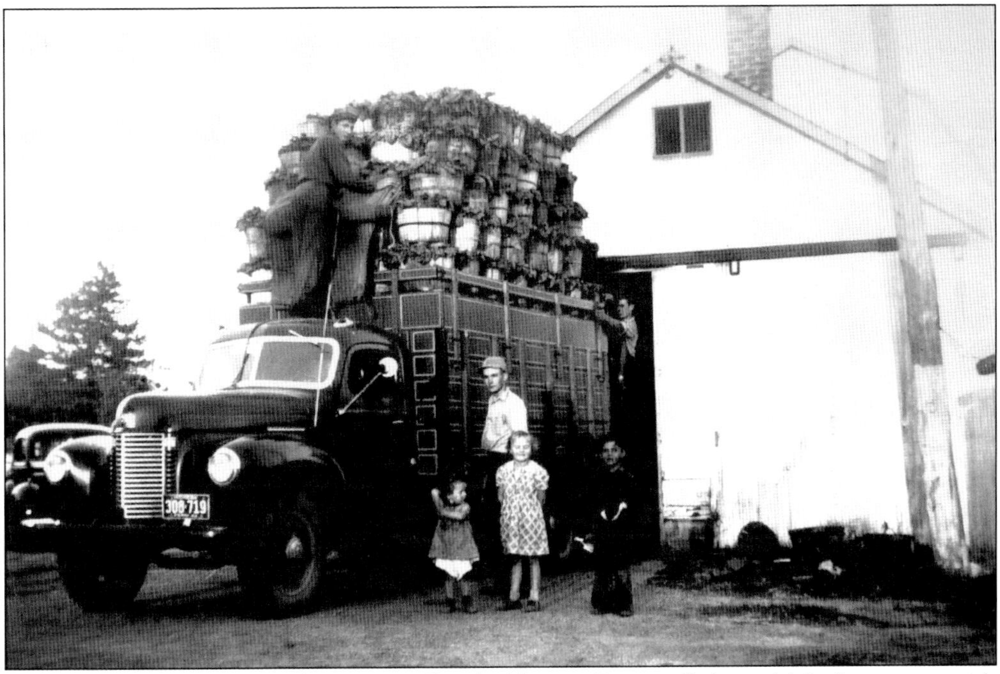

SPINACH. The Vandenbroucks—Norm, Butch, Harvey, Donna, Bob, and Marilyn—pose with their truck full of spinach bushels ready to be delivered to the C. F. Smith Company in Detroit to be sold in its grocery chain. The farm was on Hall Road, east of Schoenherr Road, where the Lakeside Mall is now. The Vandenbroucks had 11 children. In this 1944 photograph, Norm is standing on the cab of the truck, Butch is in the back, and Harvey stands with the younger children.

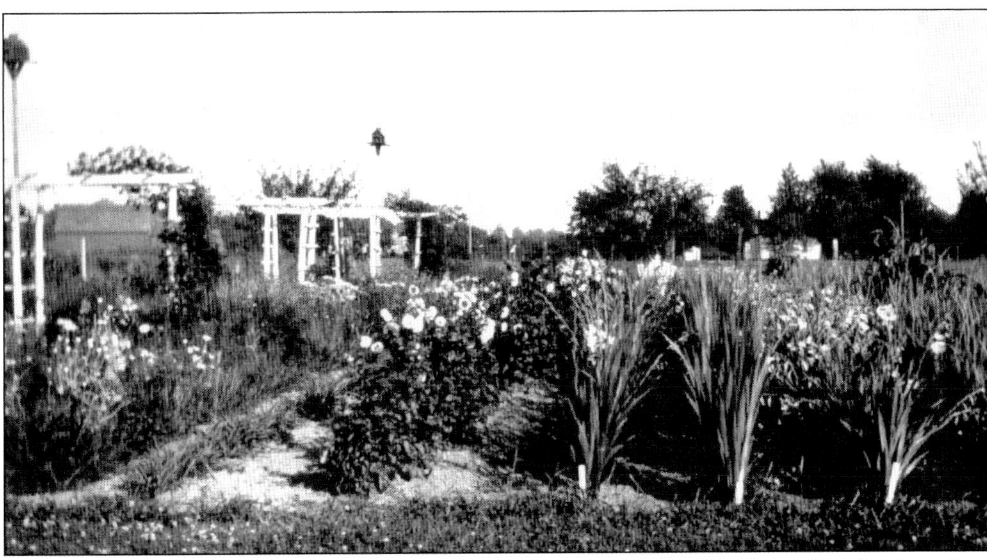

HOLZHAUER FLOWER GARDENS. The Holzhauers came out to Utica Road on a Sunday drive from Detroit in 1916 and spotted property northwest of Kleino Road. They fell in love with the spot and ended up using it as a weekend and summer home. Becoming permanent residents in the 1930s, they raised flowers and bulbs for sale at a roadside stand and also sold to greenhouses in Mount Clemens. This view is from the 1920s. (Photograph courtesy of Irene Holzhauer Hoffman.)

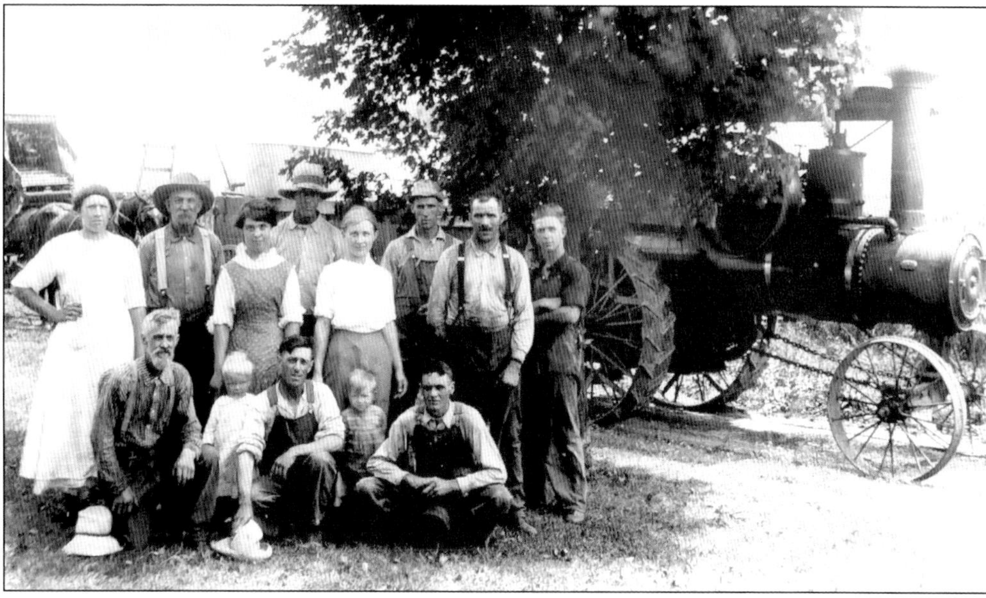

HARVEST GROUP, HAFF FARM. Harvest time was a busy and social time on the farm. Neighbors and relatives took turns helping at each other's farms. The host farm supplied famously ample meals, and the borrowed steam thresher was the center of attention. A group poses around 1916 at the Haff Farm on Dequindre Road south of Hall Road. From left to right, they are (seated) Lorenzo Haff, Evelyn Behrendt, Edwin Haff, Vera Haff, and unidentified; (standing) Meta Reinhold, George Renshaw, Alvina Behrendt, Archie Brown, Adela Behrendt Haff, Elmer Moore, Gust Ellman (owner of the thresher), and William Behrendt. (Photograph courtesy of Lawrence Haff.)

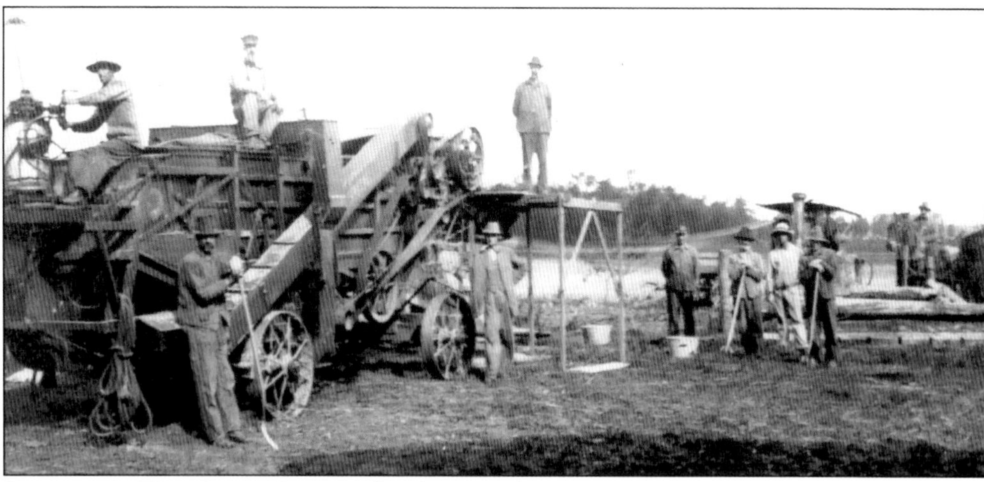

SEPARATOR, HAFF FARM. Using a threshing machine or a separator was heavy, dusty work but brought farm men together like nothing else. Here on the Haff farm around 1916, the men take a break for a photograph. Edwin Haff (blower tender) is seated on the far left; his father, Lorenzo Haff (with beard) sits up on the separator; August Behrendt, Edwin's father-in-law, stands near right wheel of machine. Neighbors helped one another out at this season, and the whole process might have taken two weeks. The Haff farm is on Dequindre Road, south of Hall Road, and still stands. (Photograph courtesy of Lawrence Haff.)

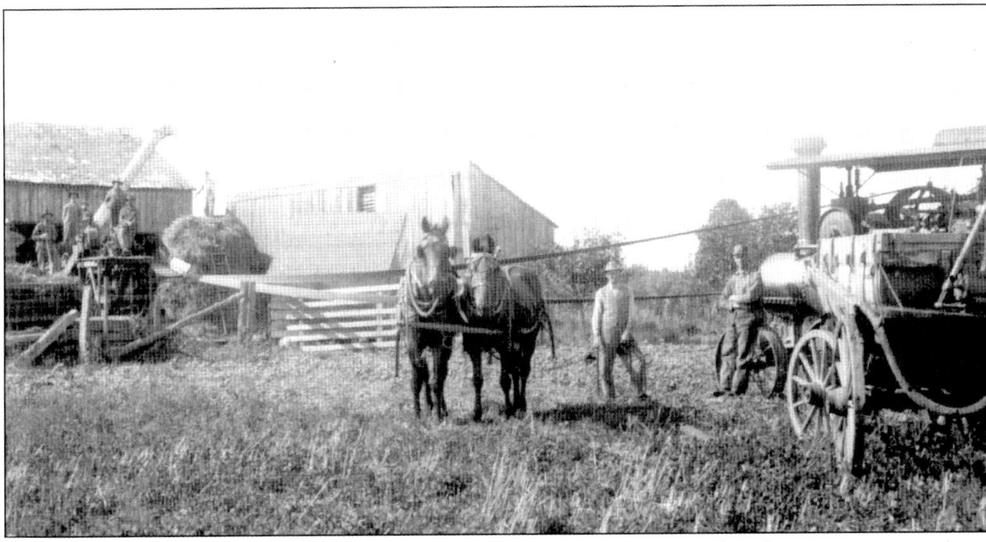

THRESHING. Few things inspired more enthusiasm than the steam threshing rig coming down the road. Pictured at the Haff farm around 1916 is Lorenzo Haff standing atop the pile of hay in the background. Neighbor George Renshaw and other men help. The glory days of steam threshing lasted only about 40 years, from about 1890 to 1930. Changing technology brought it to a close. (Photograph courtesy of Lawrence Haff.)

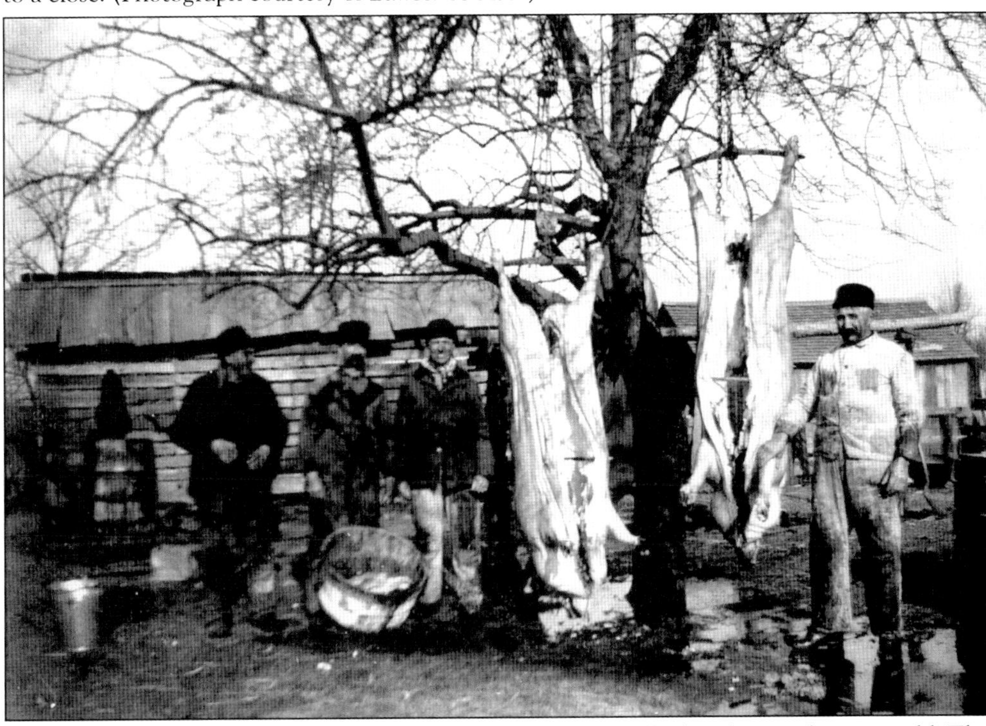

DRESSING HOGS. Hog-butchering time always came in the fall after the weather was cold. This 1900 photograph shows a group on the Ahrens farm on Clinton River Road west of Hayes Road. Usually the whole family was involved in this chore, each handling a different part of the many steps in processing and smoking the meat to be used by the family over the coming year. (Photograph courtesy of Eleanor Ahrens.)

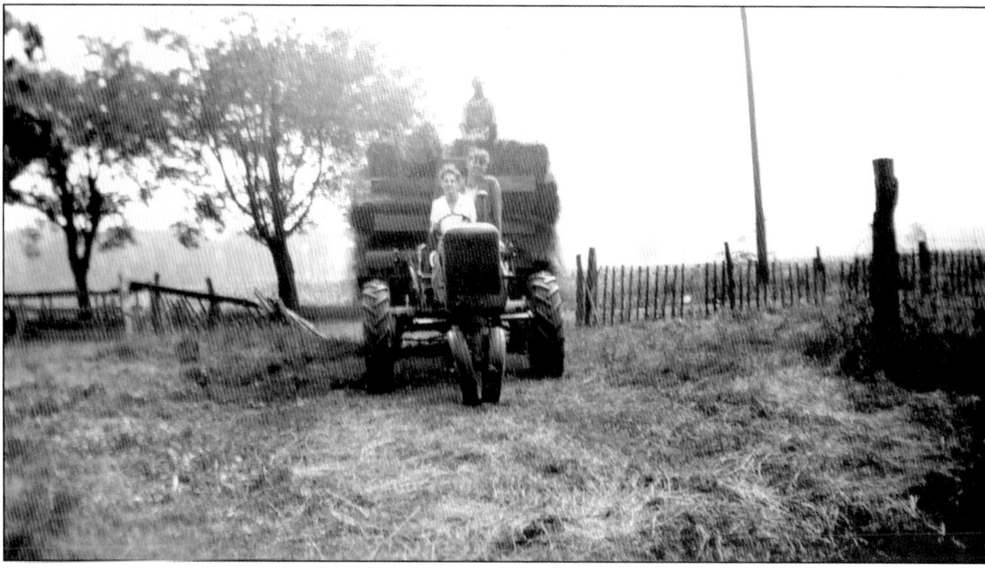

DRIVING THE TRACTOR. Eleanor Ahrens drives the tractor pulling the hay wagon in from the field around 1945. Her father, Otto Ahrens, sits atop the bales to make sure all goes well. Otto had only daughters, so the Ahrens girls did work that other farm girls did not. (Photograph courtesy of Eleanor Ahrens.)

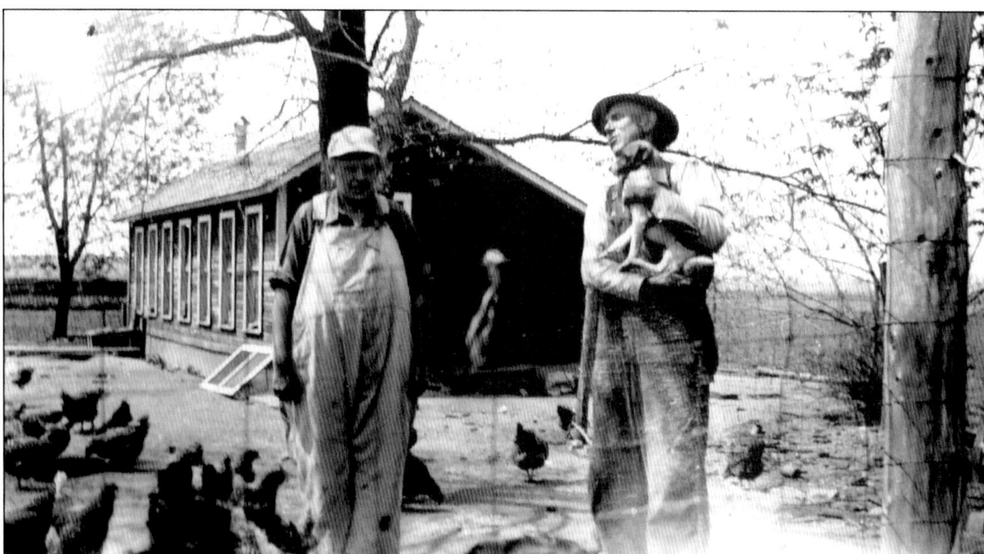

CHICKEN YARD. The handsome chicken coop in the background belongs to Bill Glawe, on the right. Meta Redcap stands to the left while the chickens go pretty much where they want to. The Bill and Ada Glawe farm, pictured here around 1930, was on Schoenherr Road, north of Canal Road. (Photograph courtesy of Jeannette Glawe.)

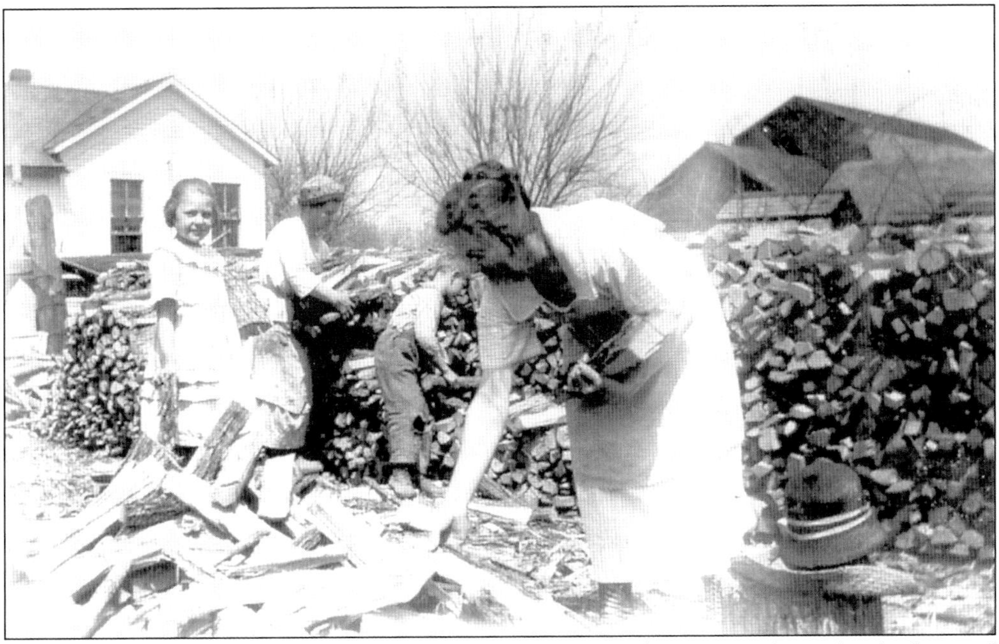

PILING FIREWOOD. Family members pitch in on the Kleino farm to neatly stack split firewood around 1920. The farm was located on Kleino Road north of Utica Road. Pictured from left to right are Marion Kleino, her mother Martha Kleino, Tom Couser, and his mother Lilly Couser. (Photograph courtesy of Armin "Duane" Kleino.)

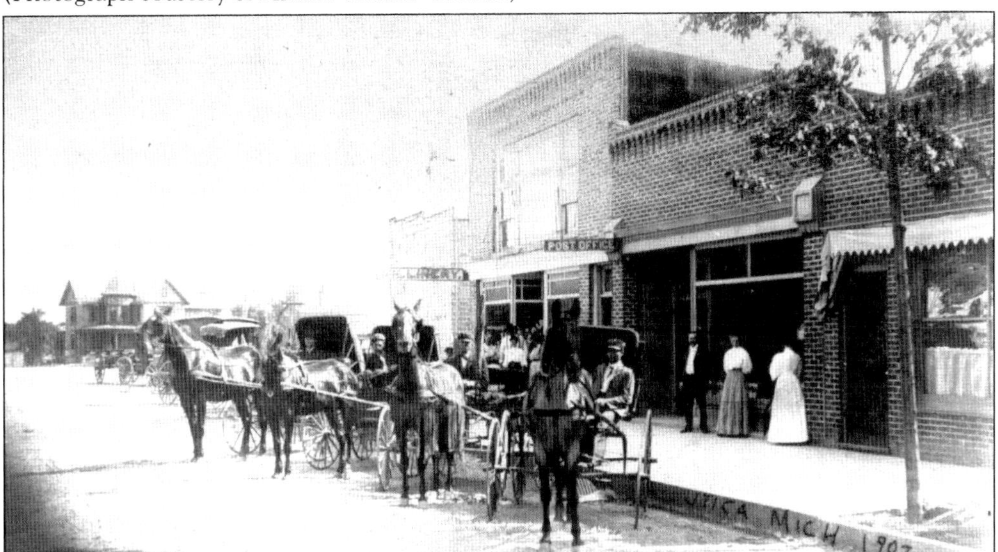

READY TO DELIVER. Herman Barg of Shelby (left) and Charlie Hacker of Utica and Sterling Township (right) pose in the buggies used to deliver mail and packages on their RFD routes for the post office. Charlie delivered the mail to much of Sterling Township for 30 years, navigating the muddy roads first with a horse and buggy, then a motorcycle, and finally an automobile. Farm families often ordered household goods through catalog companies such as Montgomery Ward and Sears and Roebuck. The Utica Post Office, seen here in 1907, was on Cass Avenue and is the storefront in the center. (Photograph courtesy of Rose Bower Hacker.)

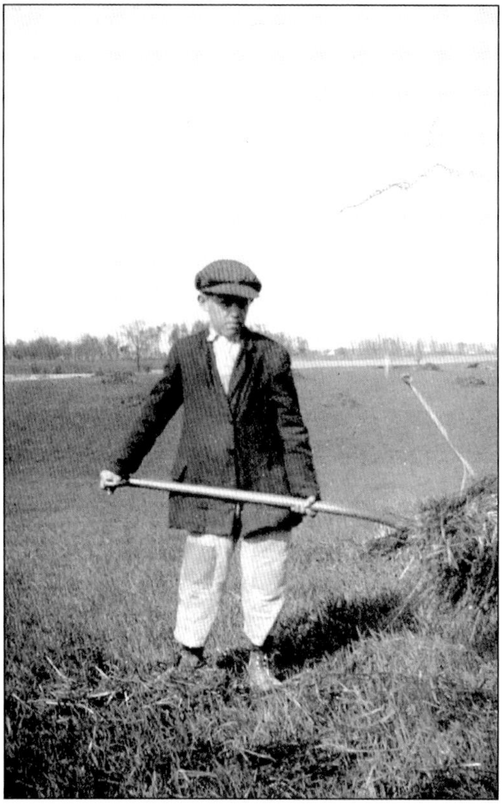

MELVIN KLEINO. Melvin Kleino poses with a pitchfork on the family farm, located on Kleino Road north of Utica Road, around 1915. Melvin was typical of area farm children who helped out with farm chores as soon as they were able, usually around early grade-school age. Children often had duties in the morning before school and then again later in the day. Their chores depended on the kind of farming the family did, temperament, and the needs of their parents. Melvin was the son of Louis and Martha Kleino. (Photograph courtesy of Armin "Duane" Kleino.)

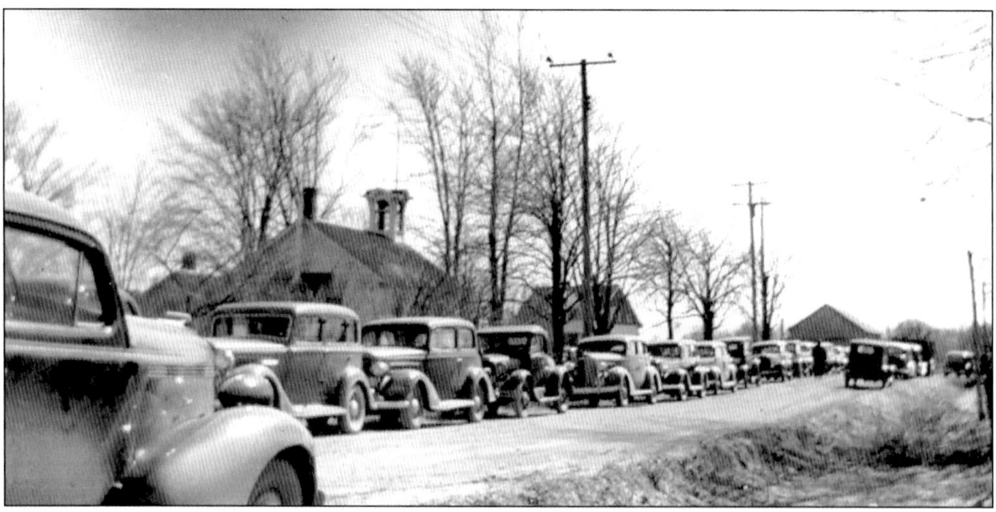

KLEINO FARM AUCTION. After the 1939 death of Louis Kleino, the family auctioned off farm equipment that would no longer be used. The sale drew quite a crowd. The Kleino family continued living here on Kleino Road for a short time and then moved down Utica Road to Fraser. The building with the cupola is the old Maple Grove School, which burned down in 1942. (Photograph courtesy of Armin "Duane" Kleino.)

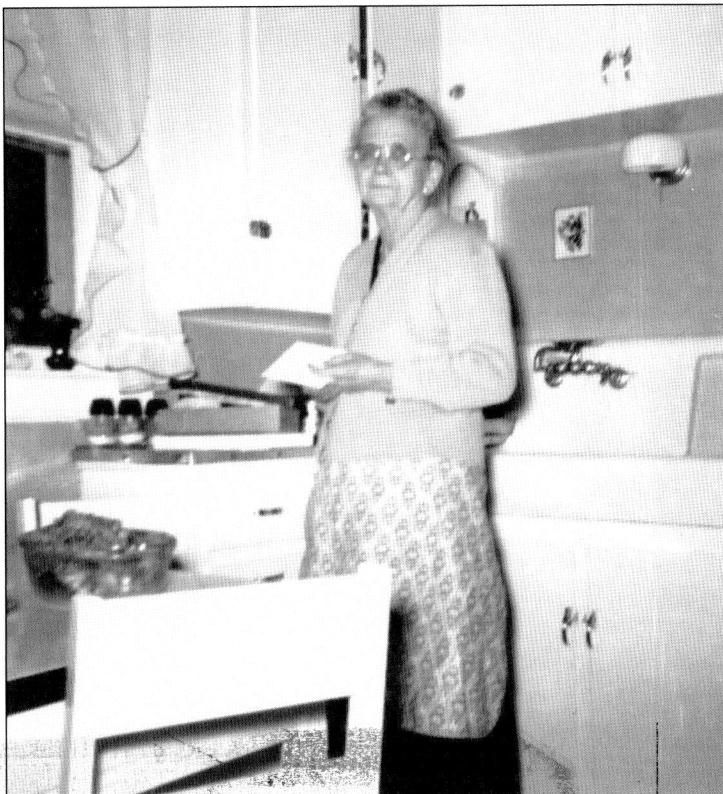

In the Kitchen. Albertine Juengel Wilbrett pauses in her tidy kitchen for a quick snapshot sometime during the 1950s. The home, built in 1924 and located on the corner of Schoenherr and Hall Roads, was home to the widowed Albertine and her son Arnold, his wife Cecelia, and their children. (Photograph courtesy of Cheryl Wilbrett Snay.)

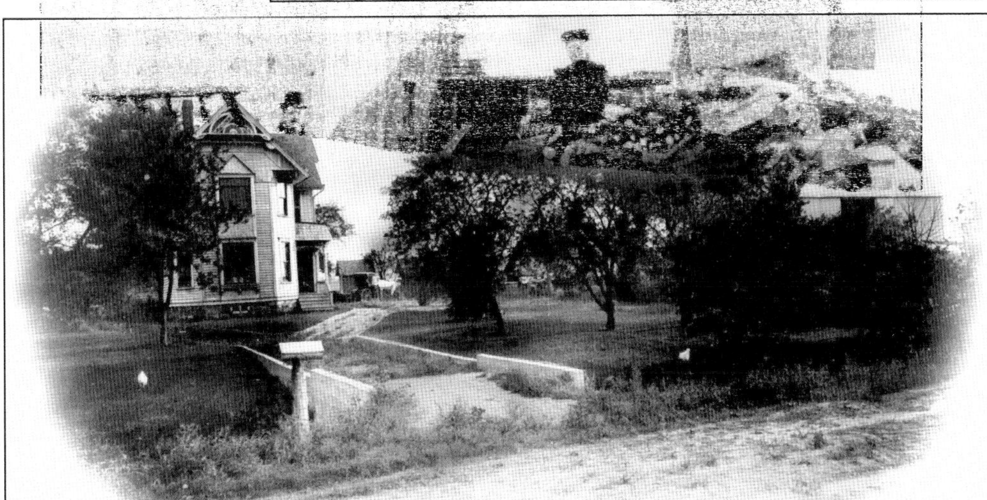

John Doebler House and Barn. John Doebler and Martha Schulz Doebler started their married lives in a log cabin and after seven years built this house on Canal Road west of Schoenherr Road in 1892. The round-roof barn was built in 1909. The barn was the most modern in the county at the time and almost the largest. The home, still standing, was also large: five large bedrooms, a parlor, and a kitchen that could seat 20 people. The couple raised three children there and sold the farm in 1926 after retiring to Utica. The "ditch" that runs alongside the road (crossed by a small bridge at their driveway) is what was left of the old Clinton-Kalamazoo Canal. (Photograph courtesy of Wallace Doebler.)

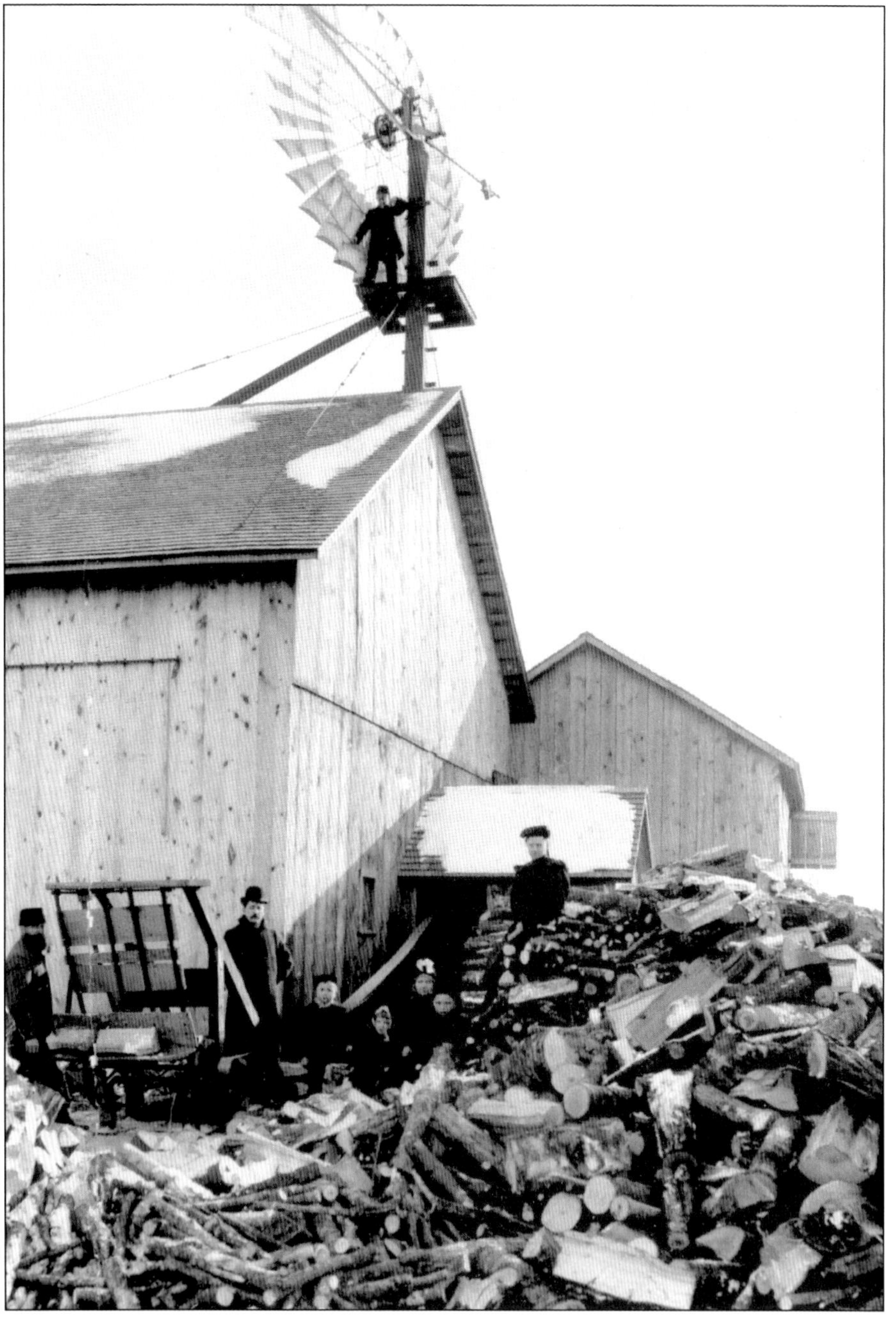

NEW WINDMILL. This 1898 photograph was taken to display the wonders of the new 14-Star Power Mill that John Doebler bought for his farm on Canal Road. The mill, mounted on top of the barn, was used to grind feed, pump water, run a grindstone, and saw wood, as the 50 cords of wood piled around attest. The large barn was moved to the neighboring Glawe farm in 1909 and replaced with an ultramodern round-roof barn. Pictured, from left to right, are John Doebler (with the beard he was known for); an unidentified agent from the windmill company; Agnes, Ada, and Herbert Doebler (John's children); Edgar Schulz (cousin); and Martha Doebler. (Photograph courtesy of Wallace Doebler.)

Three

SCHOOLS AND CHURCHES

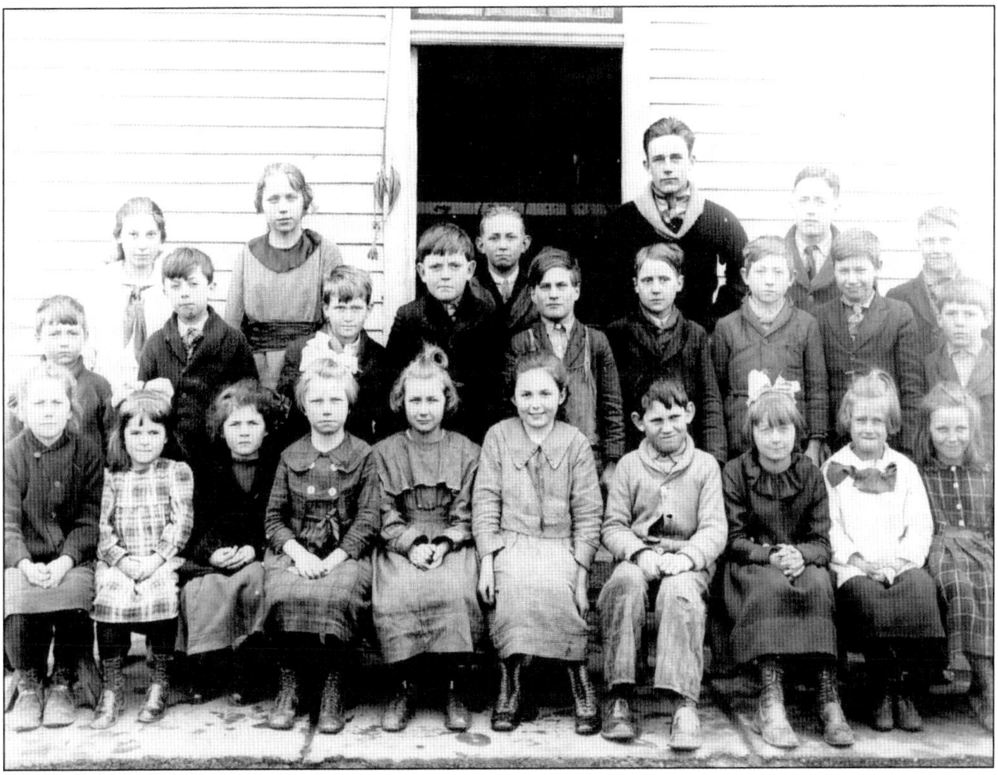

PLUMBROOK STUDENTS. This *c.* 1920 photograph shows Van Dyke and Plumbrook Roads area farm children. From left to right are the following: (first row) Edna Fiebelkorn, Thelma Meitzner, Irene Meitzner, Sadie Stolzenfeld, Mary Meyer, Gertrude Schneider, Arthur Meitzner, Myrtle Weier, Evelyn Meyer, and Marie Clauw; (second row) Carl Lieberenz, Norman Weier, Henry Maas, Elmer Sipple, Norman Hartline, Theodore Maas, Elmer Schiebel, Dave Meyer, and Adolph Meitzner; (third row) Victoria Schiebel, Margaret Stolzenfeld, Otto Maas, Norman Gelier, Roland Maas, and Joe Maas.

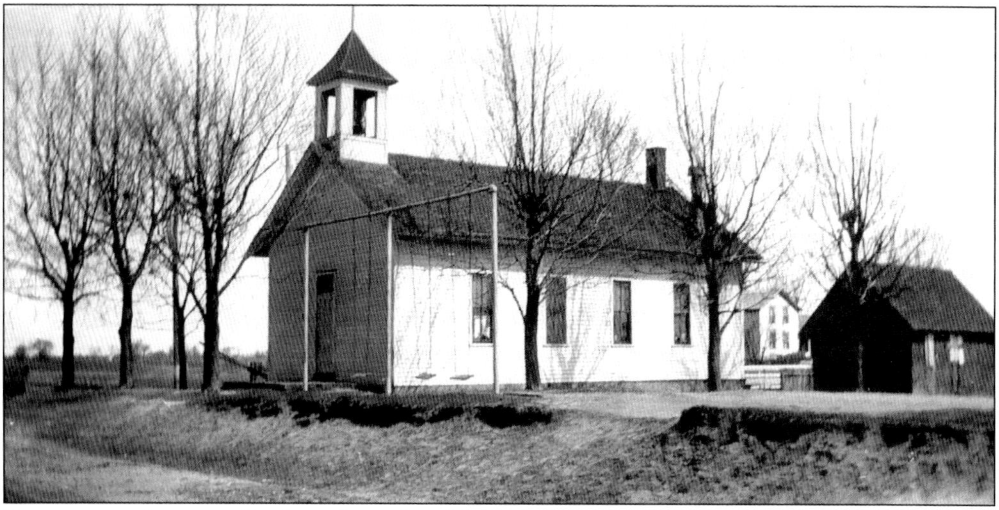

PLUMBROOK SCHOOL. Students from the 17 Mile Road and Van Dyke Avenue area went to this one-room school, located on the southwest corner of the intersection. The building is shown as it looked in the 1927–1928 school year. Recess at Plumbrook offered time to play games and use the swings or seesaw. The school was on the corner of the Lieberenz farm, and their family often had the young teacher as a boarder in their home, which can be seen back behind the school. Plumbrook was Sterling District No. 2, and served students up to the eighth grade, as did all the country schools in Sterling Township. If students wanted to continue their education after that, they had to find a ride to Utica High School. (Photograph courtesy of Helen Cope Beuthin.)

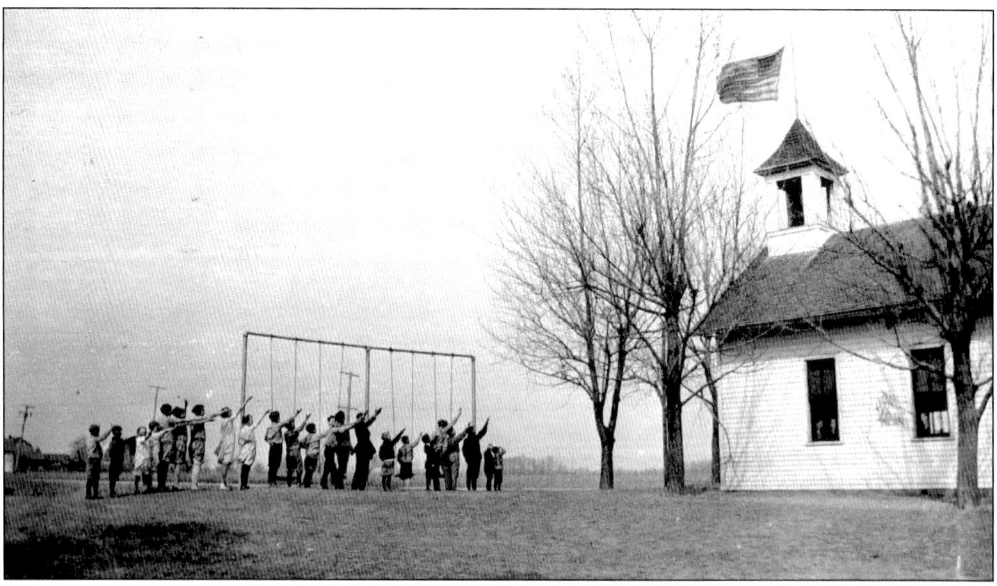

TO THE FLAG. In the years prior to World War II, the Pledge of Allegiance began with the hand over the heart, and when the phrase "to the flag" was said, the arm was extended toward the flag, palm upward, and remained so during the rest of the pledge. With the war, the outstretched arm became associated with Nazism, and the pledge was changed so that the hand remained over the heart the entire time. Pictured are students from Plumbrook School, at Van Dyke Avenue and 17 Mile Road, reciting the pledge in 1927. (Photograph courtesy of Helen Cope Beuthin.)

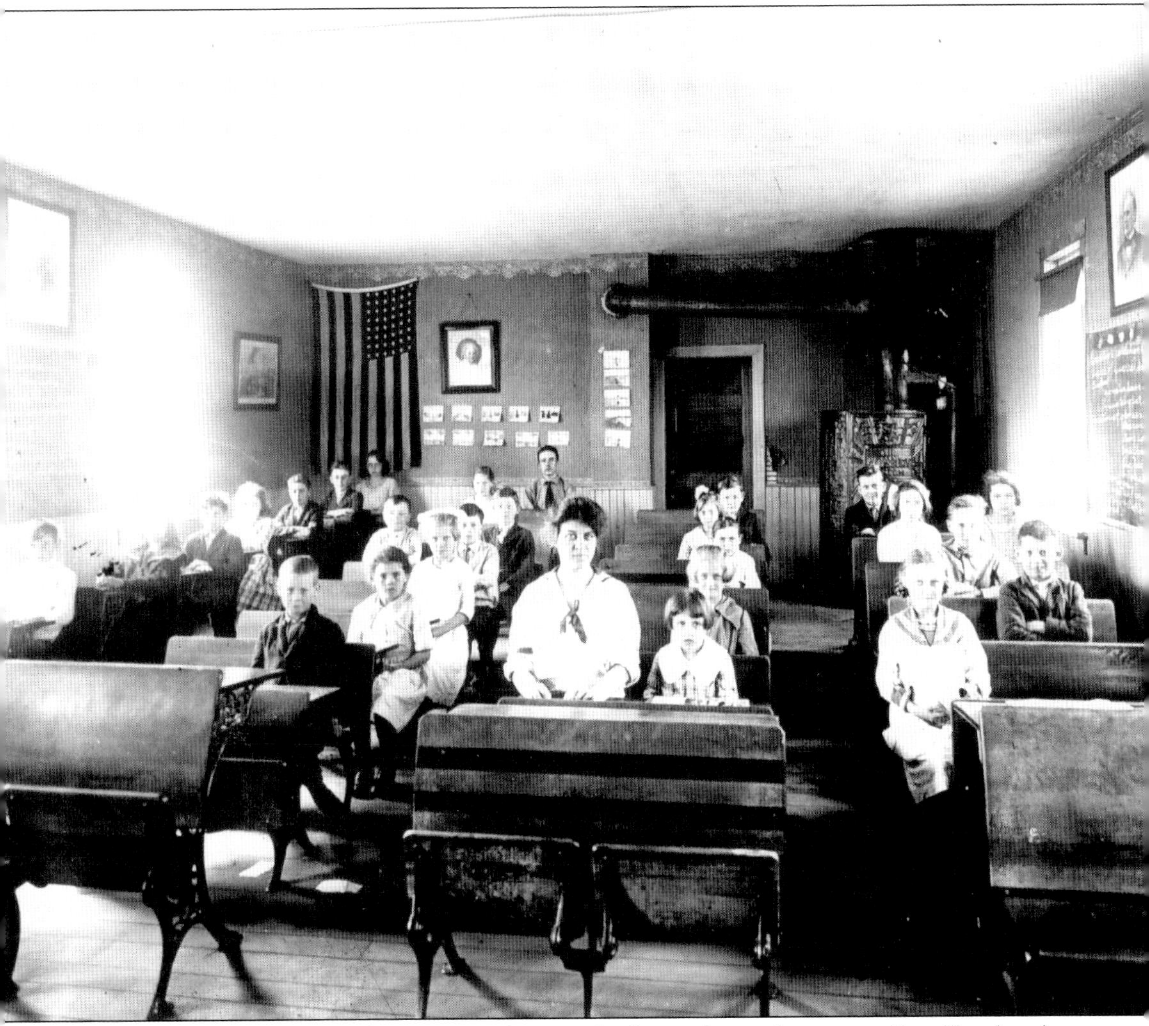

PLUMBROOK CLASSROOM. This *c.* 1920 photograph shows the students attending Plumbrook School, located on the southwest corner of Van Dyke and Plumbrook Roads. Blackboards, presidential portraits, and a U.S. flag show that some things do not change over the years. This school was remembered by many to be one of the better equipped in the area. Teachers often changed every year or so, and two from this era were Margaret Harvey and Eleanor Diselrod. The older girl in the front row could be the teacher, or just an older student. A Plumbrook teacher from the 1930s, Ethel Cope, reported having 60 students here, so the pictured group is a bit sparse, either because of population shifts, or a low attendance day due to farm duties. Games played at recess during the warm weather included fox in the clover, baseball, and dog and deer, while winter weather brought attention to the heating stove in the corner.

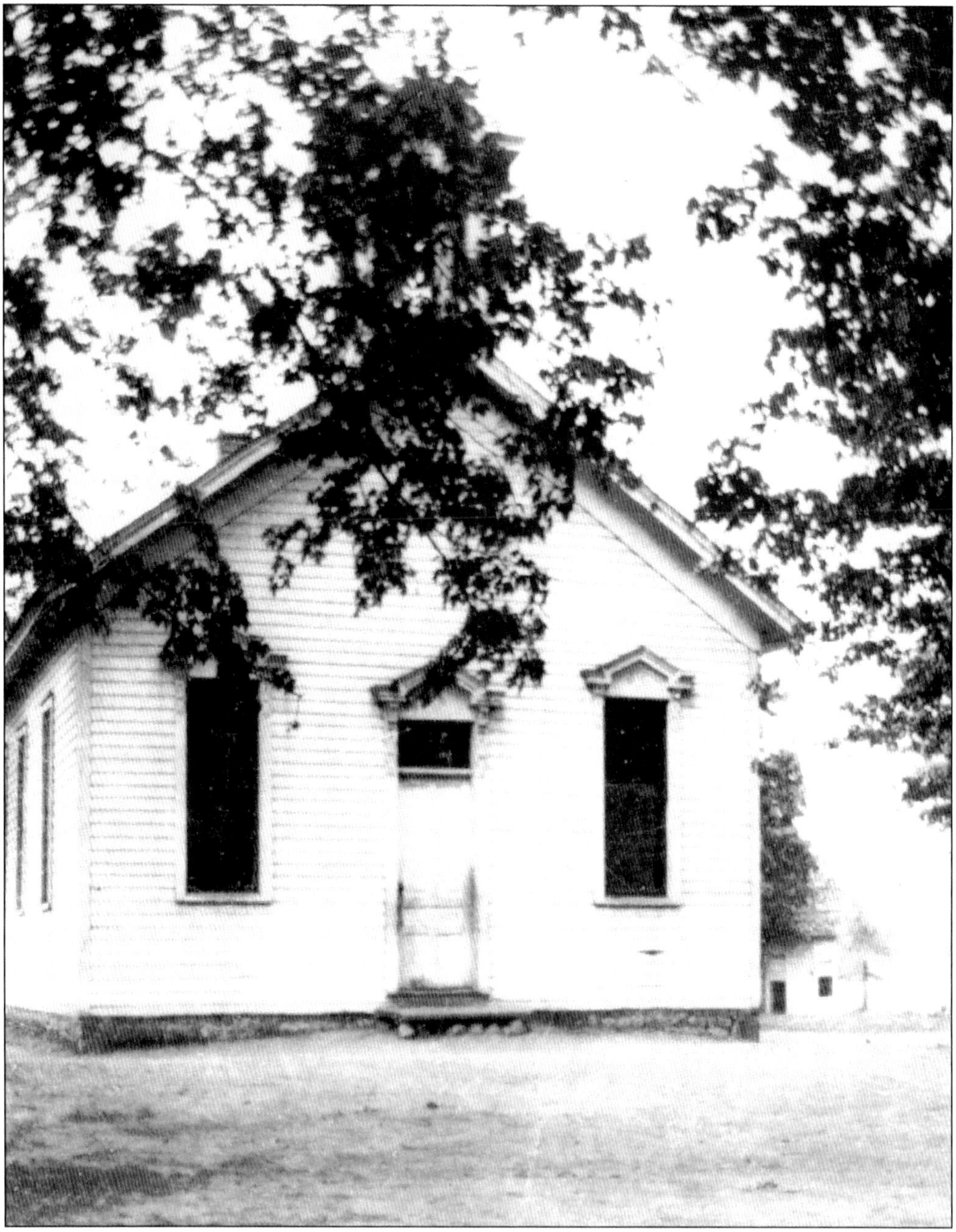

MAPLE GROVE SCHOOL. Sterling School District No. 3, Maple Grove, was located on the corner of Utica and Kleino Roads. A school had been on this site since 1838, but the building pictured in this *c.* 1920 photograph was built in 1873 to replace the original. It was used as a one-room country school steadily, except for a few years during the Depression, when costs forced students to all move into a second newer building on the site. By 1937, they were back to using both buildings. The final end came for this structure one night after a Christmas program in December 1942, when a fire broke out near the furnace, completely destroying the school. The newer building, undamaged by the fire, continued to be used for educational purposes until the 1980s and was demolished in 2004. (Photograph courtesy of Armin "Duane" Kleino.)

IRENE FREIDHOFF, MAPLE GROVE TEACHER. Irene Freidhoff taught at the Maple Grove School (Sterling District No. 3) beginning in 1919 as a 17-year-old young woman. It is not known how long she taught there, but most teachers only stayed a few years. She had about 30 students enrolled, ages 5 through 15, ranked beginner through eighth grade. This photograph is from 1920. (Photograph courtesy of Armin "Duane" Kleino.)

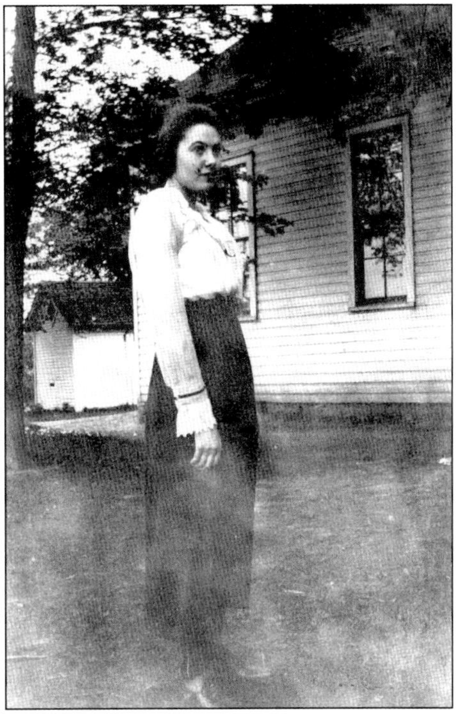

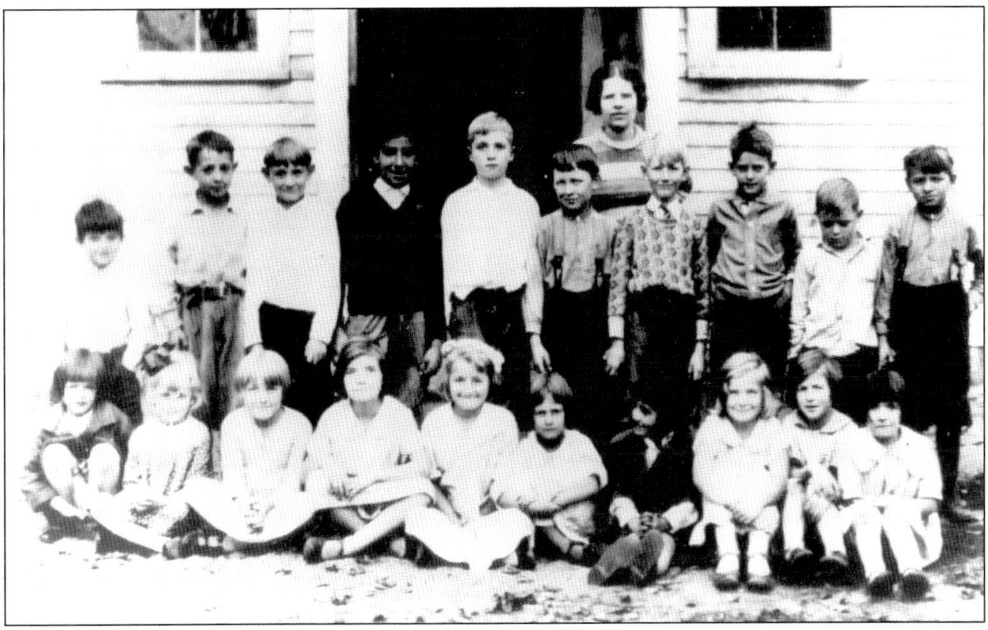

MAPLE GROVE STUDENT PORTRAIT. A day in May 1932 was portrait day for grades one through four of the Maple Grove School (Sterling District No. 3). Teacher Francis Wagner stands behind her students. From left to right are the following: (first row) Jean Schulz, Ila Liebenow, Norma Kleino, Esther Fox, Eleanor Borski, Marie DeBlouw, Alice Yessian, Elaine Fox, Aileen Drake, and Jean Swank; (second row) Glenn Drake, Maurice DeBlouw, Leo Hellebuyck, Harry Yessian, Edward Ochylski, Norman Bobcean, Elmer Buelow, Eugene O'Brien, Jack Curtis, and Melvin Bobcean. (Photograph courtesy of Edward Ochylski.)

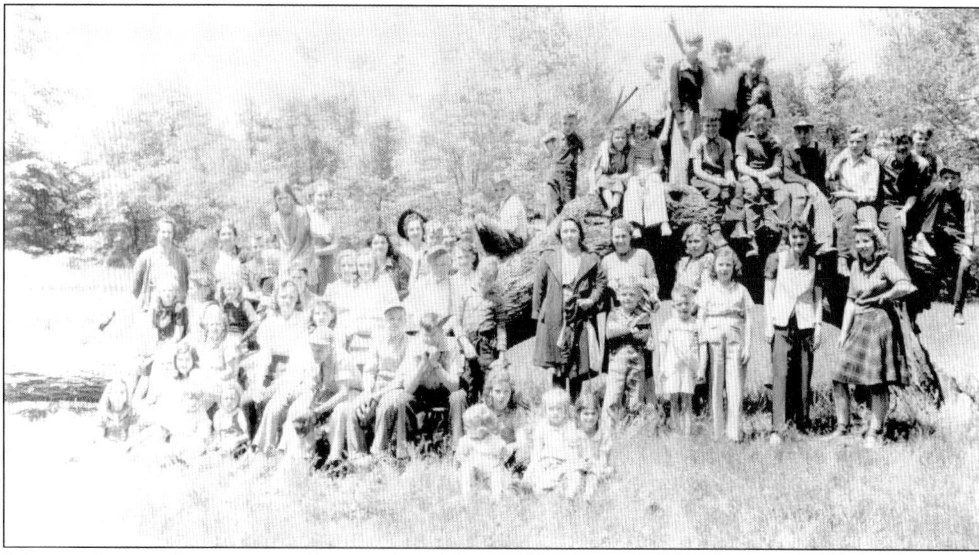

MAPLE GROVE STUDENTS. About 60 children and a few women pose on a fallen tree in this photograph from the 1940s. The event may have been a school picnic, which Maple Grove School (Sterling District No. 3) usually hosted at the end of the school year. The country school was located at the corner of Kleino and Utica Roads. A schoolhouse had been on that corner since at least 1838. (Photograph courtesy of Merle Peters.)

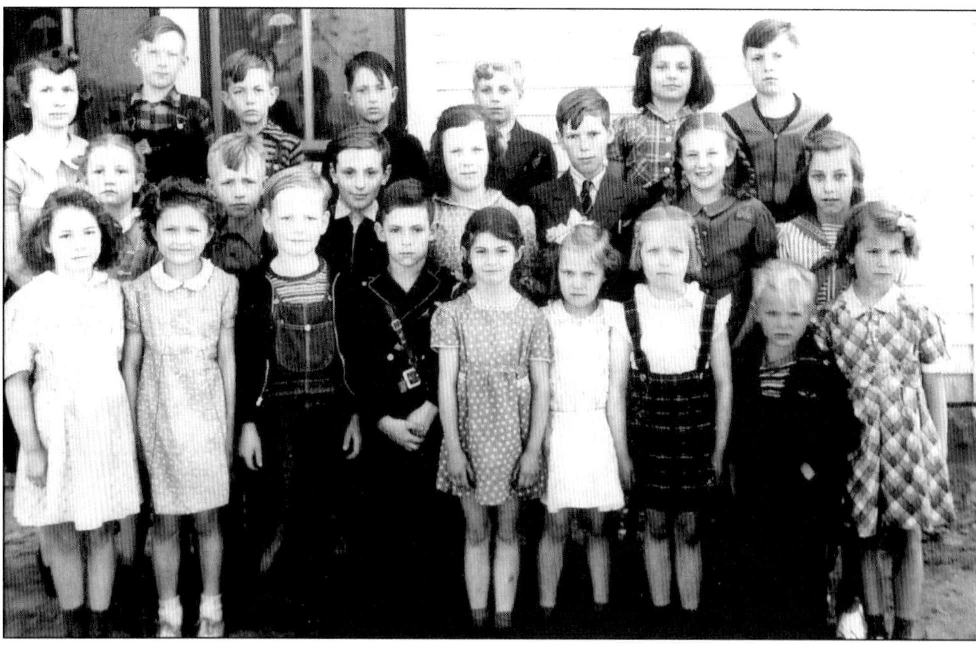

PICTURE DAY. Students from the Utica and Kleino Roads area pose on May 19, 1942. From left to right are the following: (first row) Nancy Eastman, Anna Zinni, Robert Knapton, Robert White, Janet Drake, Audrey Kleino, Alice Rice, James Wiegand, and Elaine Wiegand; (second row) Anna Starkey, Nancy Tieme, George Wiegand, Kathleen Daly, Burton Kimball, Edward Botapy, and Betsy Knapton; (third row) teacher Dorothy Schmidt, Leroy King, David Buckley, Lester Eastman, Ronald Wiegand, Betty Rice, and Arthur Boglio. (Photograph courtesy of Armin "Duane" Kleino.)

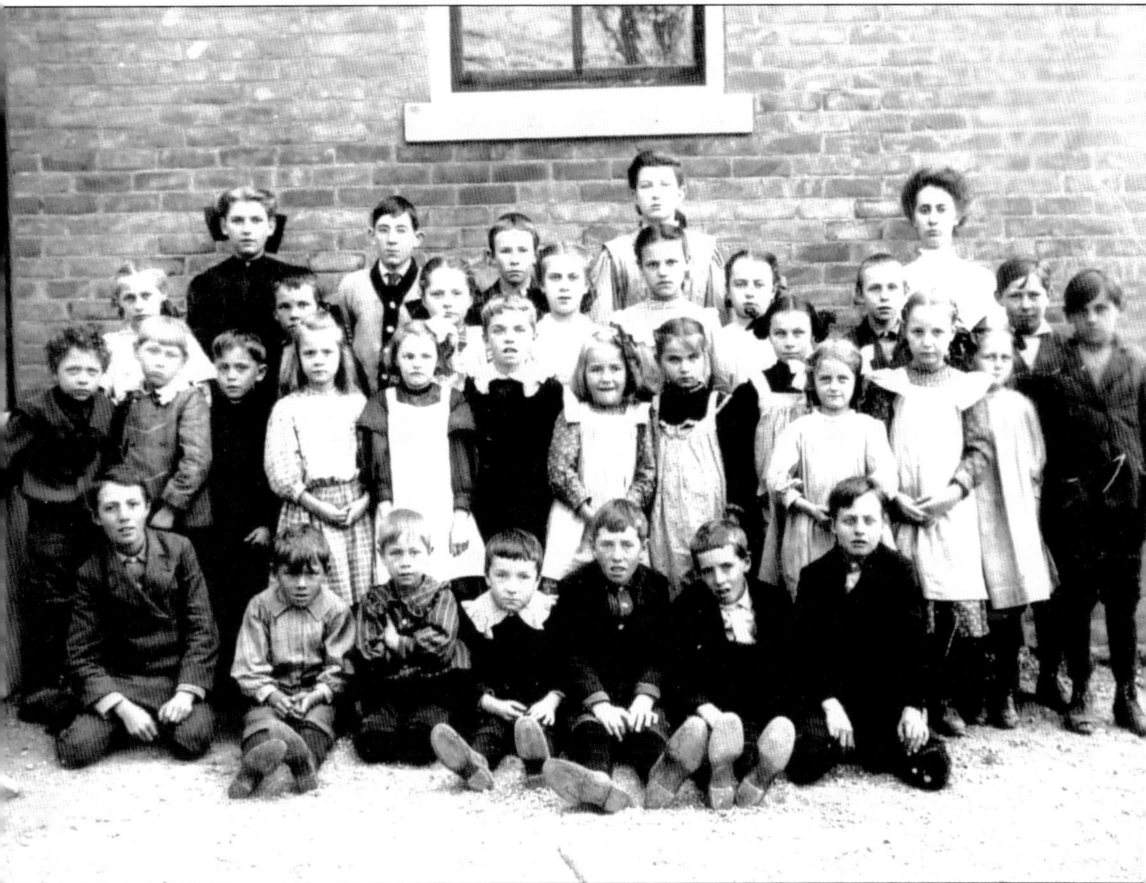

BURR SCHOOL STUDENTS. The Burr School, located on Ryan Road north of 18 Mile Road, was founded in 1845 to service the children of the northwest area of the township. Pictured are students and their teacher in front of the school in 1908. It was the only brick schoolhouse in the township and was named after the Burr family who supplied the bricks for construction from their brick and tile yard on 18 Mile Road near Ryan Road. The one-room brick structure was used into the 1950s, even after a new modern wing was added in 1951, but was demolished around 1960. The Burr School District No. 1 was the last district to join in consolidation with the Utica Community Schools in 1956. A modern school building with the Burr name occupies the same site today.

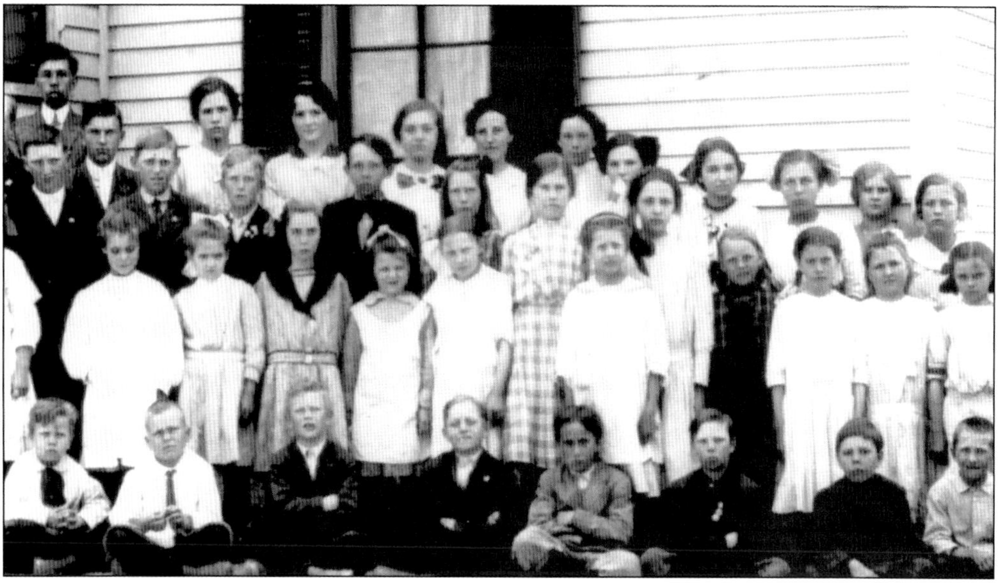

BERZ SCHOOL STUDENTS. Sterling School District No. 4, Berz School, was located on the southwest corner of Mound and 15 Mile Roads. It was a two-room country school, serving students up to the eighth grade. It was named for the Berz family, who were prominent farmers in southern Sterling Township back to 1860, owning large areas of land, including 100 acres on that corner. In this c. 1910 photograph, brothers Elmer and Arnold Measel (seated third and second from right) pose with unidentified students. Elmer remembers teachers May Peck and Harriet Mellow from his time there. May Peck had an elementary school named after her in Warren. (Photograph courtesy of Elmer Measel.)

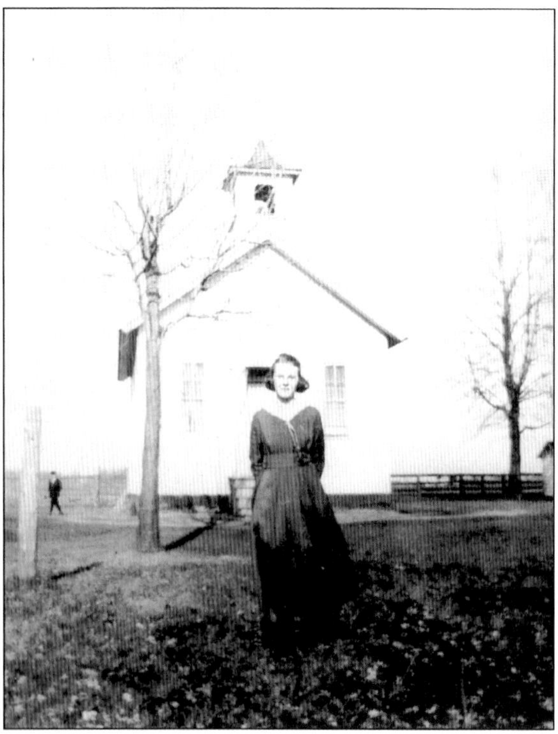

FOX SCHOOL. This *c.* 1917 photograph shows Meta Ahrens, a Sterling Township teen from down Clinton River Road, posing in front of the Fox School, located on Clinton River Road east of Hayes Road. The school was actually in Clinton Township, but Sterling Township students who lived near the eastern boundary attended also. The building survived until the 1980s, when fire destroyed it. Meta, on the other hand, lived to be 101. (Photograph courtesy of Armin "Duane" Kleino.)

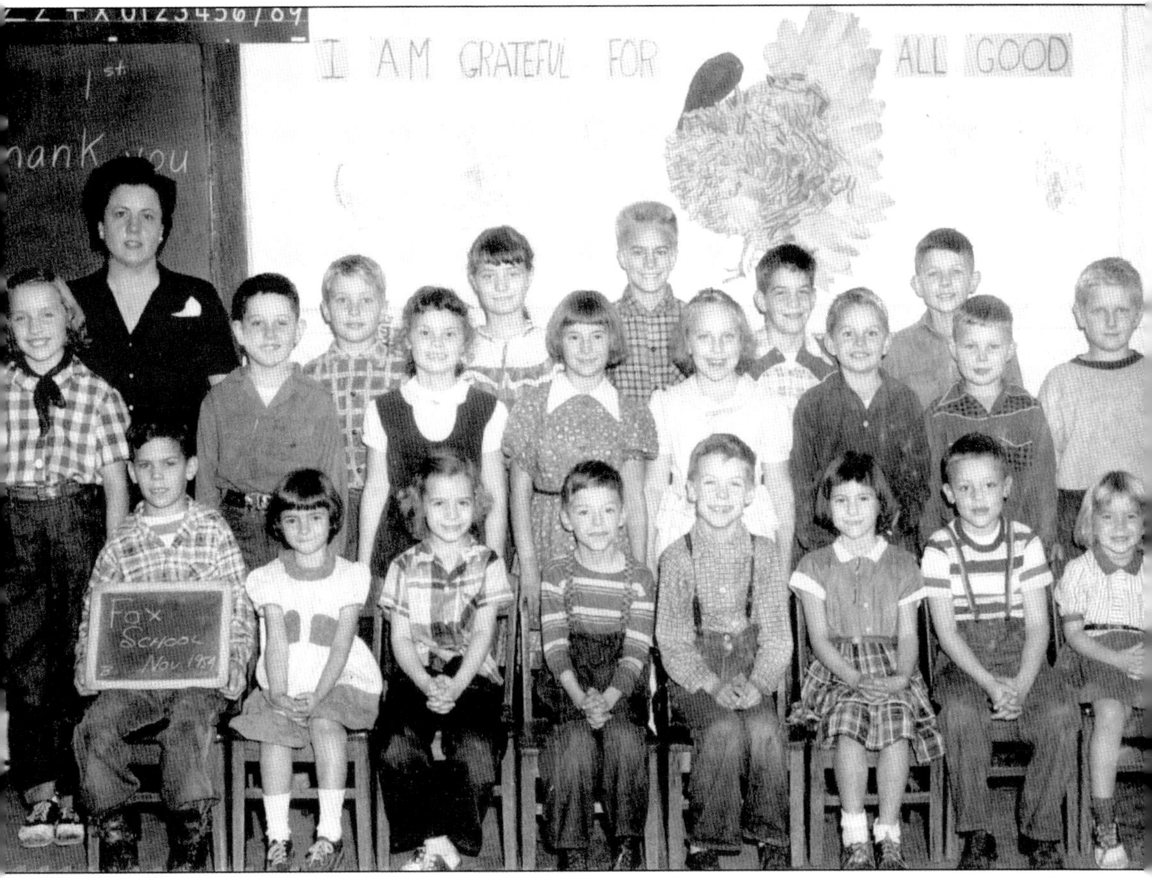

Fox School No. 1 Students. There were two Fox Schools during this era. Both were located on Clinton River Road east of Hayes Road. School No. 1 included first grade through fourth and was located just east of Resurrection Cemetery. School No. 2 included fifth grade through eighth and was just west of the cemetery. Both were one-room country schools with no indoor plumbing. Pictured in 1954 are, from left to right, the following: (first row) John Kempt, Faye Morton, Elizabeth Fleming, Tommy Zoldos, Billy Sharpe, Brenda Morton, Skip Valentine, and Cynthia Wolgosz; (second row) Carol Randazzo, Ed "Buzz" Martin, Nancy Valentine, Linda Morton, Diane Nieman, Don Wolgosz, Greg Loury, and Vincent Loury; (third row) teacher Mrs. Schmidt, Charles Young, Rozinna Primesburger, Rod McIntosh, Michael Briley, and Dan Phillips. (Photograph courtesy of Michael Briley.)

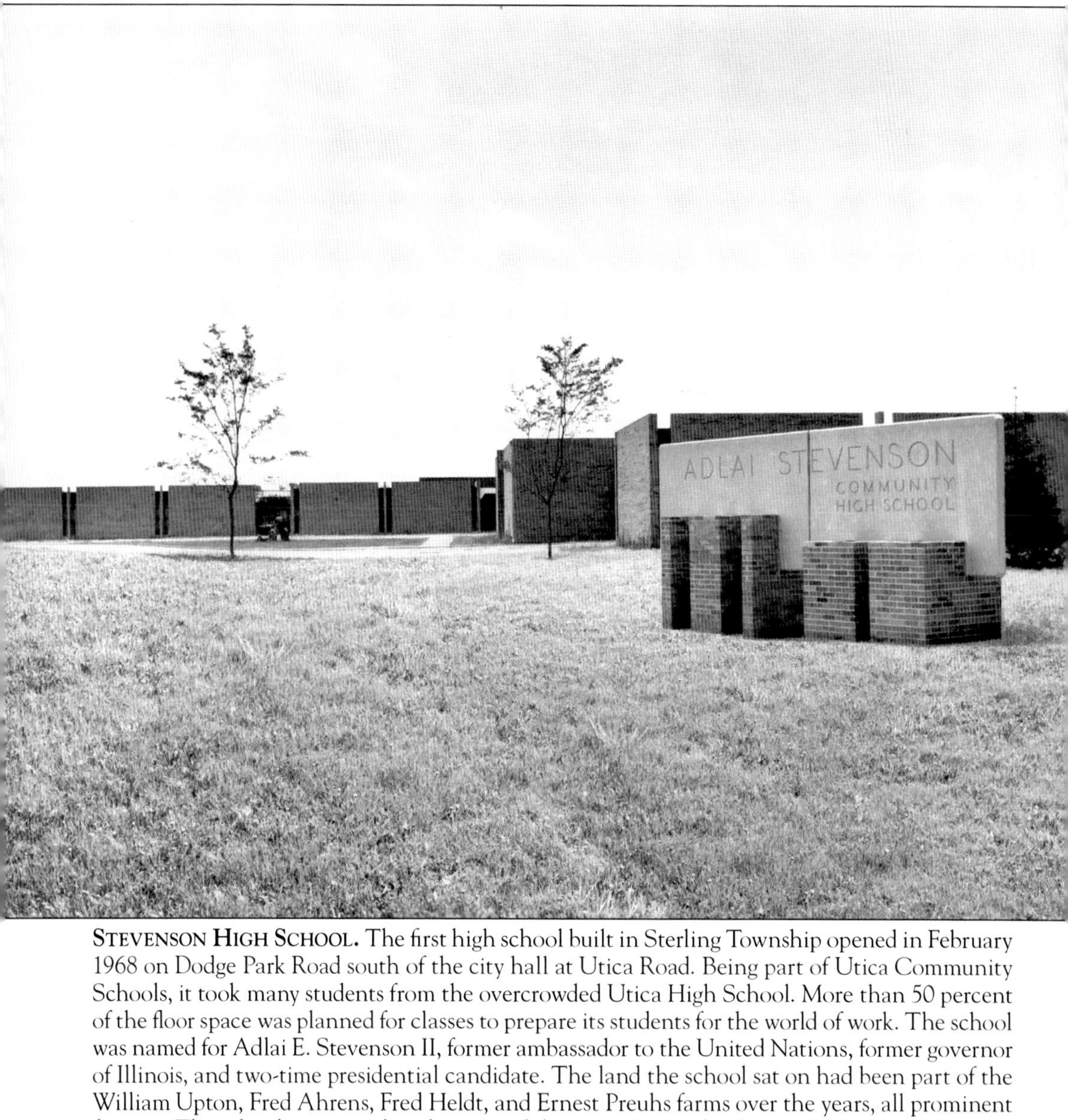

STEVENSON HIGH SCHOOL. The first high school built in Sterling Township opened in February 1968 on Dodge Park Road south of the city hall at Utica Road. Being part of Utica Community Schools, it took many students from the overcrowded Utica High School. More than 50 percent of the floor space was planned for classes to prepare its students for the world of work. The school was named for Adlai E. Stevenson II, former ambassador to the United Nations, former governor of Illinois, and two-time presidential candidate. The land the school sat on had been part of the William Upton, Fred Ahrens, Fred Heldt, and Ernest Preuhs farms over the years, all prominent farmers. The school is pictured at the start of the 1968–1969 school year. (Photograph courtesy of the Utica Sentinel.)

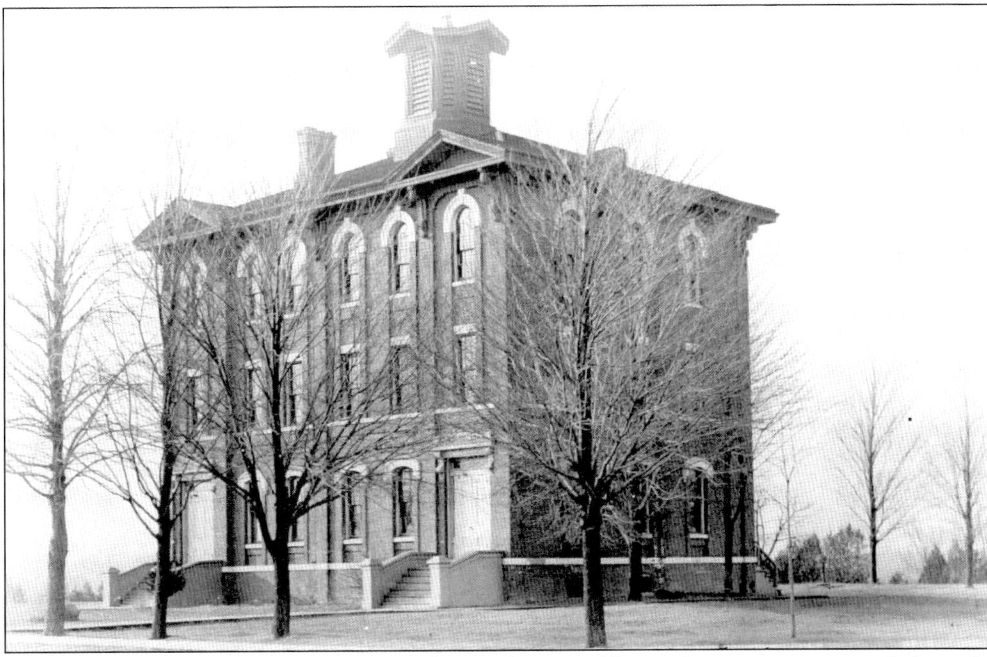

UTICA HIGH SCHOOL. If Sterling Township students could pass the state exam in eighth grade, they were allowed to continue their education. That usually meant going to Utica High School, in the village of Utica. Township students had to pay tuition, get their own rides into town, and be able to be spared on the farm, so it was special to be able to enroll here, before the system changed in the 1940s. This view of the school, which actually accommodated grades 1 through 12, is from around 1907. The school opened in 1860.

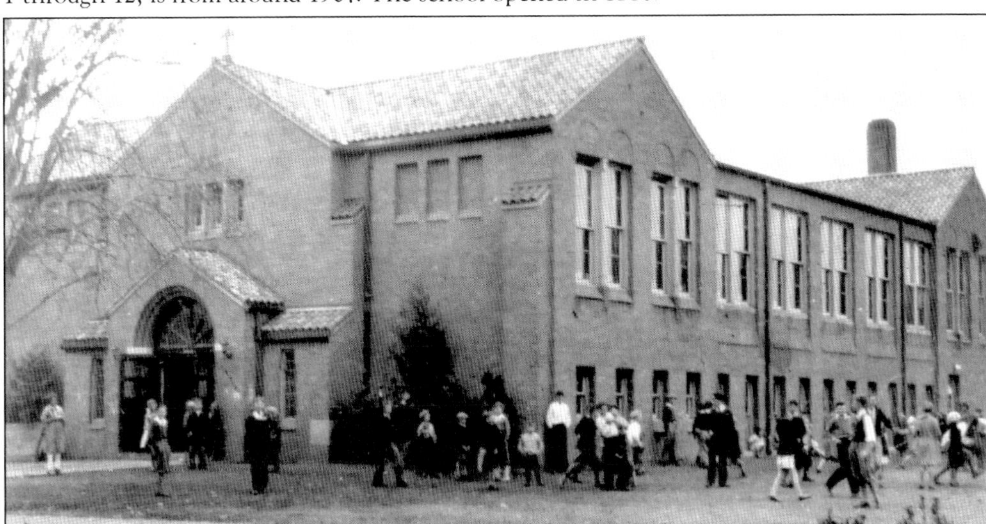

ST. LAWRENCE CATHOLIC SCHOOL. Pictured around 1940, St. Lawrence was the only Catholic school in the area at the time. The St. Lawrence Parish covered 80 square miles during the 1940s and served the growing Catholic community made up of the increasing Belgian, Polish, and Italian populations of Sterling and Shelby Townships and Utica. The grade school opened in 1930, and the high school in 1954. The school, located in Utica, still operates, although the high school closed in 1971. (Photograph courtesy of Evelyn Vogler Nowalski.)

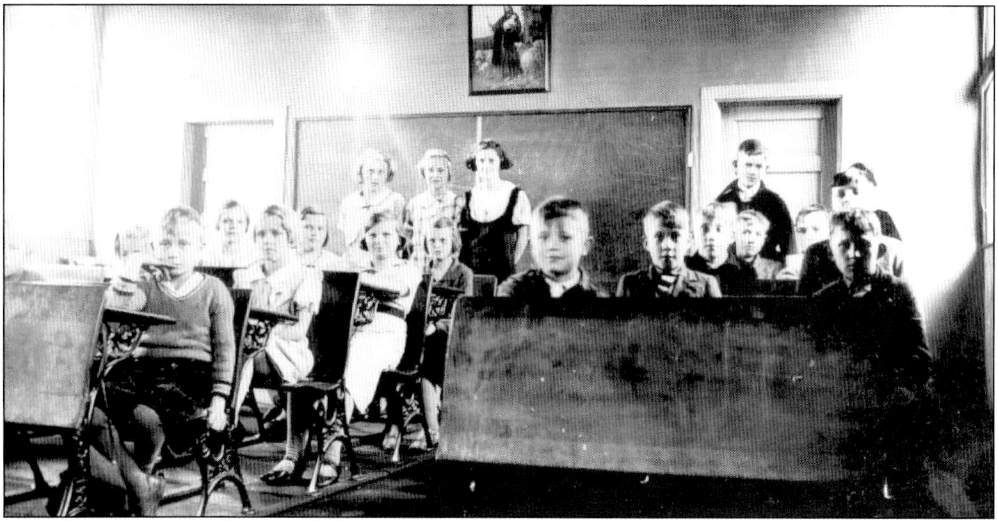

ST. PAUL CLASSROOM. What was probably the entire student body at St. Paul's at the time poses in the classroom around 1935. This building was the original church, built in 1879, and was used as the school from 1890 until 1959, when a new school building was built. School services were discontinued by the church for a time, from 1936 to 1946, but the school is still operating on Hayes Road today.

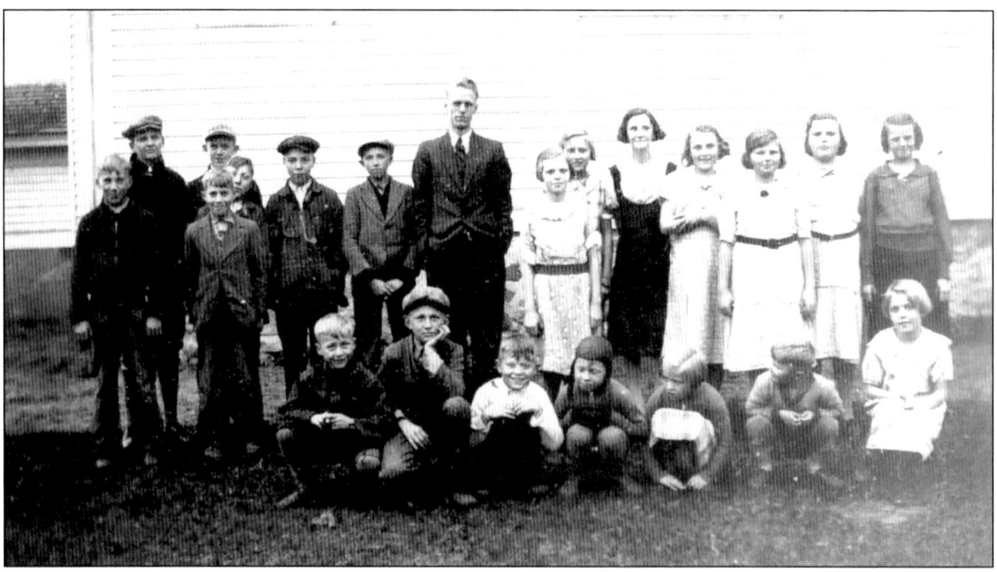

TEACHER AND STUDENTS. The same students from the classroom photograph pose with their teacher, Hugo Quitmeyer, outside St. Paul Lutheran Church, around 1935. Arnold Krentz was pastor at this time, his tenure being from 1923 to 1941. Krentz also acted as the school's teacher for some periods.

TEACHERS AT ST. PAUL LUTHERAN SCHOOL. James and Carolyn Wanagat, teachers at St. Paul, look over a paper while arithmetic textbooks wait to be passed out to students for the new 1967–1968 school year. The school at that time was located on Hayes Road at Canal Road and was built in 1959, replacing the 1879 building, which had served as the church's school since 1890. Education was offered through the eighth grade. (Photograph courtesy of the Utica Sentinel.)

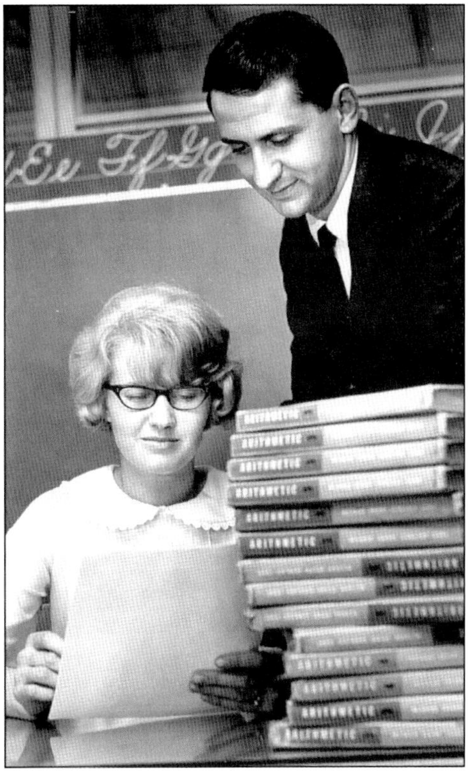

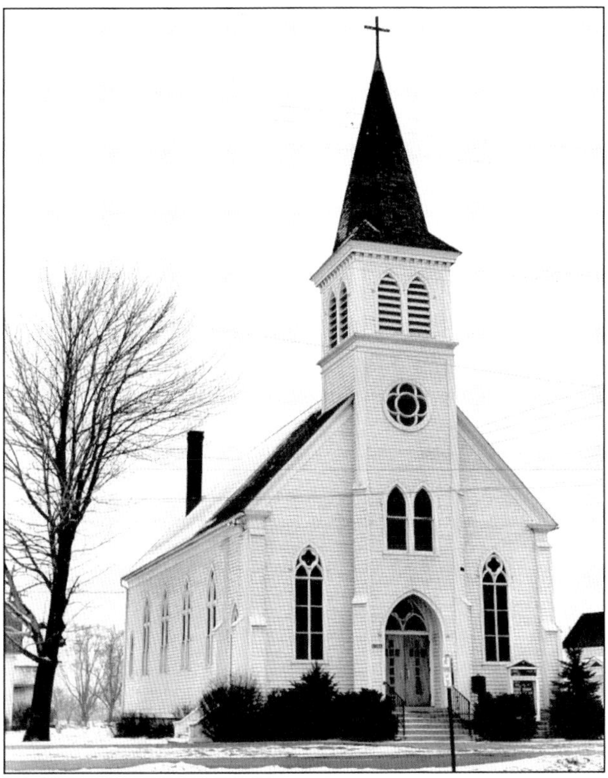

ST. PAUL LUTHERAN CHURCH. The congregation was founded in 1875 by immigrants from northern Germany. This structure, built in 1901 after lightning struck and burned the previous church, is seen as it looked in 1966. All services were held in German until 1925. Attempts to save the church from a road-widening project at its site on the corner of Canal Road and Hayes Road by moving it to Dodge Park to be used as a nondenominational chapel and museum failed. The church was demolished in 1989. A new church building replaced it. St. Paul's church and school was a very important part of the German Lutheran community that made up a large part of Sterling Township.

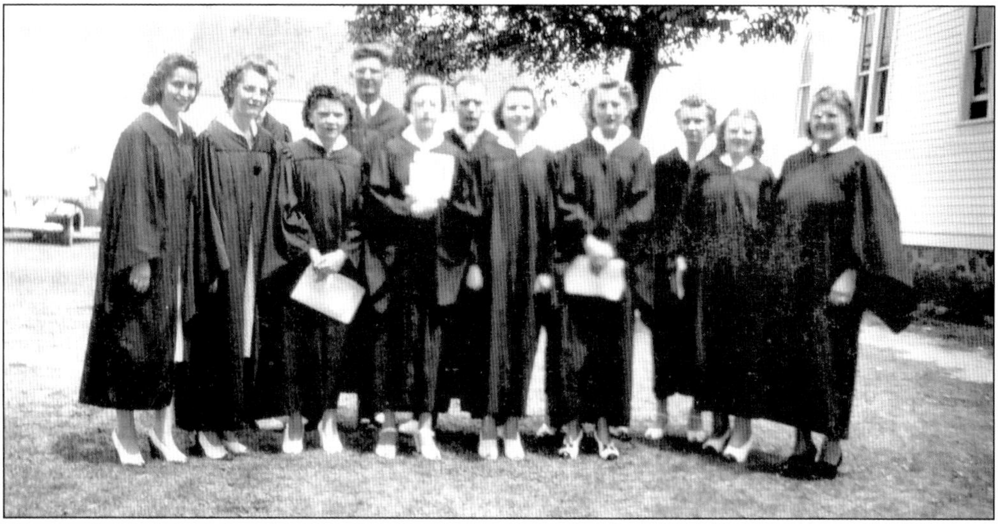

Choir Group. The St. Paul Lutheran choir group poses next to the church in this *c.* 1940 photograph. Magdalena Krentz, the wife of Pastor Arnold Krentz, was director of the choir at the time. The choir was one of many vital activities within the church community. The church provided social solidarity for the isolated farm families by offering a Ladies Aid, Men's Club, Walther League, Sunday school, ice-cream socials, and an annual harvest dinner. It was the heart of the German Lutheran community. The church was located on Canal Road at Hayes Road.

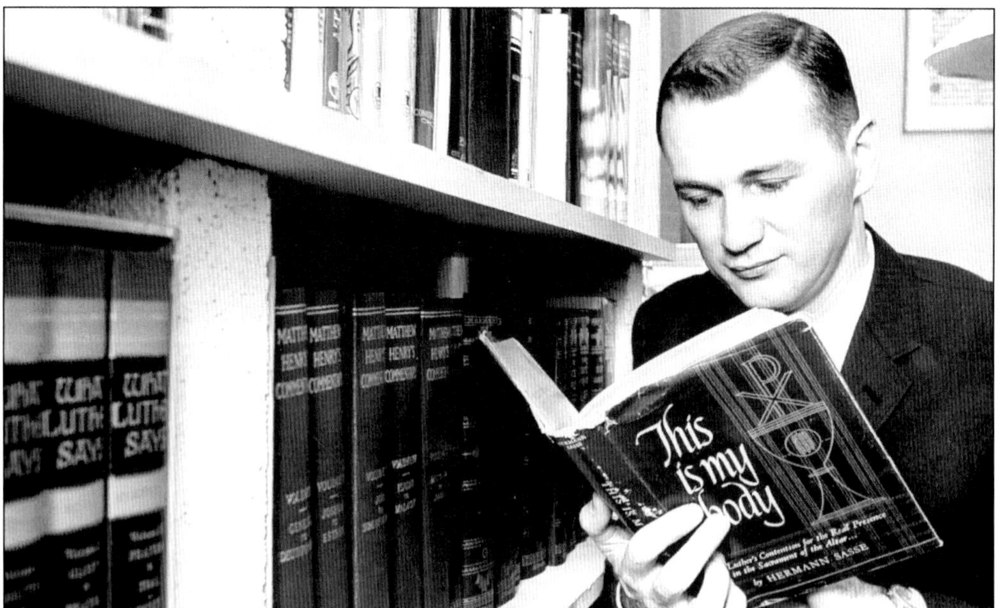

Reverend Pinchoff of St. Mark Lutheran. Some members of Ascension Lutheran Church in Detroit, led by Rev. Alfred Maaske, first held services in 1963 at Sunnybrook Lanes for the new mission church, St. Mark Lutheran Church. The Sterling Township area had no churches representing the Wisconsin Evangelical Lutheran Synod, so property was purchased at 11063 16½ Mile Road, and by 1968 a new church had been constructed. Rev. Edward Pinchoff, the first full-time pastor, as seen in this 1967 photograph, led the congregation from 1965 until 1969. (Photograph courtesy of the Utica Sentinel.)

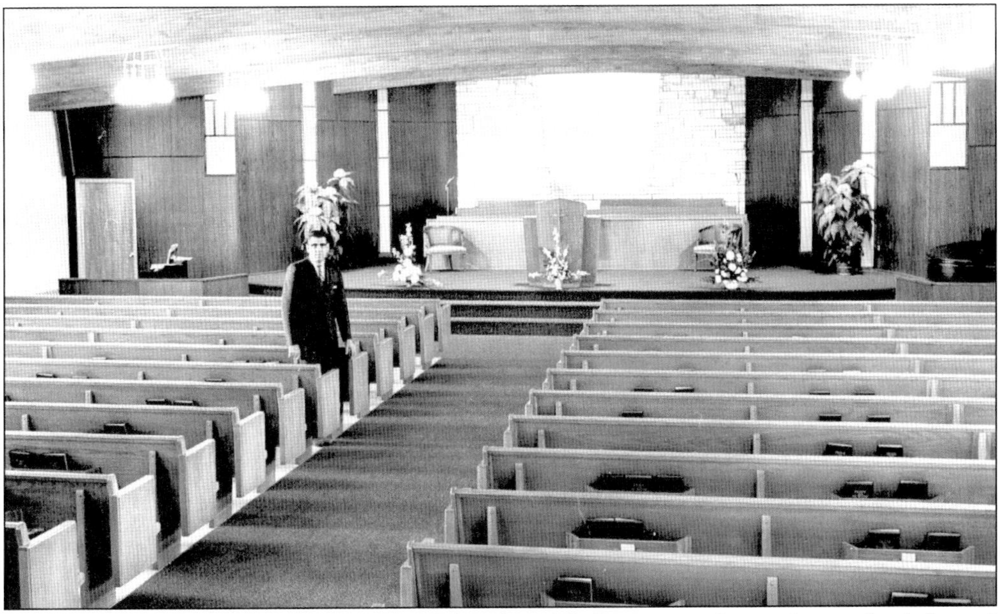

COVENANT BAPTIST CHURCH. Pastor Theodore Madonna stands in the newly dedicated addition to the original 1961 church building. The congregation began meeting at the home of Reverend Madonna in 1956. They built a small church building at 11455 Canal Road in 1961 and opened this addition in 1966. The reverend's son, Paul Madonna, is the current pastor of the church. (Photograph courtesy of the Utica Sentinel.)

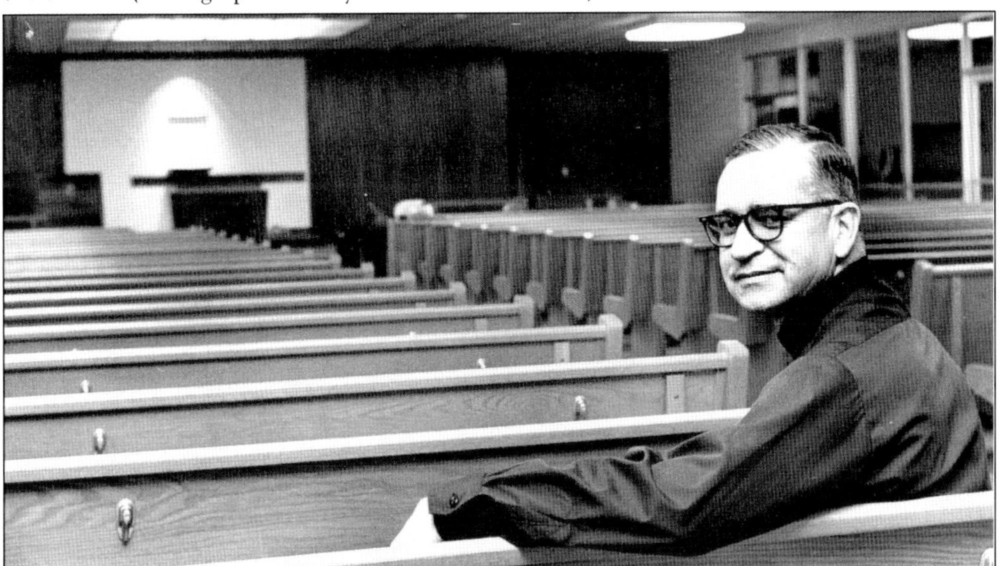

REVEREND SCHRAUDER OF ST. BLASE. St. Blase Catholic Church was founded in 1967 by Rev. George Schrauder. The part of the building pictured here, in 1968, was opened in December 1967 and used for masses until the new church was built in 1978. The original section was then used as an extra gathering space. The architecture of St. Blase is said to closely resemble St. Ephron, another Sterling Heights Catholic church. St. Blase grew from the original 40 families to become at one time the largest Catholic parish in Macomb County. The church is located at 12151 15 Mile Road at Maple Lane Road. (Photograph courtesy of the Utica Sentinel.)

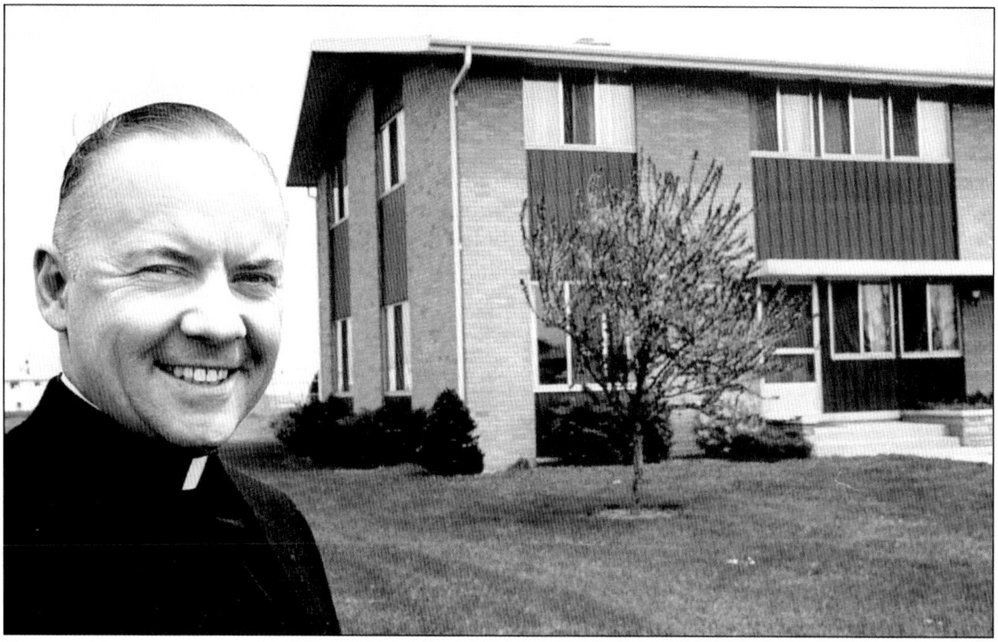

Father Partensky of St. Matthias. St. Matthias Catholic Church, located on 19 Mile Road near Goldberg, began as a mission church of St. Lawrence in 1960. Fr. Leonard Partensky was appointed its first full-time pastor. In this 1967 photograph, he poses by the rectory that was built, along with the temporary church, in 1961. Partensky served St. Matthias until 1967, when he was followed by Fr. Henry Waraksa as pastor. (Photograph courtesy of the Utica Sentinel.)

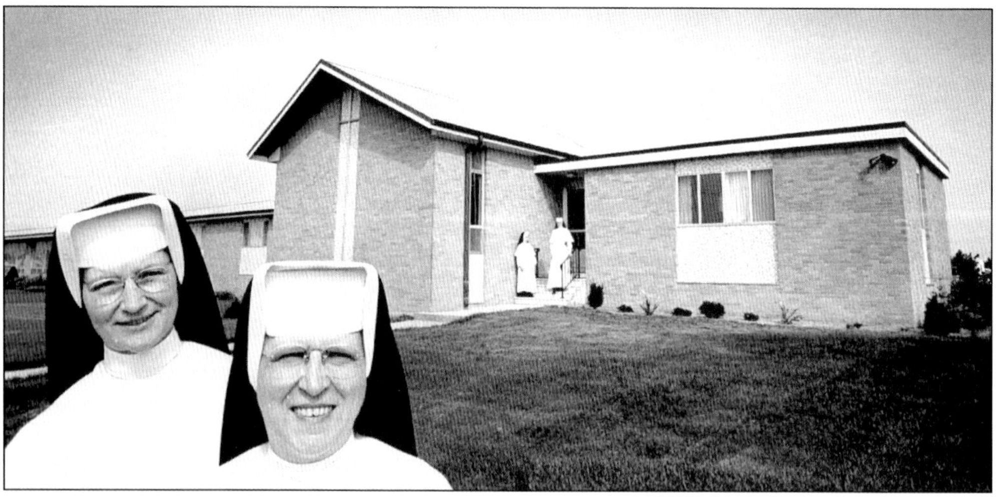

St. Matthias Convent. Happy to be in their new home, four Dominican Sisters of the Congregation of St. Rose de Lima, Oxford, pose in front of the new convent in August 1966. The convent had rooms for six nuns plus two visitor rooms, a sitting room, a dining area, and a kitchen. Pictured here are, from left to right, Sister Mary Joseph, who had been principal of St. Benedict in Pontiac; Sister Angela; Sister Delores; and Sister Mary Celeste. A building with six classrooms to be used for religious education was also opened at this time and was rented at first by Utica Community Schools to accommodate an overflow of elementary students from Dresden Elementary School. (Photograph courtesy of the Utica Sentinel.)

Four

RECREATION

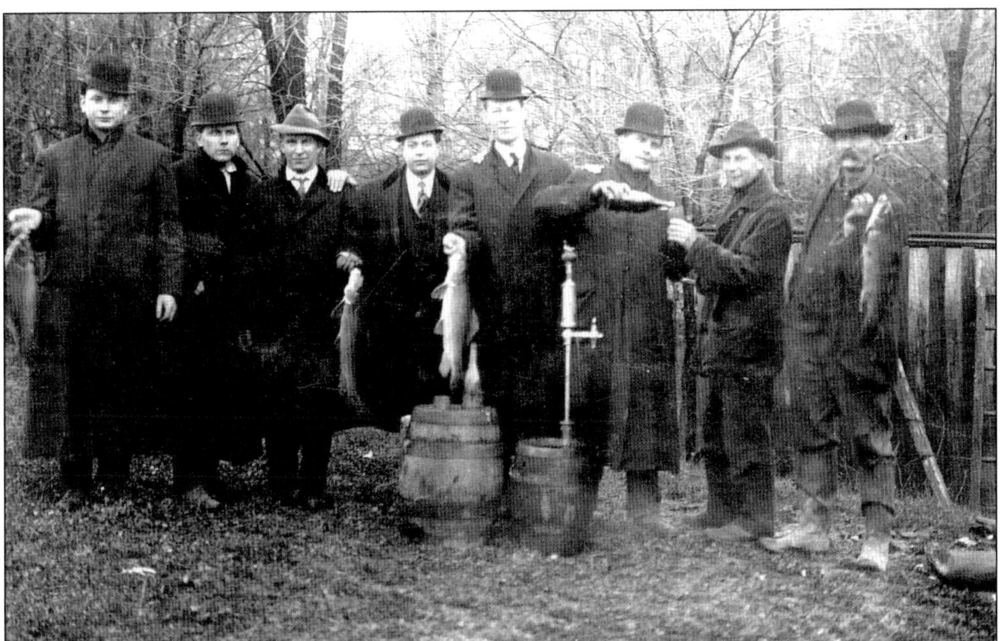

CLINTON RIVER FISHING PARTY. Formally dressed business men pose with local farmers Otto Ahrens and his father, Charles Ahrens (second and first from right). The Ahrens farm backed up to the Clinton River, just west of Hayes Road. This 1910 scene may have been an old-time equivalent to a modern golf outing. The fishing was done with nets, and the refreshments came from a bottle or a keg. (Photograph courtesy of Eleanor Ahrens.)

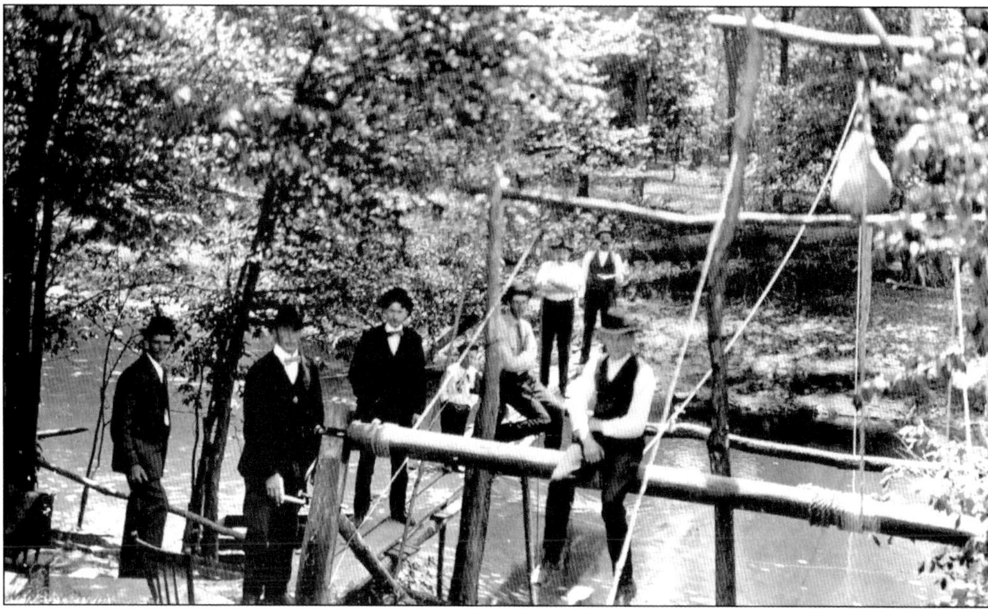

SHANTYMEN. Fishermen are enjoying a sunny day in 1910 while trying their luck at fishing with a dip net in the Clinton River. These elaborate apparatuses made from tree limbs were not uncommon along the river. In this view, the net appears to have been lowered into the water, while the bow-tied man in the foreground has his hand on the crank. A number of these men are from the Ahrens family, with Charles Ahrens at the far end of the dock. (Photograph courtesy of Eleanor Ahrens.)

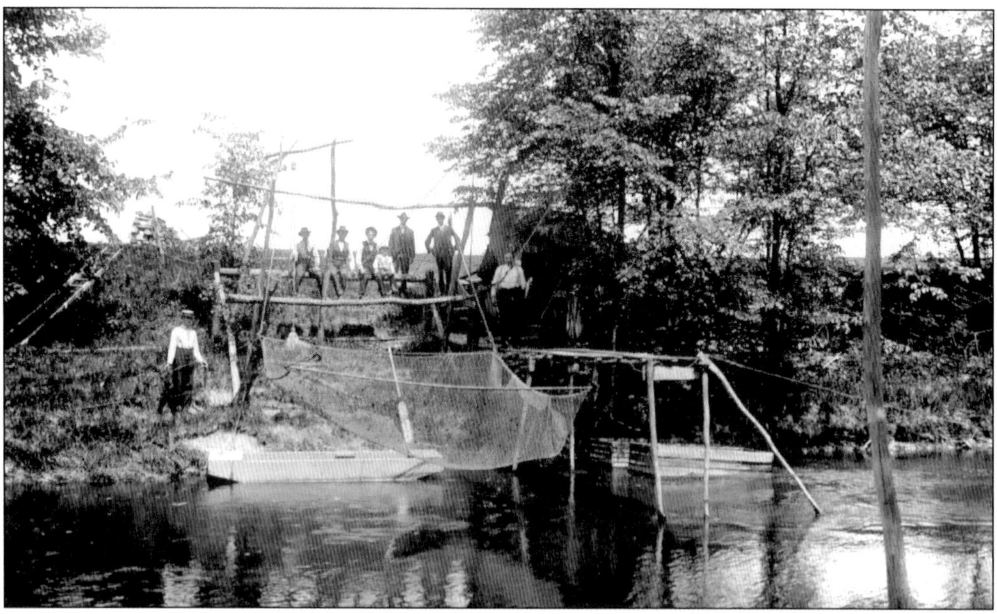

RAISING THE NET. The same group is seen from the other side of the river, but the only thing in the net seems to be the paddle for the skiff. They might have hoped for mullet, suckers, and red horse, fish commonly caught in dip nets in the area at that time. The shanty on the bank provided shelter and a place to play cards while waiting for the fish to cooperate. (Photograph courtesy of Eleanor Ahrens.)

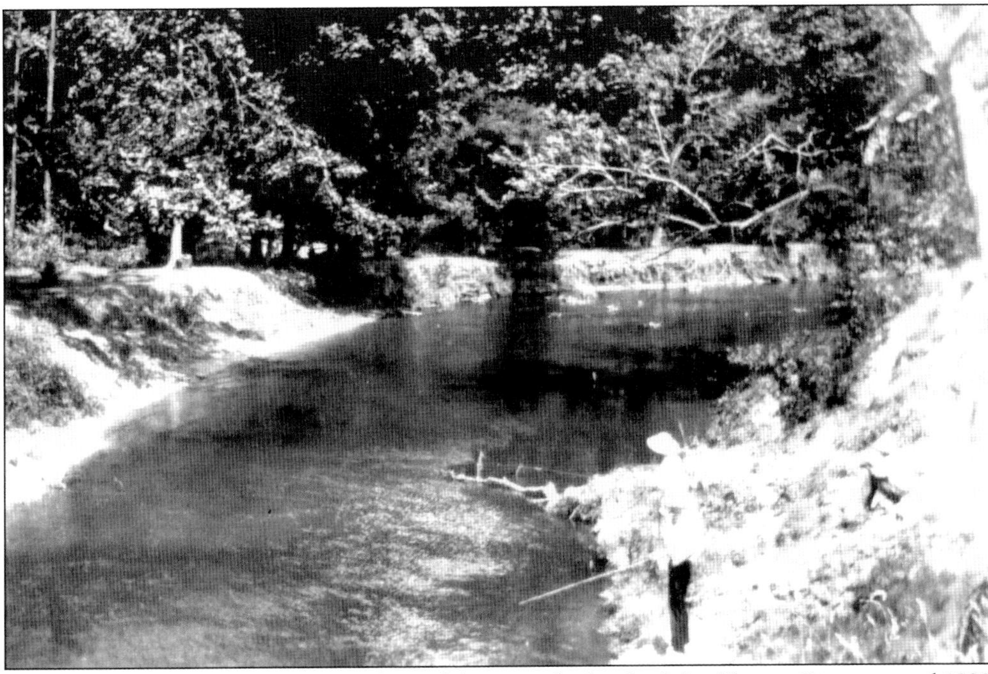

ARE THE FISH BITING? Three people are fishing on the bank of the Clinton River around 1920. Along with dip nets, fishing was also done with poles, as seen here, and sometimes at night from a small boat with lanterns and spears, as one resident remembered. The water looks clear and clean and must have been a relaxing way to spend a summer afternoon.

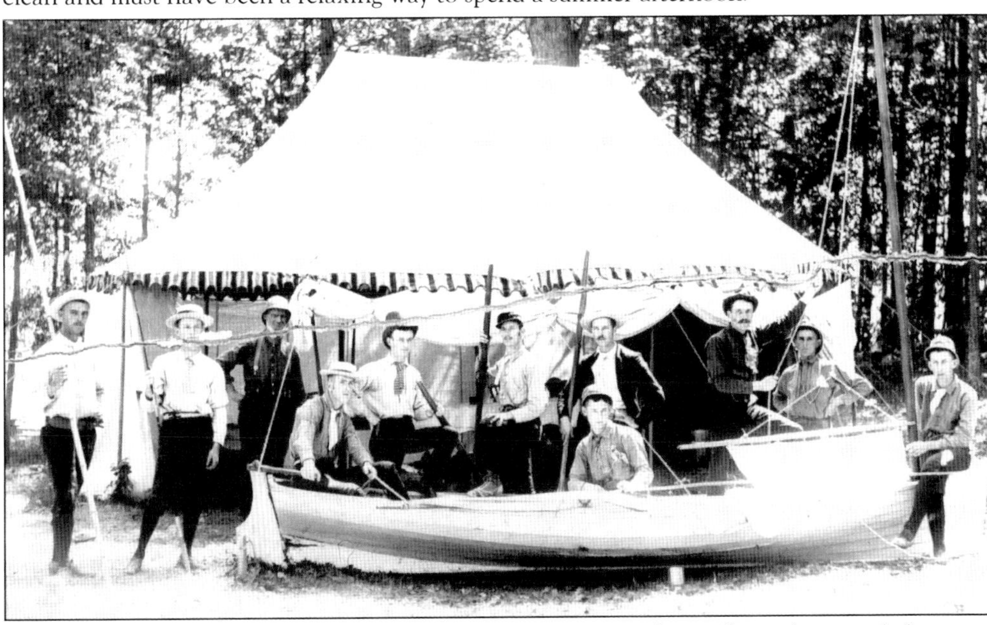

YOUNG MEN WITH A SAILBOAT. This genteel group poses with a sailboat that may belong to a boating club. The fine tent behind them could have sheltered their afternoon meal. Not much is known for sure about this *c.* 1885 photograph other than Frank Upton, son of the wealthy and prominent Sterling Township farmer William Upton, is at the far left. (Photograph courtesy of Marjorie Upton DeFrancis.)

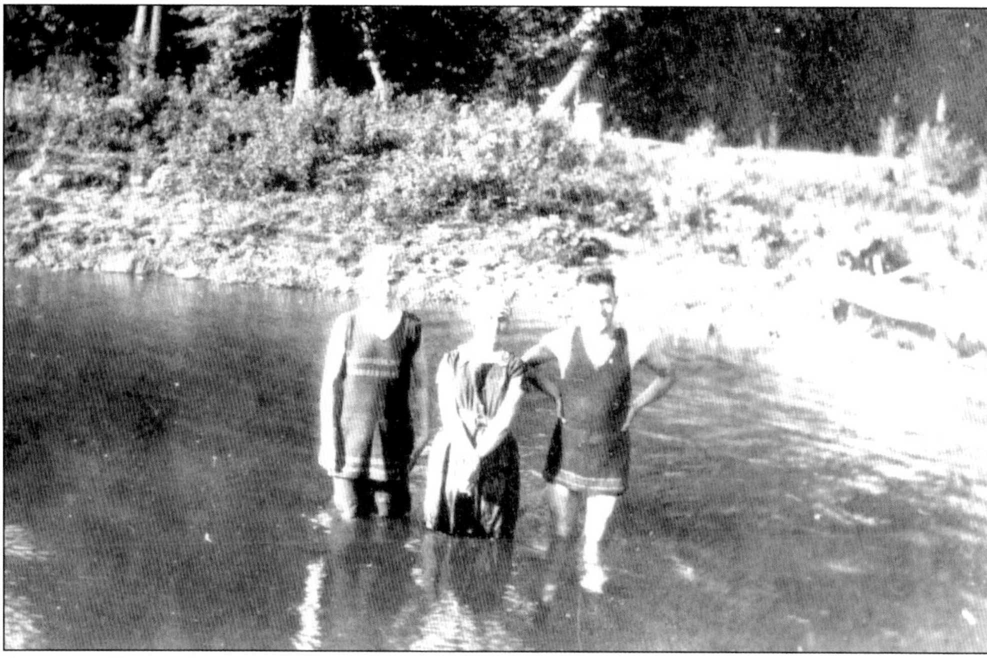

CLINTON RIVER SWIMMING. In this scene from the 1920s, a group pauses in their summertime fun. This spot on the Clinton River was on the Holzhauer property on Utica Road west of Kleino Road. The Holzhauers lived part-time in Detroit and part-time in Sterling Township, where the family raised flowers to be sold in Mount Clemens. The river was popular with swimmers, boaters, and fishermen, as the water was clean and clear, often drawing visiting relatives from Detroit who enjoyed what the countryside had to offer. (Photograph courtesy of Irene Holzhauer Hoffman.)

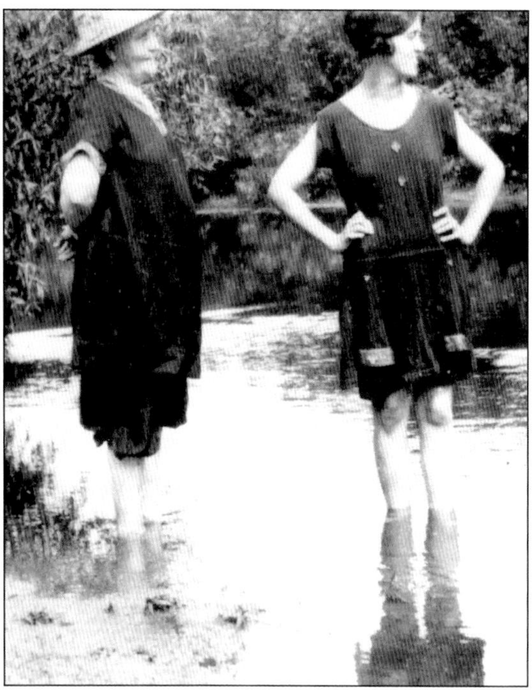

BATHING BEAUTIES. Anna Holzhauer and her daughter Irene Holzhauer Hoffman enjoy wading in the clear water of the Clinton River around 1920, which ran behind their home on Utica Road, west of Kleino Road. The women's bathing suits were the style of the time; even a man's bathing suit covered most of the body. (Photograph courtesy of Irene Holzhauer Hoffman.)

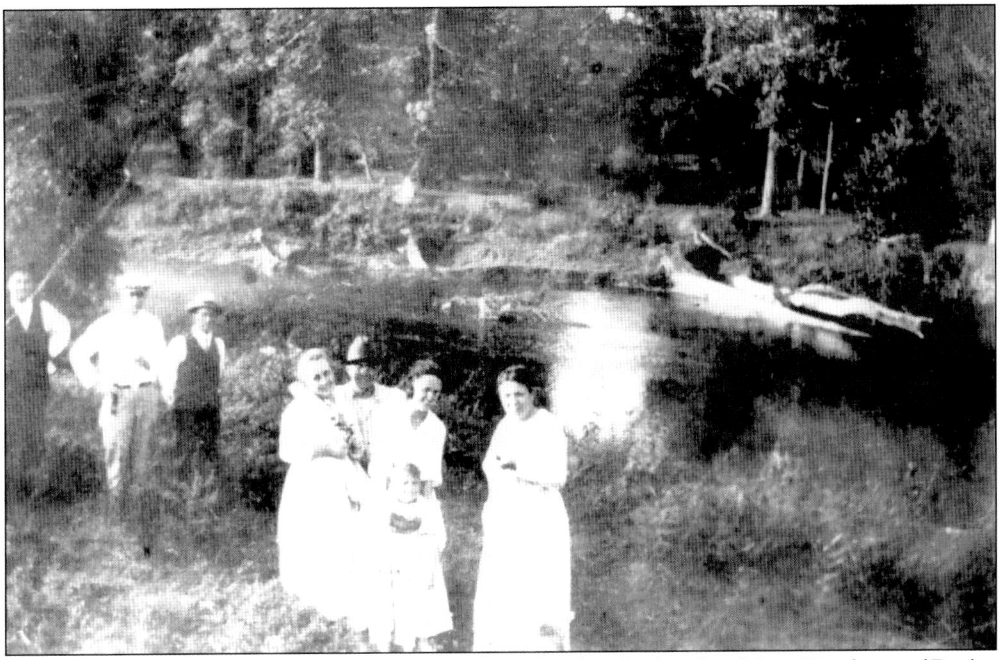

RIVERBANK. Pictured around 1918 is the Holzhauer family, who lived on Utica Road east of Dodge Park Road. Their property backed up to the Clinton River, which made a nice focal point for the many friends and family who visited them on weekends. Fishing, swimming, or just enjoying the pleasant sounds of the river were all options. Pictured, from left to right, are four unidentified people, Fred Holzhauer (property owner), Irene Holzhauer (Fred's daughter), Harriet Holzhauer Klagge, and an unidentified child in front. (Photograph courtesy of Irene Holzhauer Hoffman.)

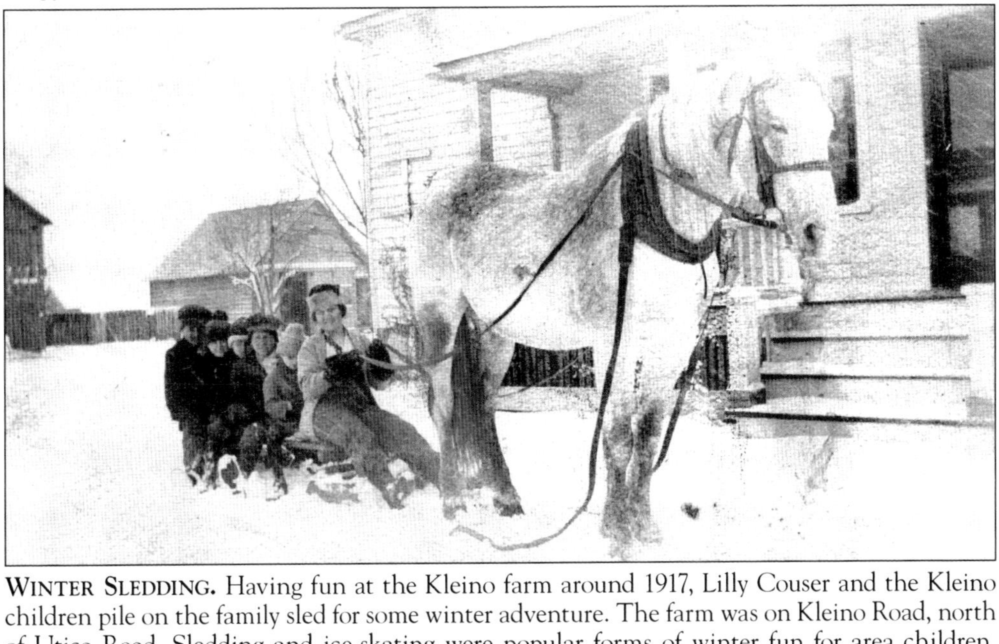

WINTER SLEDDING. Having fun at the Kleino farm around 1917, Lilly Couser and the Kleino children pile on the family sled for some winter adventure. The farm was on Kleino Road, north of Utica Road. Sledding and ice-skating were popular forms of winter fun for area children, especially along the Clinton River, the old Clinton-Kalamazoo Canal, and other area creeks. (Photograph courtesy of Armin "Duane" Kleino.)

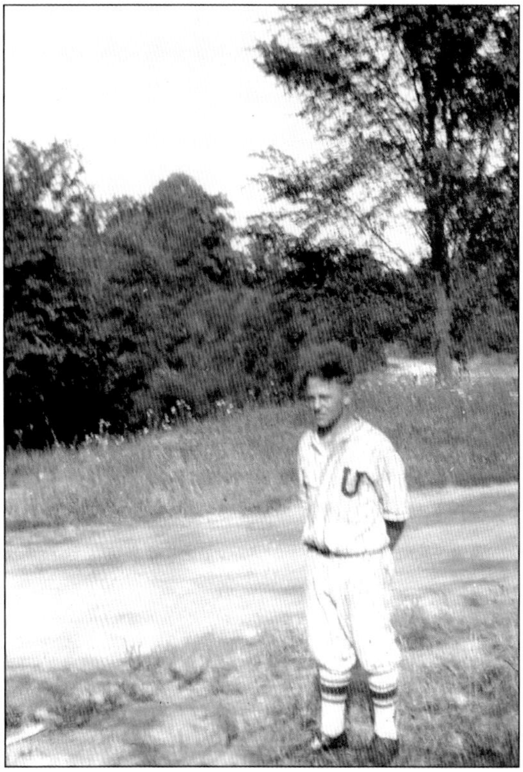

GO UTICA! Pictured is Melvin Kleino, of Kleino Road in Sterling Township, all suited up for a Utica High School baseball game around 1924. Baseball was very popular in the area; the village of Utica even had their own team to compete with other communities. A number of local boys went on to play professional baseball or football, the most famous being Duane "Duke" Maas, the son of Fred and Mabel Maas. Duke pitched for the Detroit Tigers, Athletics, and Yankees from 1955 to 1961. He got his start as a boy throwing rocks at their Dodge Park Road farm, located across from the current Heritage Junior High School. His home still stands. (Photograph courtesy of Armin "Duane" Kleino.)

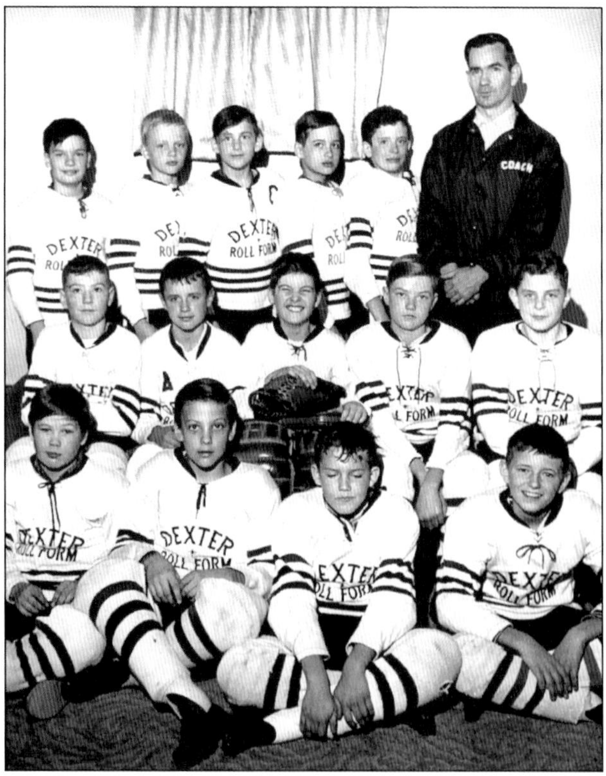

STERLING HAWKS. Pictured are the January 1968 Hawks, a peewee hockey team organized by the fledgling Sterling Township Parks and Recreation Department. Sponsored by Dexter Roll Form, a manufacturing company based in Warren, Michigan, these boys are some tough-looking opponents.

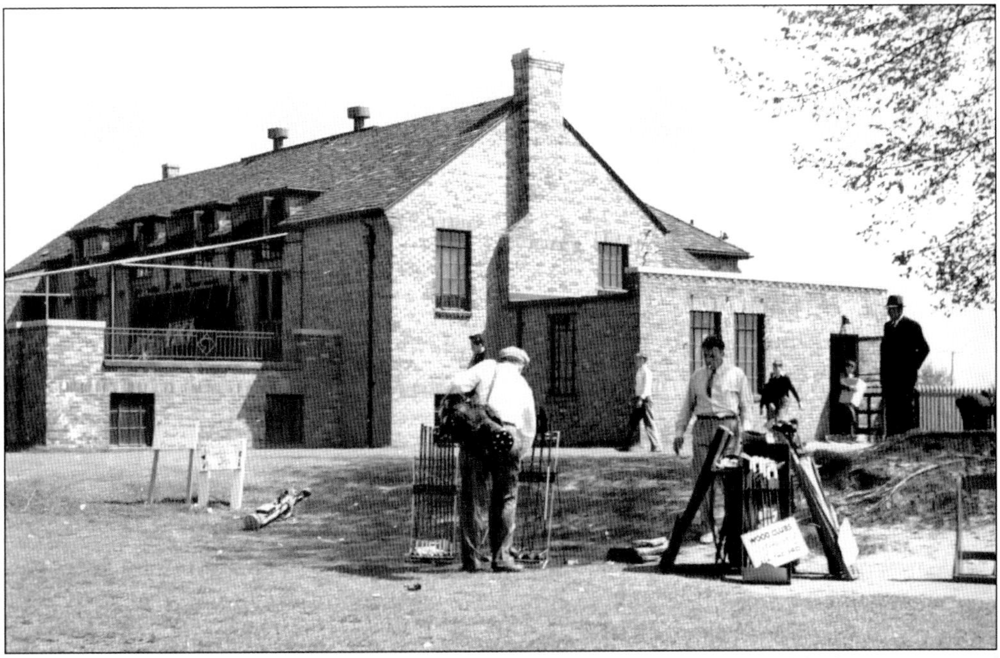

RAMMLER CLUBHOUSE. This 1940s photograph taken at Rammler Golf Club shows a group of golfers checking out clubs for sale. Area courses drew golfers from far and wide. Also, for locals who preferred not to work on the farm, the courses offered employment outdoors or in the kitchens. (Photograph courtesy of Paul Duda, Rammler Golf and Country Club.)

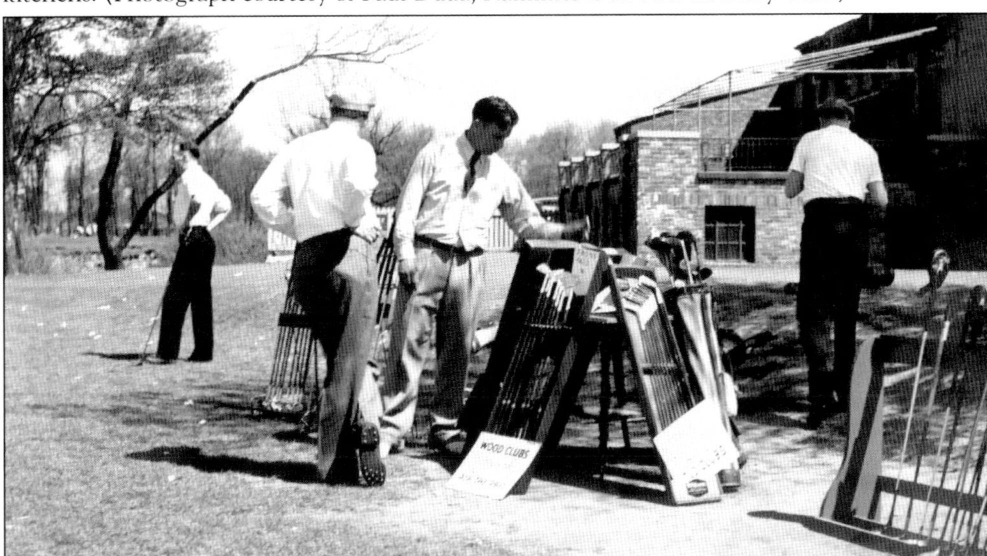

ASK THE PRO. These stylish gentlemen are enjoying signs of spring at Rammler Golf Club during a golf club sale in the 1940s. The course, located at 38180 Utica Road east of Schoenherr Road, was built in 1929 on land that was originally the Rice family farm. Township farms gave birth to a number of golf courses during the 1920s in order to provide the wide-open spaces needed for the newly popular sport of golf. Other township courses started about the same time were Maple Lane, Plumbrook, Sunnybrook, and the now defunct Clinton Valley Country Club. (Photograph courtesy of Paul Duda, Rammler Golf and Country Club.)

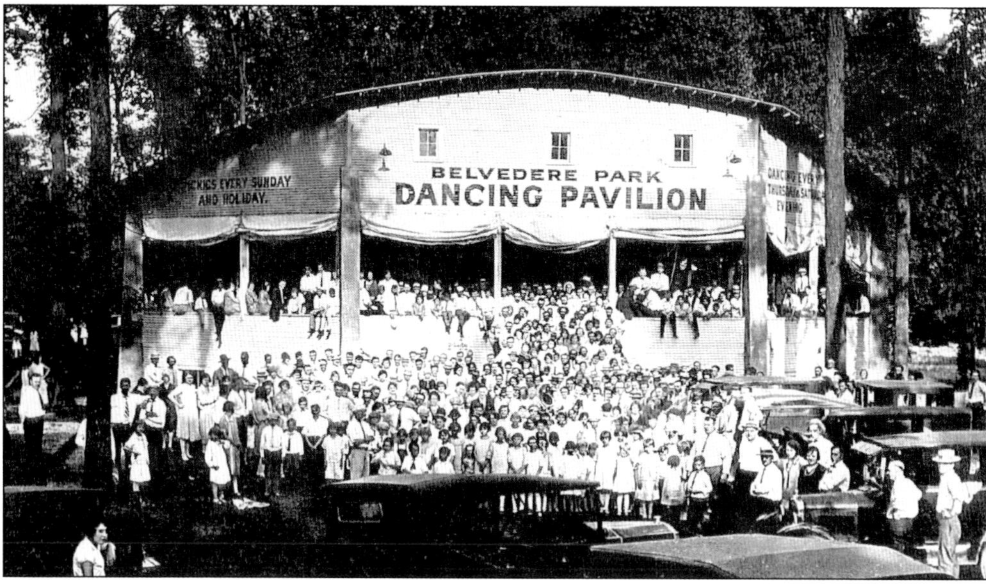

BELVEDERE PARK DANCE PAVILION. Belvedere Park was located along the Clinton River, on Utica Road, west of Hayes Road. The park was owned and run by Edward Ochylski as a private park from the early 1920s until it was dismantled in 1941. The park was one of a number of Polish parks located at sites along the Clinton River and its tributaries. The parks were favored by Detroit area Polish groups who drove up for summer recreation and bootleg beverages. World War II gas and tire rationing brought an end to the summer jaunts and to the private park tradition in the Clinton River area. This scene is from the mid-1920s. (Photograph courtesy of Edward Ochylski Jr.)

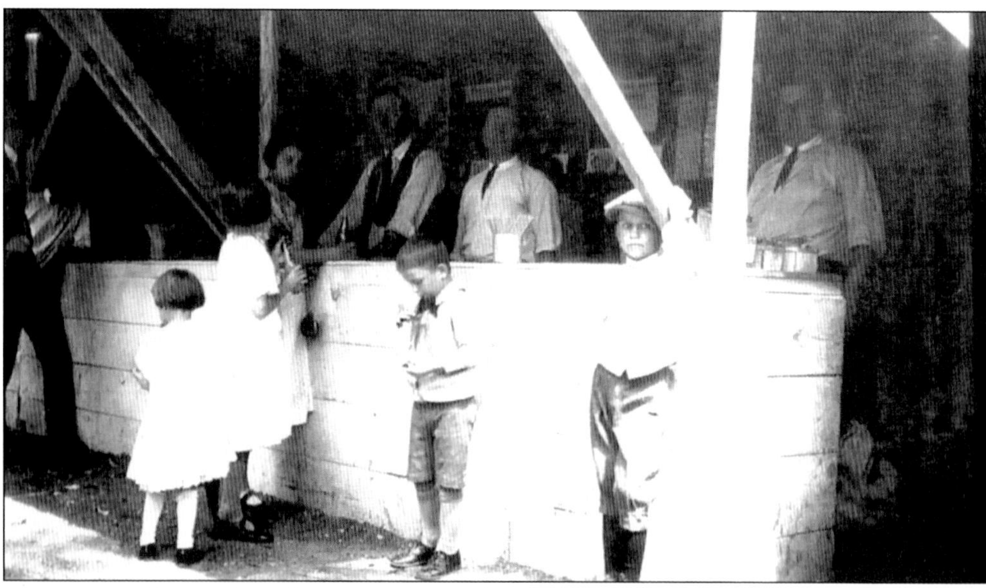

CONCESSION STAND. Root beer, strawberry, cherry, rock and rye, grape, and cream soda were the choices of Faygo pop. Candy, ice-cream cones, and hot dogs rounded out the menu for lucky children at Belvedere Park in 1926. For the older folks, there was beer. The icehouse stored ice from the Clinton River to keep the refreshments cold. (Photograph courtesy of Edward Ochylski Jr.)

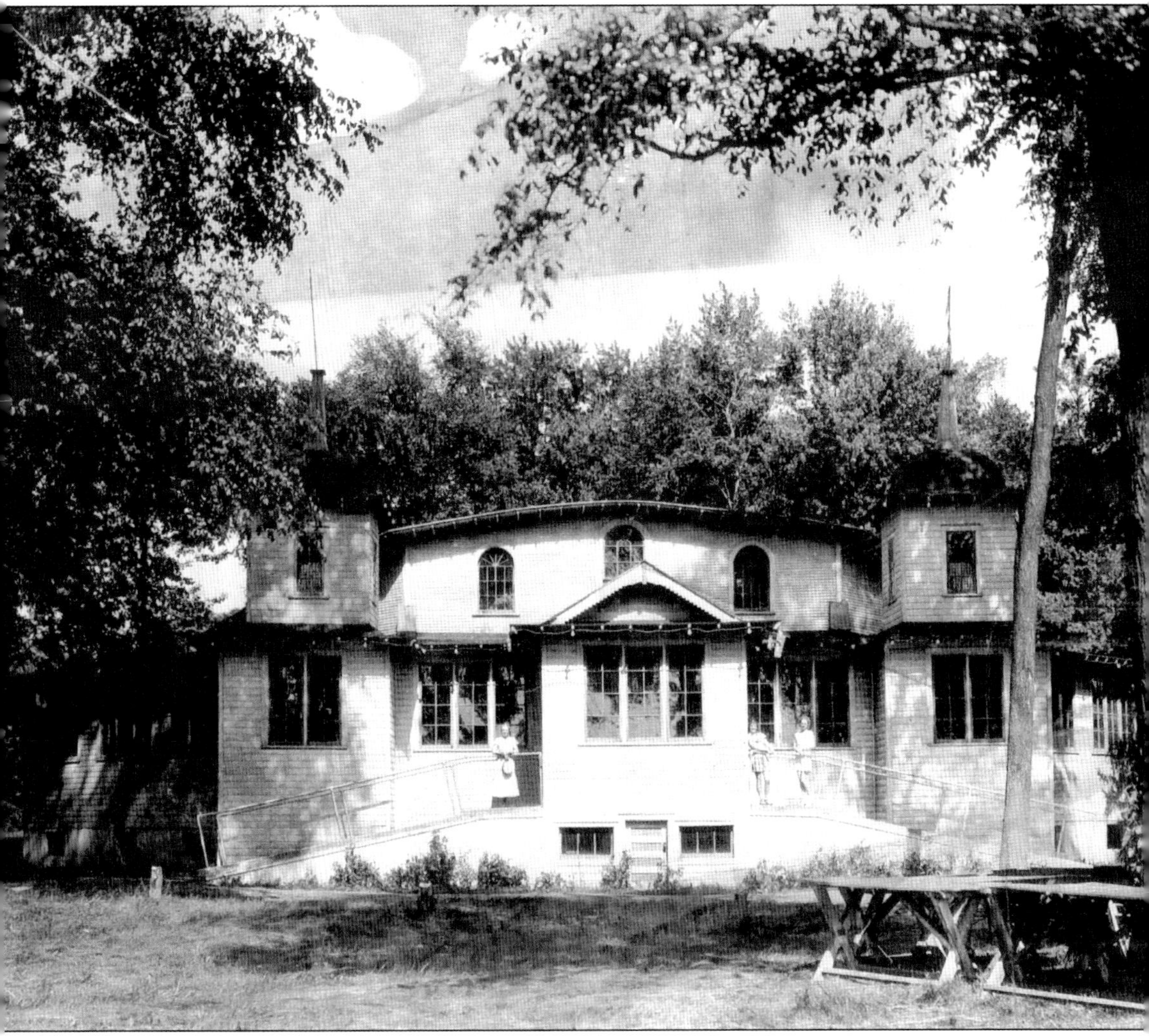

IMPROVED BELVEDERE DANCE PAVILION. An addition surrounds the original structure in this *c.* 1930 photograph. The only all-weather dance hall in the area, and the second largest in Michigan, featured a maple dance floor and bleacher seats. Acrobats, talent shows, and contests provided entertainment in addition to the dancing. The inclined concrete ramps were used to bring in pianos and stage props to be used by the large professional bands complete with audio systems that were employed by the park. Outdoor activities were plentiful too, including airplane rides, decorated car contests, barbecue pits, pony rides, and alligator wrestling. During Prohibition, raids by the Macomb County Sheriff's Department and even federal agents were commonplace here and at other private parks in the area, but business always went on as usual. Sterling Township's Belvedere Park, named after a famous park in Warsaw, Poland, finally succumbed in 1941 to declining business and was dismantled, the wood being sold to build buildings and attractions at Green Glen Park, another Polish park in the area that lasted longer. After the park was out of business, the Ochylski family went on to make a name for themselves in the meatpacking industry. (Photograph courtesy of Edward Ochylski Jr.)

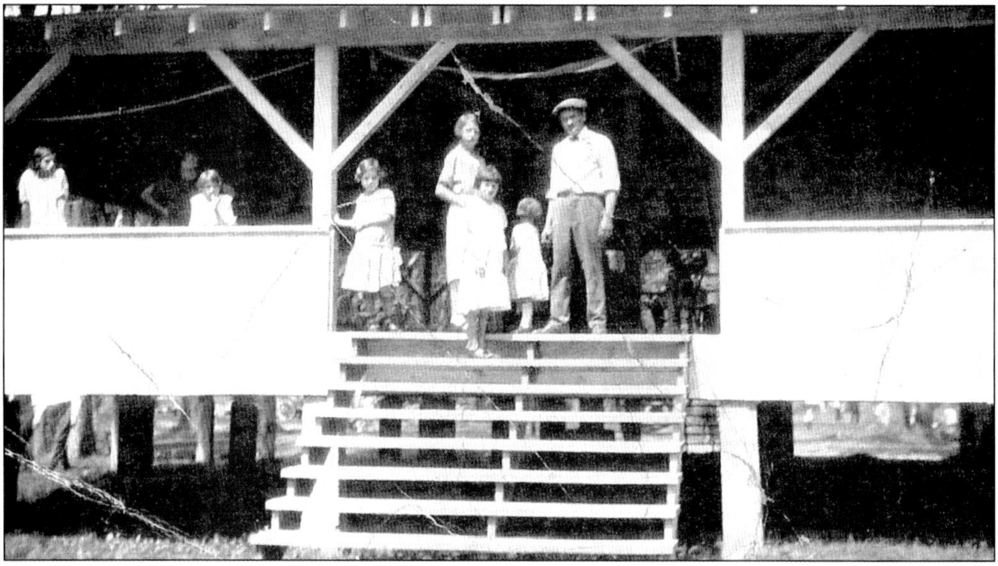

BELVEDERE CASINO BUILDING. One of the first buildings in the park, the 75-foot square casino building was originally used for dancing. Later, after a separate dance pavilion was erected, it became a place for eating and drinking, with slot machines scattered about. Amenities included a 60-foot oak bar, polished maple dance floor, and an orchestra stage. This 1924 photograph shows Ed Ochylski Sr. (the owner) with some of his children. The pillars supporting the structure up off the ground were to protect it from the annual spring flooding of the Clinton River that plagued the area. (Photograph courtesy of Edward Ochylski Jr.)

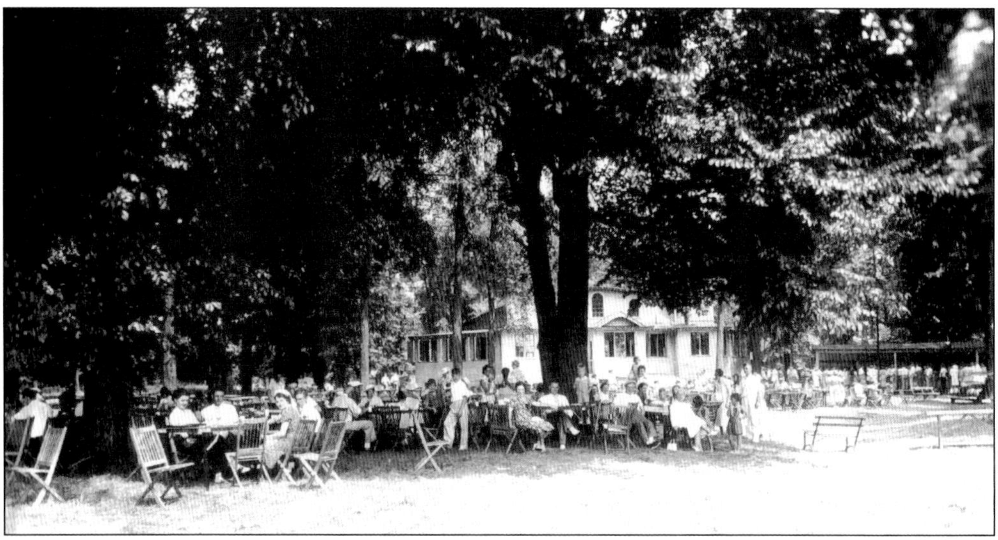

BELVEDERE PICNIC AREA. Sunday afternoon picnickers gather under the shade trees at Belvedere Park on Utica Road. Families were able to listen to music from speakers set up in the trees. The dance pavilion and concession stand can be seen in the background. Ed Ochylski, the owner of the park, was instrumental in getting electricity to this neighborhood by subsidizing the cost of running lines up from Roseville along Utica Road during the later 1920s. This photograph, taken around 1937, depicts a time when park operations were shifting from families just driving up from Detroit and paying their $1 entrance fee, to the park being rented by the day to groups, churches, and unions for their picnics. (Photograph courtesy of Edward Ochylski Jr.)

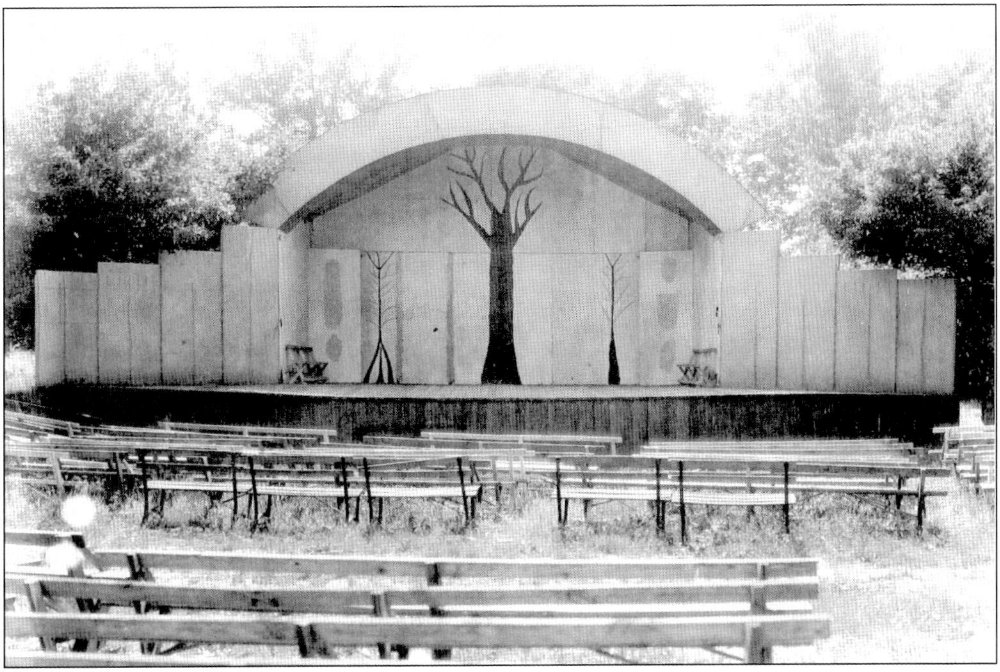

BELVEDERE BAND SHELL. By 1940, hard times were falling on the park; the band shell sits in disrepair. Gas rationing brought on by the war limited turnout. In its heyday, the shell, built in 1933, seated 1,500. It was used for concerts, choral groups, and politicians. (Photograph courtesy of Edward Ochylski Jr.)

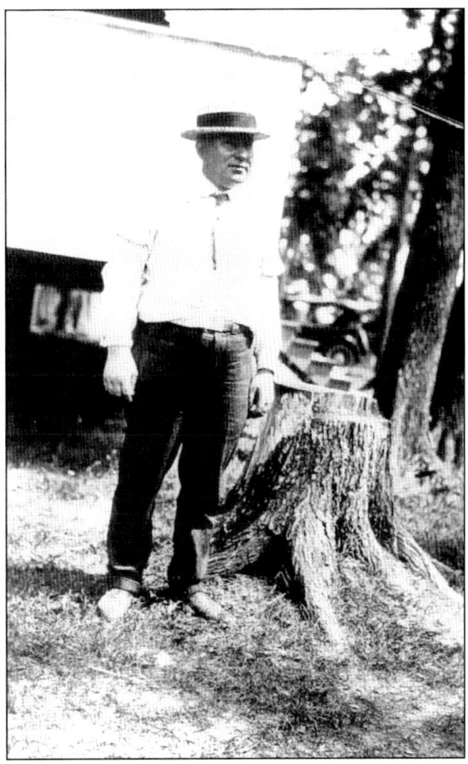

EDWARD OCHYLSKI. Pictured around 1925 is the owner of Belvedere Park. Overcoming many hardships, he and his wife raised six children during the time he lived in the township—Helen, Arthur, Edward Jr., Evelyn, Bernice, and Diana. (Photograph courtesy of Edward Ochylski Jr.)

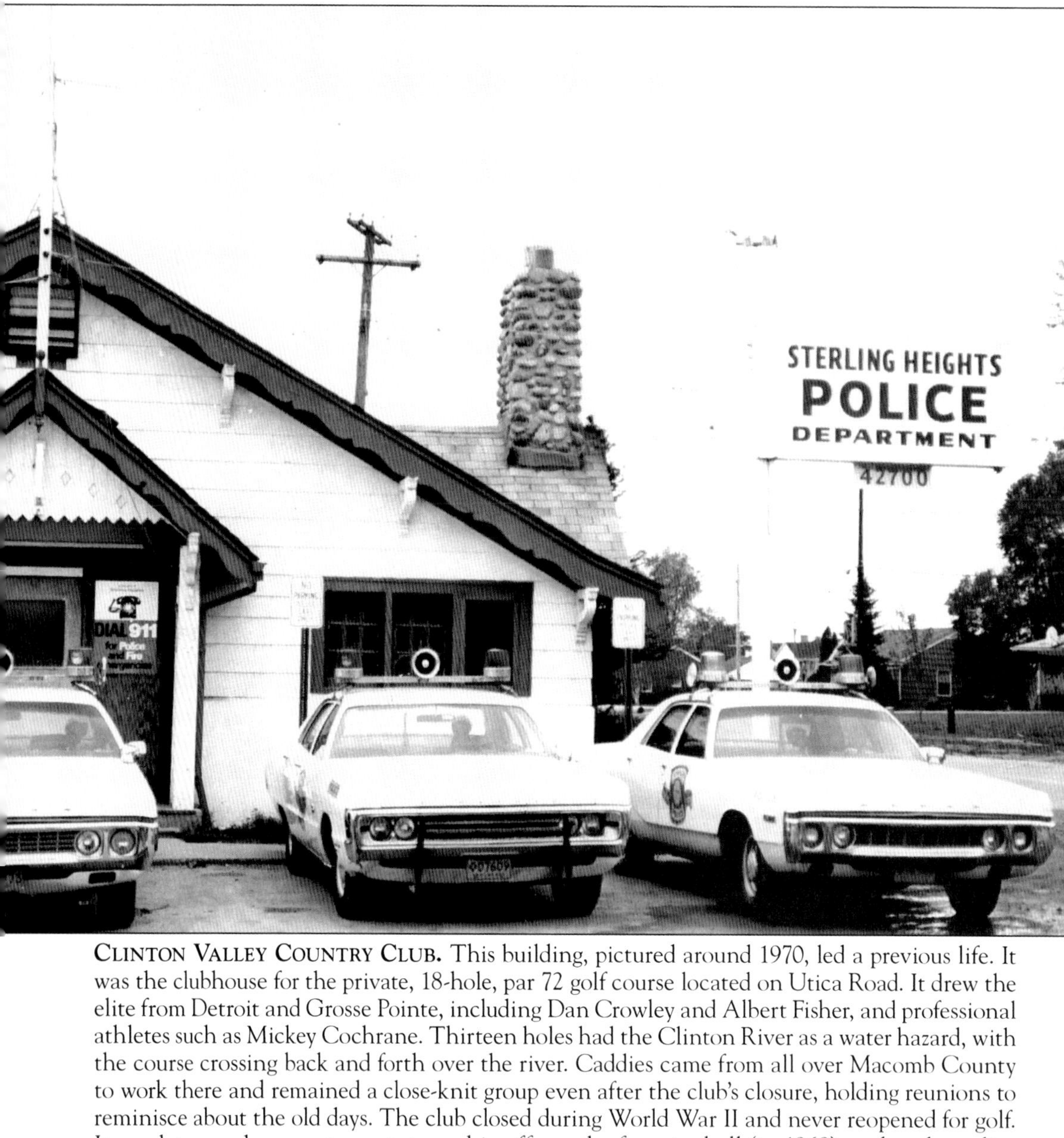

CLINTON VALLEY COUNTRY CLUB. This building, pictured around 1970, led a previous life. It was the clubhouse for the private, 18-hole, par 72 golf course located on Utica Road. It drew the elite from Detroit and Grosse Pointe, including Dan Crowley and Albert Fisher, and professional athletes such as Mickey Cochrane. Thirteen holes had the Clinton River as a water hazard, with the course crossing back and forth over the river. Caddies came from all over Macomb County to work there and remained a close-knit group even after the club's closure, holding reunions to reminisce about the old days. The club closed during World War II and never reopened for golf. It was later used as a restaurant, township offices, the first city hall (in 1968), and as the police department. It was demolished in the late 1970s and became the site of the Nature Center.

Five

BUSINESS

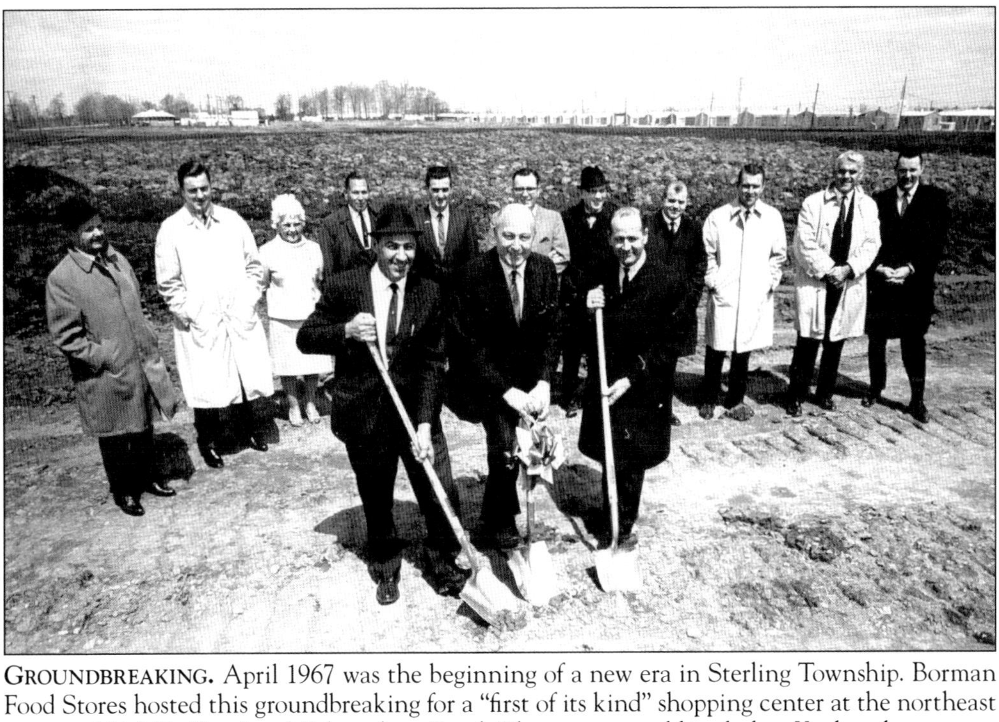

GROUNDBREAKING. April 1967 was the beginning of a new era in Sterling Township. Borman Food Stores hosted this groundbreaking for a "first of its kind" shopping center at the northeast corner of 14 Mile Road and Schoenherr Road. The center would include a Yankee department store, Farmer Jack grocery store, and an Arnold drugstore, all owned by Borman. The men in front are township supervisor William Valusek, an official from Borman's, and Warren mayor Ted Bates. The row behind includes treasurer Richard Brown, clerk Robert Evans, industrial coordinator Leo Keitz, planning commissioner Nellie Floodquist, and representatives from Borman, the bank, and Warren Consolidated Schools. The center opened in November 1967. (Photograph courtesy of the Utica Sentinel.)

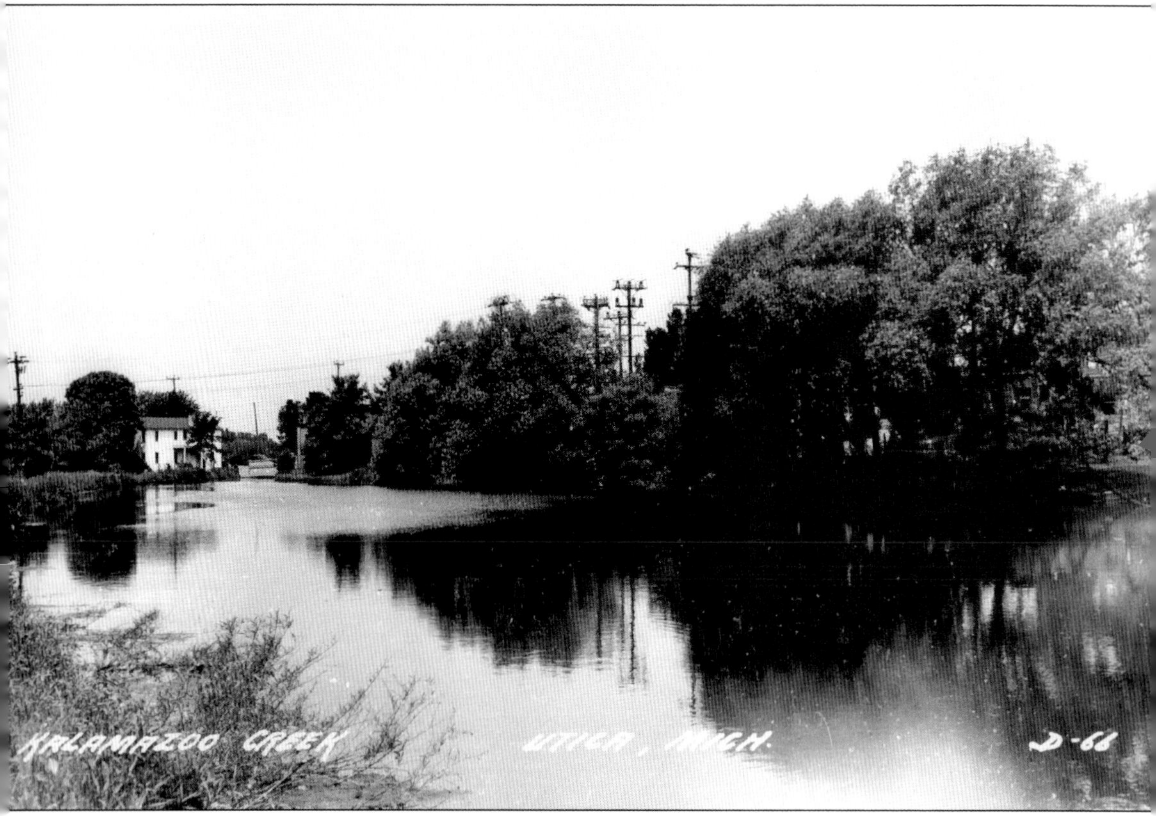

CLINTON KALAMAZOO CANAL. In 1838, the State of Michigan began building this canal, which would enable settlers to cross southern Michigan by boat from Lake St. Clair to Lake Michigan. They started in Mount Clemens and got as far as Rochester by 1843, when money ran out and the project was abandoned. With the coming of railroads, support for the canal vanished. Canal Road was the towpath (a path mules or horses used to tow the boats along) to the portion of the canal that ran through Sterling Township. Portions of the canal near the village of Utica were still large and easy to identify in spite of having been abandoned. This photograph was taken near Utica around 1910. Children were known to enjoy ice-skating in these areas during the winter and used them for swimming before the water eventually became too stagnant.

Hacker Sawmill. The Chris Hacker farm on 16 Mile Road, west of Mound Road, had a small sawmill, as seen in this 1951 photograph. Before the coming of gasoline engines, steam engines, or electricity, farmers had to depend on large sawmills located at waterpower sources. In the 1880s, these small neighborhood sawmills began to appear, not requiring waterpower. Chris Hacker is on the far right. His son Marvin Hacker is guiding the log, and Forrest Pease watches from behind.

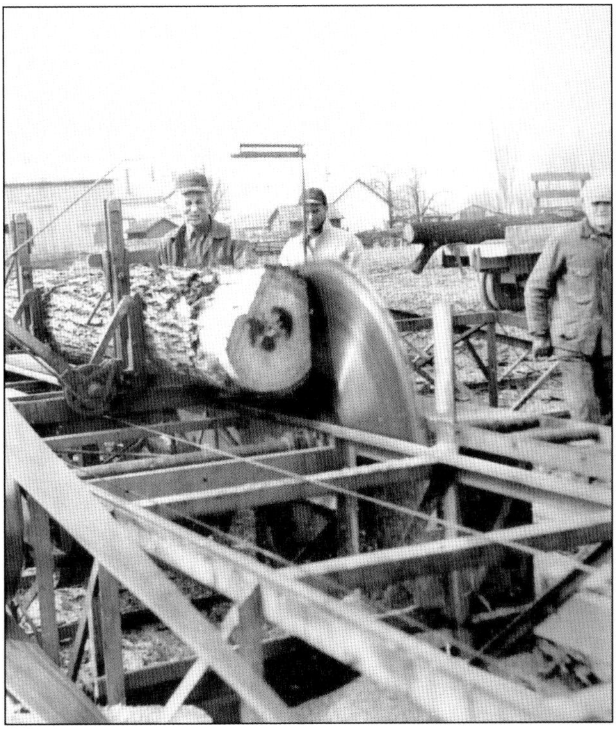

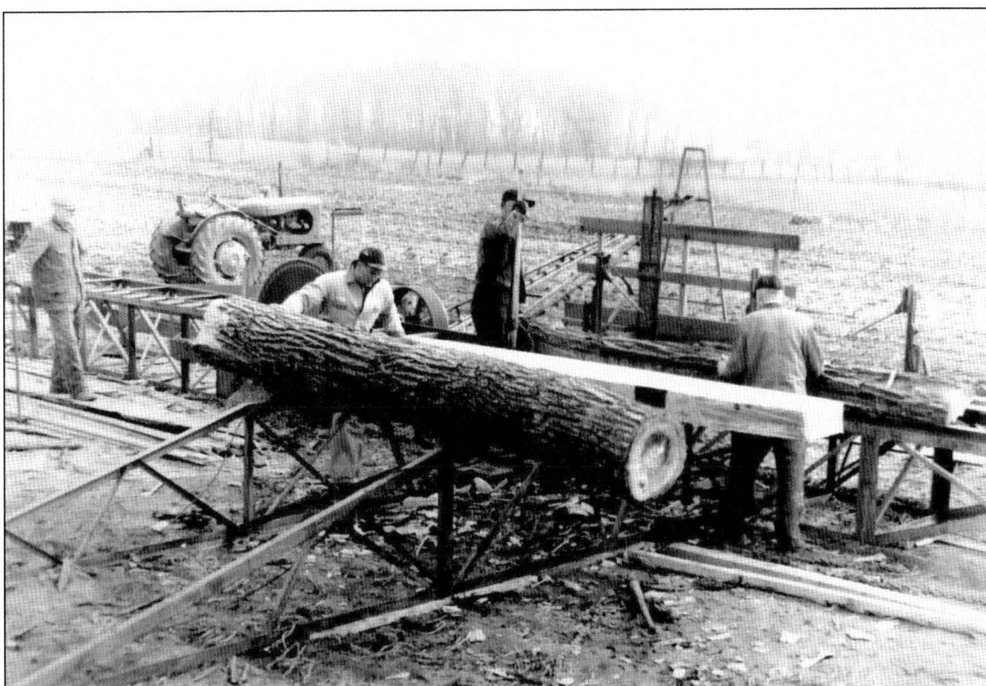

A Log Is Rolled Up. The Hacker sawmill in 1951, like other small sawmills, could convert logs from trees on area farms into lumber for farm buildings and fences. Pictured from left to right are Chris Hacker, Forrest Pease, Marvin Hacker (Chris's son), and Fred Hacker (Chris's brother).

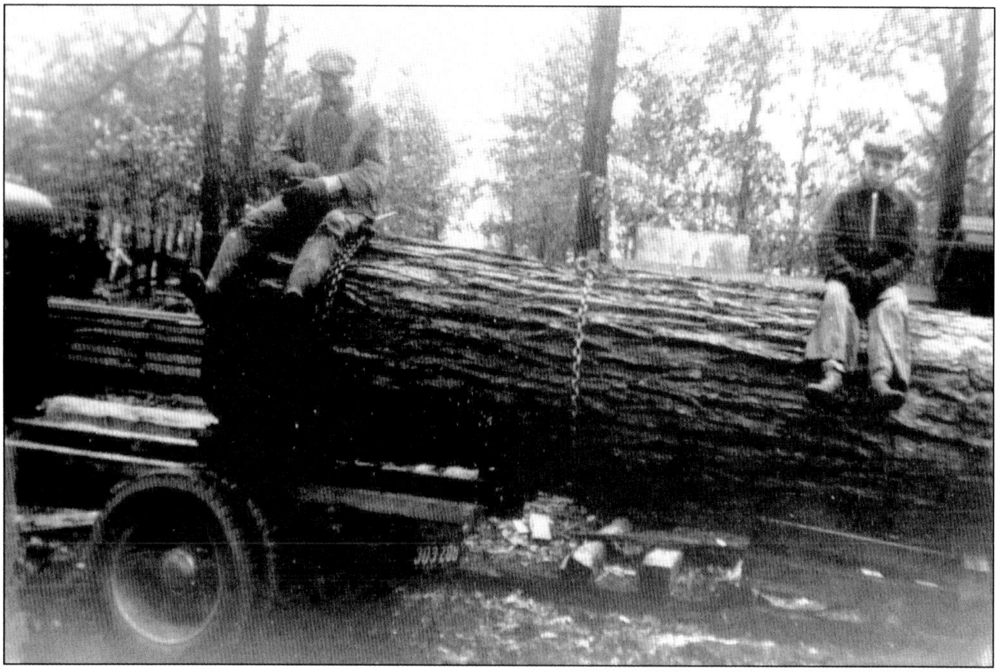

RIDING THE LOG. What a huge tree this must have been. Members of the Hacker family grab a ride on this tree headed to the sawmill around 1940.

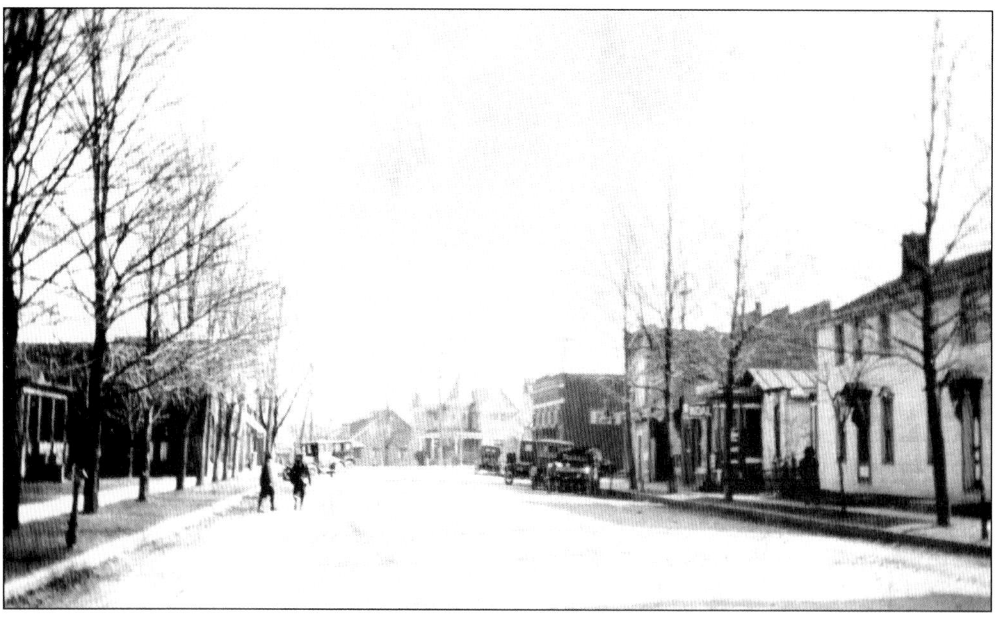

CASS AVENUE IN UTICA. Since Sterling Township had no business center, farmers who lived in the northern half of the township considered the village of Utica, located on the northern boundary of the township, to be their downtown. This *c.* 1920 scene shows Cass Avenue (an extension of Clinton River Road), one of the main thoroughfares in town. Saturday night brought throngs of farm families into town for shopping, banking, and socializing. Fraser, Warren, Center Line, Rochester, and Mount Clemens also drew the township's rural residents.

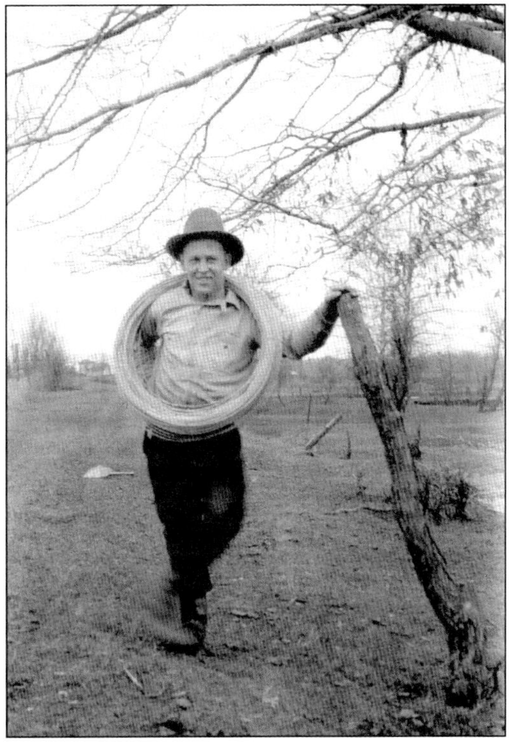

WORKING ON THE PHONE LINES. Telephone service began in rural areas of the township during the 1920s. Pictured around 1940 is Melvin Kleino, whose father, Louis Kleino, co-owned the Riverside Roadway Telephone Company along with Kenneth Rice and four other area farmers. The business installed and repaired the iron phone lines used at the time, which needed constant repair due to corrosion. Melvin went on to own a television-repair business in Fraser and was very active in the Fraser Lions Club, civic, and St. John Lutheran Church activities. (Photograph courtesy of Armin "Duane" Kleino.)

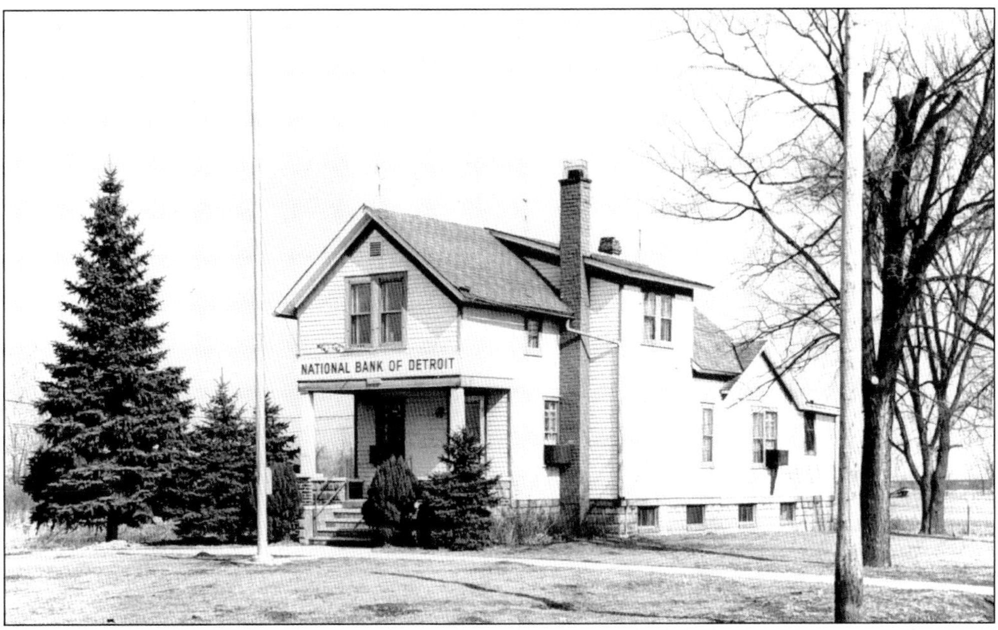

BANK IN A HOUSE. This is the Fred Hacker farm as it looked in 1957, a few years after Fred and his wife, Anna Zirbel Hacker, retired to Utica. For two years, the home served as a branch of the National Bank of Detroit until a new modern bank, still standing, was built next door in 1957. This building is believed to be the first bank in the rural part of the township. The property, on Mound Road between 16 and 17 Mile Roads, has recently been used to house offices. (Photograph courtesy of Jim Boehmer.)

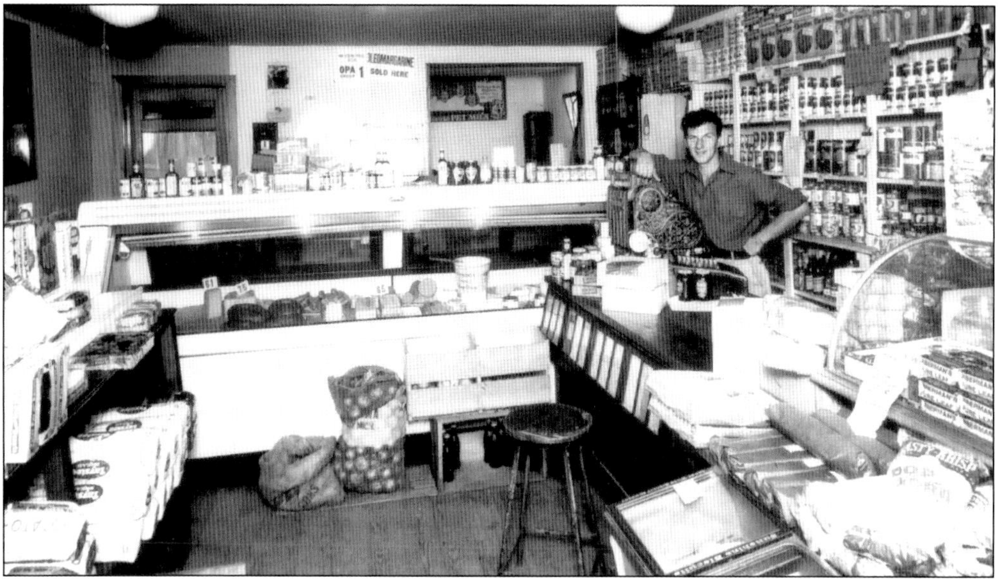

EDDIE'S MARKET. Eddie Nowalski poses behind the counter of the family store around 1945. His parents, Peter and Alexandria, were familiar with Sterling Township because of the many Polish parks in the area. They moved their Detroit grocery business to a spot on Mound Road south of Hall Road (currently in the shadow of the Wal-Mart across the street), adding a store onto an existing house. The store, run by Eddie and his wife, Evelyn, was a popular spot to pick up a few groceries, some of their famous homemade Polish sausage, or some friendly conversation. The store, one of the earlier commercial businesses in the township, was still run by the family in 2005. (Photograph courtesy of Eddie Nowalski.)

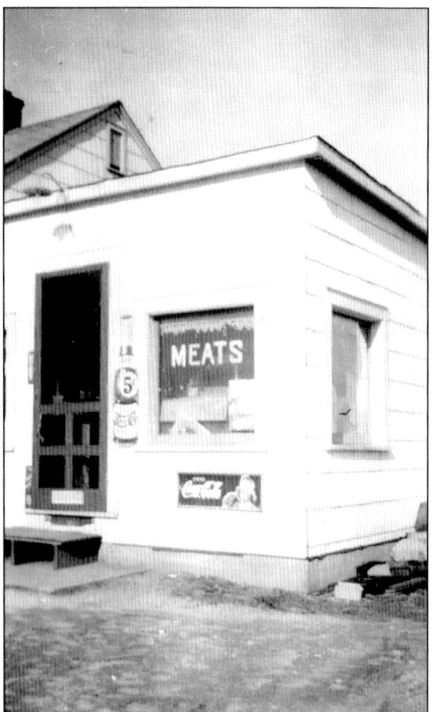

EDDIE'S MARKET. Pictured in the 1940s or 1950s is the outside of Eddie's Market. The Nowalski family ran the store and lived in the home attached to the north side of the store. Located on Mound Road south of Hall Road, the home had previously been used as a sales office for Eyster Mound Road Farms, a real estate business selling small rural lots for homes in the area. Eddie has passed away, but his wife, Evelyn, still runs the store. (Photograph courtesy of Eddie Nowalski.)

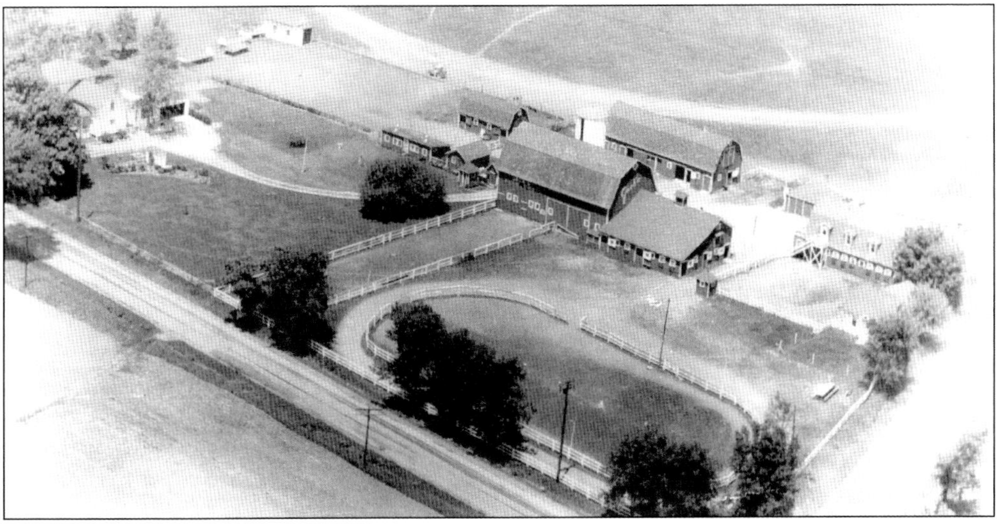

JACK'S STABLES. The 40-acre farm of George Upton on Clinton River Road was being used as Jack's Stables, as seen in this *c.* 1960 aerial photograph. Jack and Rose Fulk bred horses here, one of a number of different horse stables that offered their services in Sterling Township over the years. This one was run by the Fulks. Their son and daughter-in-law, Jack and Rita, then ran it as J&R Stables, and it was finally operated by another owner as Sterling Stables. This was one of the last stables in business in Sterling Heights. J&R moved its successful horse-breeding business to Washington Township, and the Clinton River Road site was eventually razed for a housing development. (Photograph courtesy of the Fulk family.)

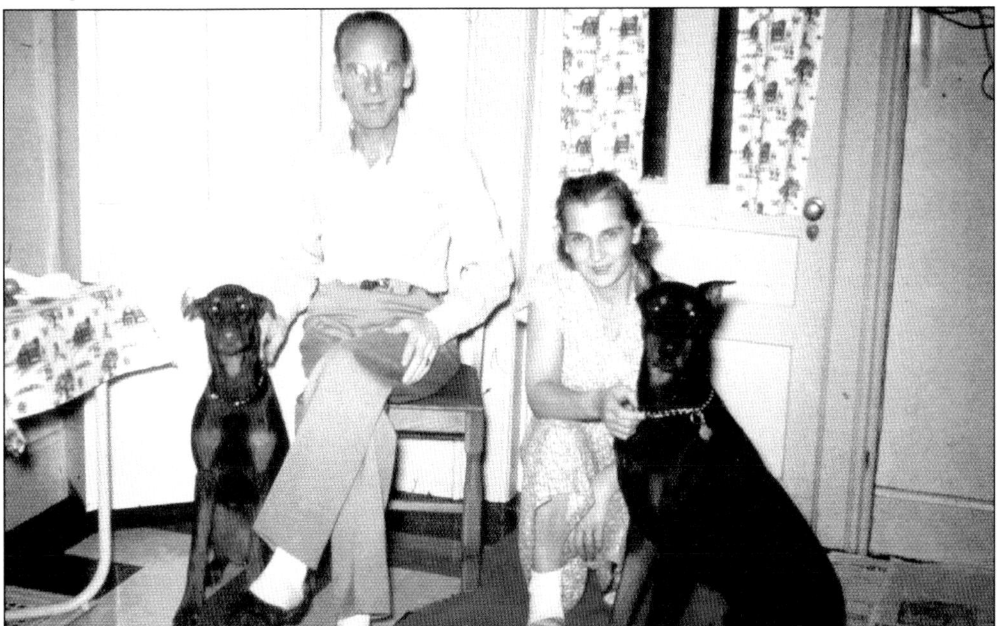

JACK AND ROSE FULK. Clarence "Jack" Fulk and his wife, Rose, sit in their kitchen at Jack's Stables, located on the northwest corner of Clinton River Road and Schoenherr Road. Jack operated the stables, located on the old George Upton farm for 32 years. The couple, horse breeders and riding instructors, are pictured here around 1958 with the family dogs, Caesar and Cricket. (Photograph courtesy of the Fulk family.)

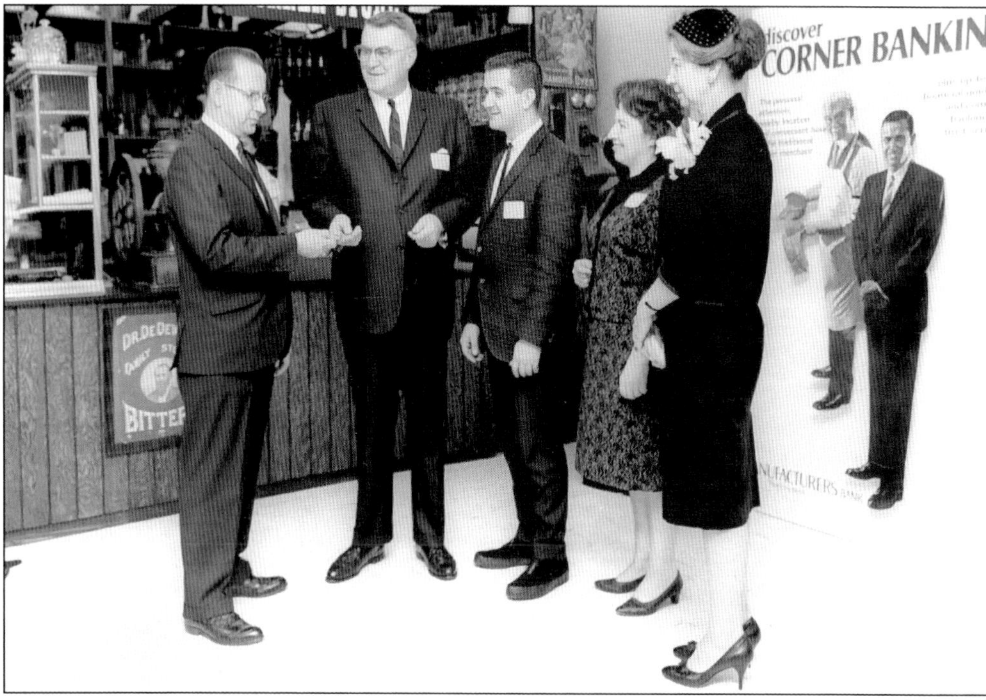

MANUFACTURERS NATIONAL BANK. It is November 1967, and another new bank has opened in Sterling Township. During the 1960s, many bank branches were popping up to serve the growing population's financial needs. This one was located on Dequindre Road near 15 Mile Road. Richard O. Brown, township treasurer, is pictured third from the left.

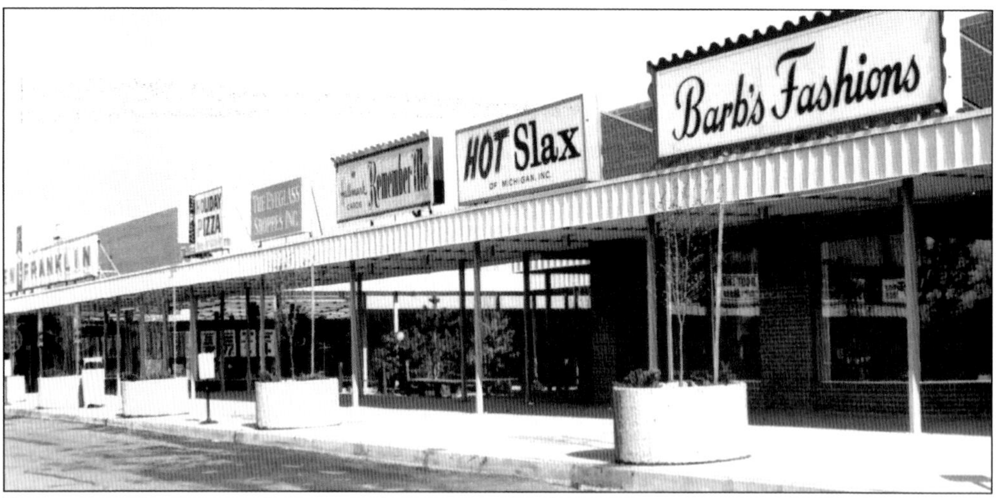

RIVERLAND SHOPPING CENTER. The center, developed by M. E. Arden Company, Detroit developers, opened in November 1967 after many years of planning. The first phase included a Kroger store, Sav-Way Drugs, and a cleaners and laundromat. A second phase included more stores, as pictured here in 1972: Ben Franklin, Holiday Pizza, Eyeglass Shoppes, Hallmark, Hot Slax, and Barb's Fashions. The owners of the center were instrumental in having Riverland Drive constructed, which provided only the second bridge over the Clinton River in the township and improved access for development. The center is located on Van Dyke Avenue, north of Riverland Drive.

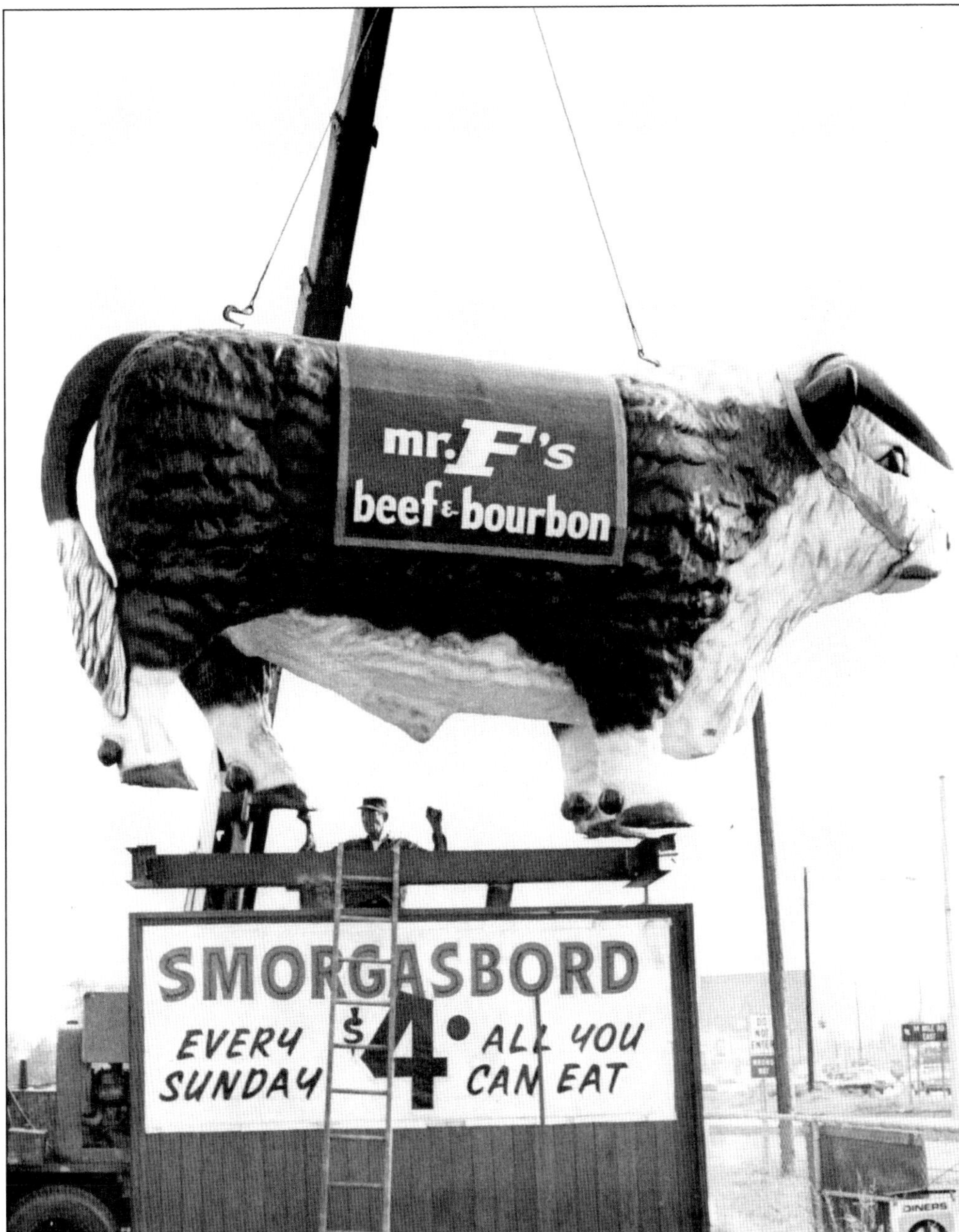

THE BULL ON THE CORNER. The 3,500-pound, 15-foot fiberglass bull on the northeast corner of Van Dyke Avenue and 14 Mile Road served as a major landmark in the area since about 1961, when Thomas Furtney purchased it as a sign for his restaurant, Mr. F's. Residents used it as an aid when giving people directions. Families took pictures of their children posing by it. Furtney previously ran another business from the location, Furtney's Rock & Roll, known as a pretty wild place, according to early township police officers. He changed the name, and the format, to a family steak house with the addition of this statue, and ran it that way until the restaurant was sold in 1988, causing much community concern over what would happen to the beloved bull. It was removed and sold to an unknown business. (Photograph courtesy of the Utica Sentinel.)

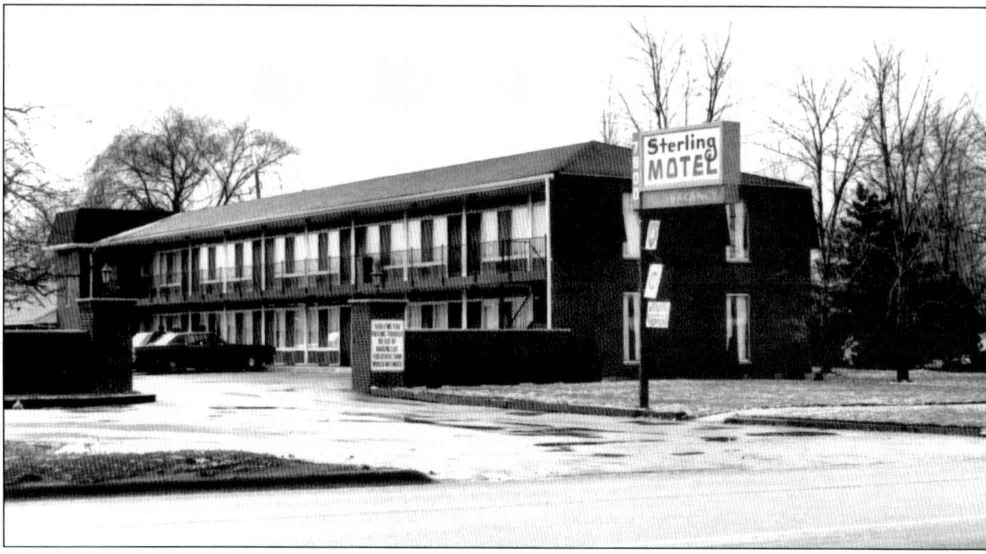

STERLING MOTEL. The Best Western Sterling Inn and Conference Center is pictured as it appeared in 1972. The Demuch Motel, as it was first named, was built by Joe Demuchowski in 1954 with 11 motel rooms on the corner of Van Dyke Avenue and 15 Mile Road. The Urquhart family bought Demuchowski out in 1960, changing the name to Sterling Motel. The wing in this view was added in 1969 by co-owners John Urquhart and Victor Martin, with more additions to follow, including a restaurant and lounge, banquet center, and Michigan's first indoor water park. By 2004, there were 250 rooms, with the original 11 rooms just a memory. The DeMuch and Sterling Motel was one of the first motels in the township. (Photograph courtesy of John Urquart.)

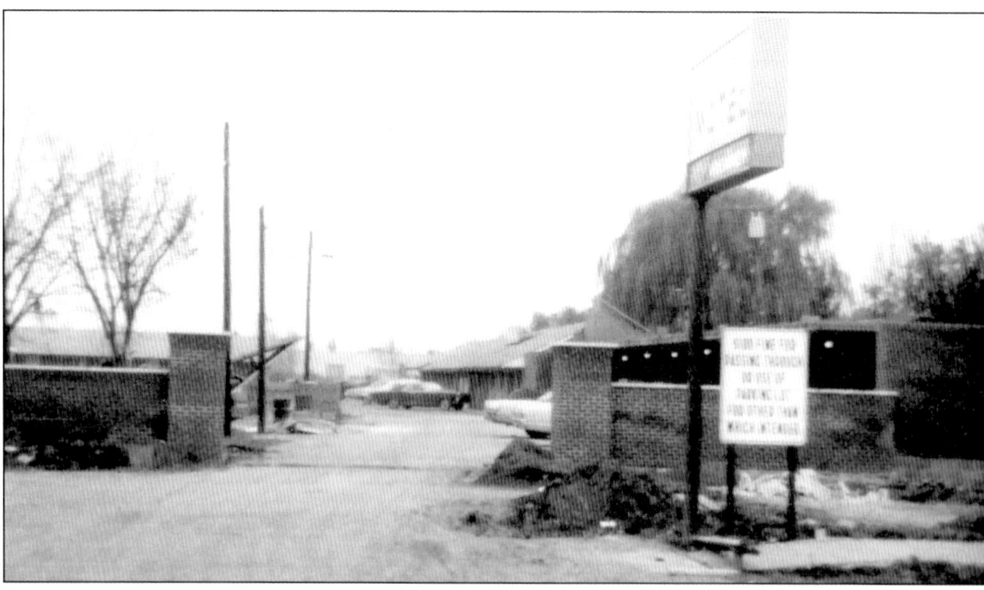

STERLING MOTEL ADDITION. One of the many additions and changes to the old Sterling Motel, owned by Victor Martin and John Urquhart, is under way here in 1969 as a two-story section is being built just beyond the sign. The first floor is in place. Part of the original one-story section of the motel can be seen farther back. This brick-fenced entry area faced 15 Mile Road. (Photograph courtesy of John Urquhart.)

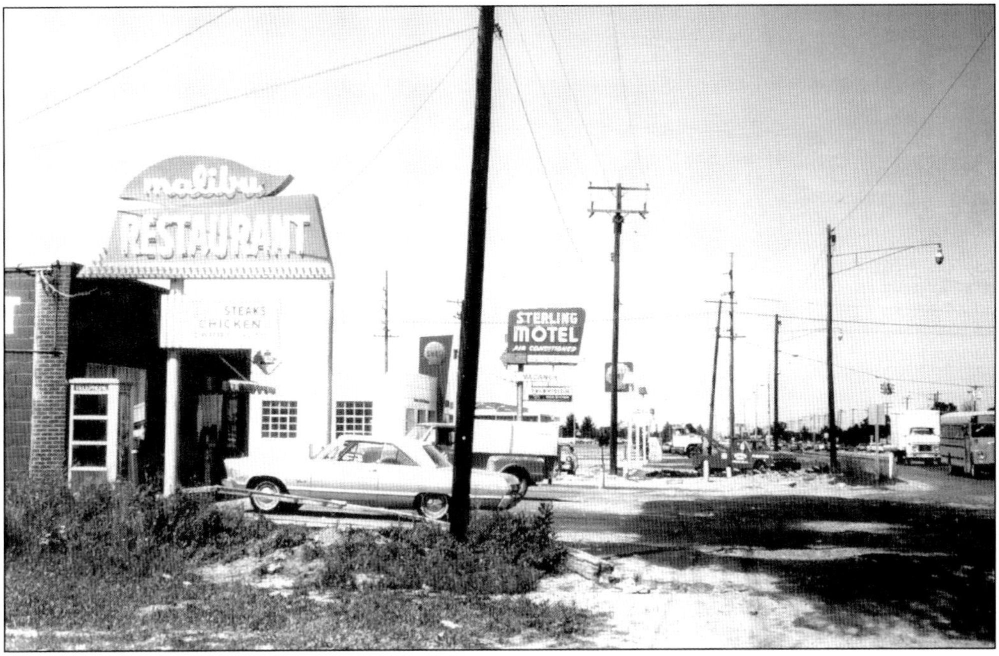

VAN DYKE AVENUE AND 15 MILE ROAD. This is what you would have seen looking north on Van Dyke Avenue just south of 15 Mile Road in 1969: the Malibu Restaurant (now gone) advertising steaks and chicken, a sign for the Sterling Motel (later the Best Western Sterling Inn and Conference Center), and a Shell service station (still there but operated by another oil company). Beyond the intersection on the left would be the Chrysler Sterling Stamping Plant. (Photograph courtesy of John Urquhart.)

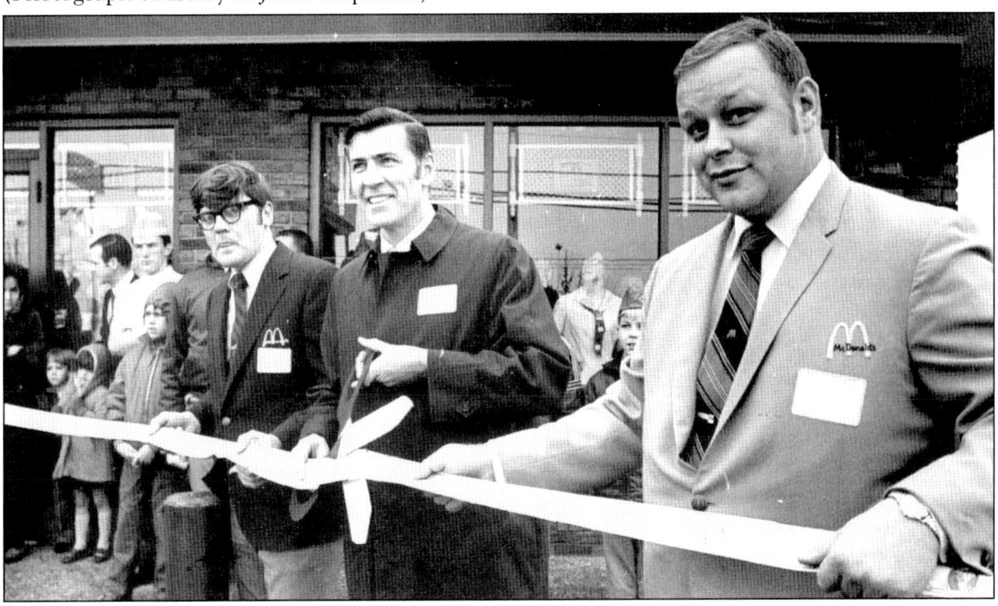

MCDONALD'S OPENING. It was a pretty exciting day on Van Dyke Avenue when McDonald's opened what was probably the first Sterling Heights McDonald's restaurant in December 1970. The city's first mayor, Jerry Donovan cuts the ribbon. Located on Van Dyke Avenue between 17 and 18 Mile Roads, it is still serving up Big Macs today. (Photograph courtesy of the Utica Sentinel.)

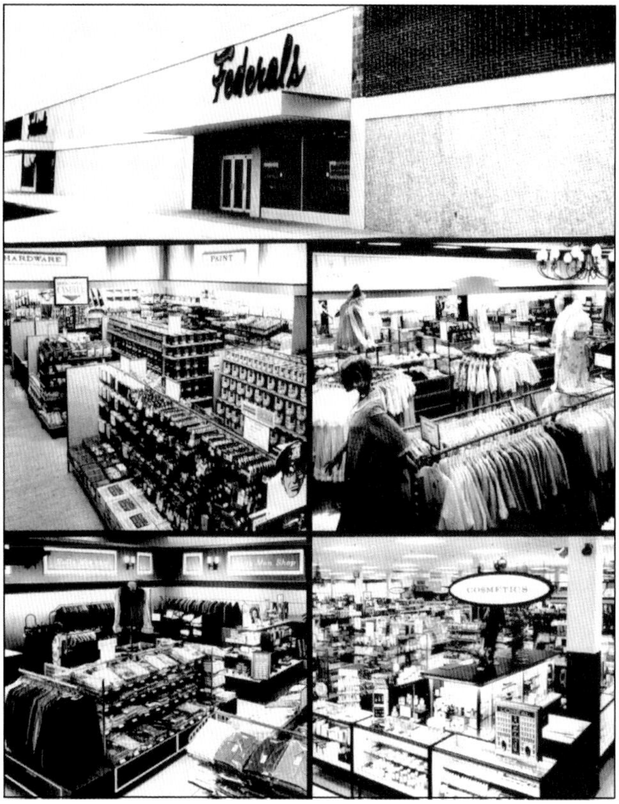

FEDERAL'S DEPARTMENT STORE. This store, as seen in the late 1960s, was located on 16 Mile Road east of Van Dyke Avenue, not far from where Meijer stands today. The building stood for another 30 years, used by a variety of business concerns.

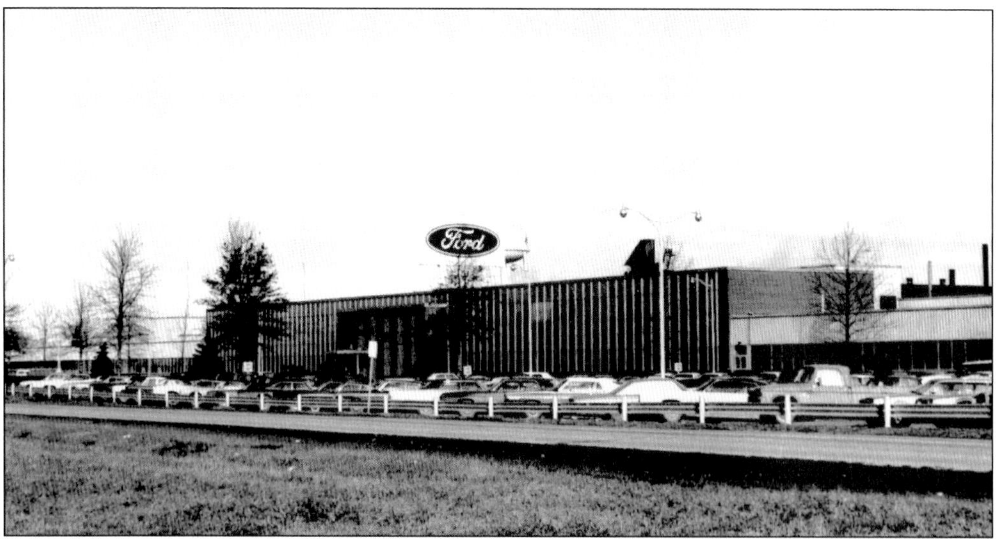

FORD STERLING PLANT. Ford Motor Company built this plant (pictured in 1972) on the northeast corner of 17 Mile and Mound Roads in 1956. Most of the property had been the Ploetz farm. By 1967, some 8,500 men and women worked in the 2.5-million-square-foot building making rear axle assemblies, suspensions, and driveshafts. Many of these workers moved up from Detroit and other areas to be near their jobs, requiring subdivisions, sewers, and water for their families. Very soon, other plants followed, and the farming community was never the same. In 2000, the plant was taken over by Visteon Corporation (a former Ford division).

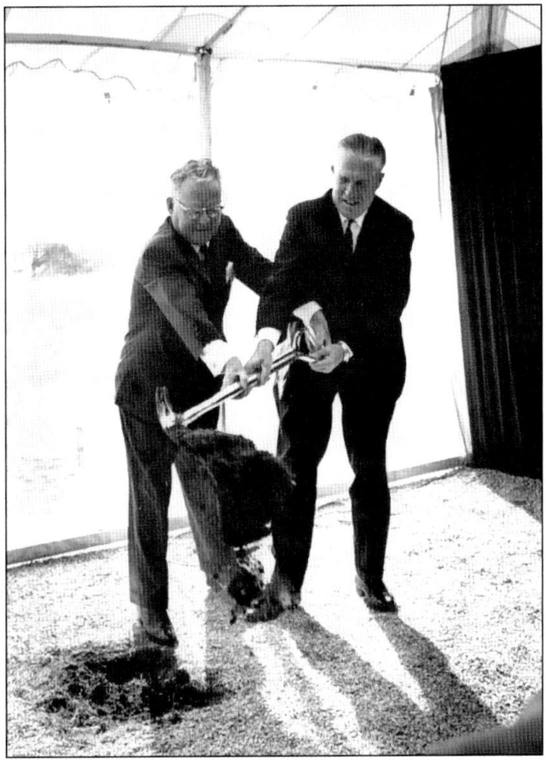

FORD VAN DYKE PLANT. It is 1966, and Michigan governor George Romney (right) and Ford Motor Company executive vice president Charles H. Patterson share a shovel in the groundbreaking for the new Ford Van Dyke Plant located on the northwest corner of Van Dyke Avenue and 18 Mile Road. The 1.6-million-square-foot facility opened in 1968, employing 1,600 workers who had transferred over from the Ford Sterling Plant, plus an additional 1,900 new jobs. The new building was run by the Transmission and Chassis Division of Ford, as was its sister plant on Mound Road. Sterling Township was excited to be boosting its industrial tax base, in addition to the added employment. (Photograph courtesy of the Utica Sentinel.)

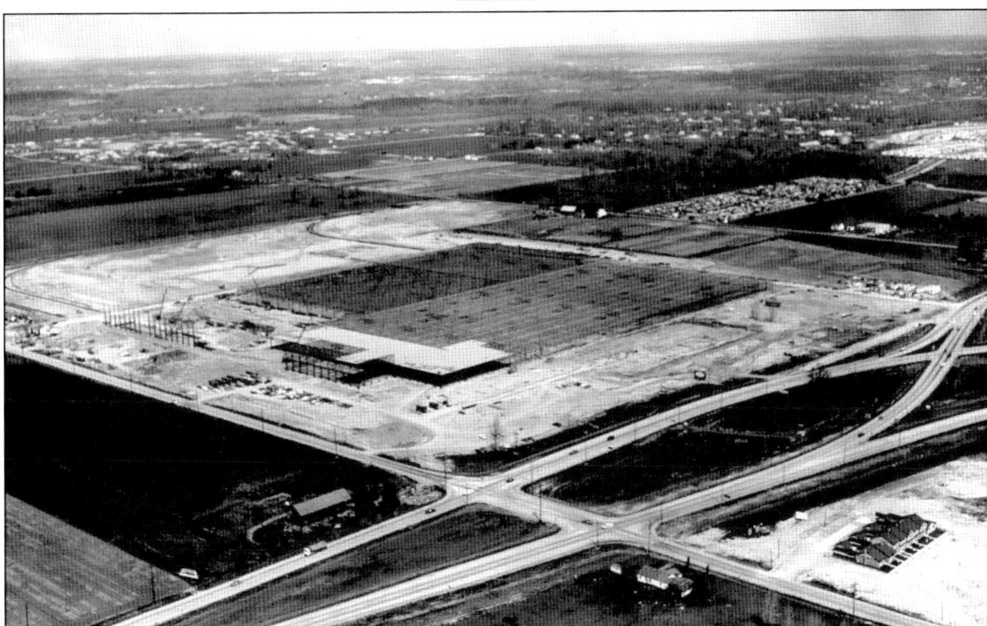

FORD VAN DYKE PLANT CONSTRUCTION. Looking northwest, this aerial view of 18 Mile Road and Van Dyke Avenue shows what was going on there around 1967. The Ford Van Dyke Plant is going up, and the northeast corner shows the first units built of the Andover Heights condominiums. The remnants of the two farms on the south side of the street are now the sites of a Fuddruckers restaurant, a Big Boy, and a bank.

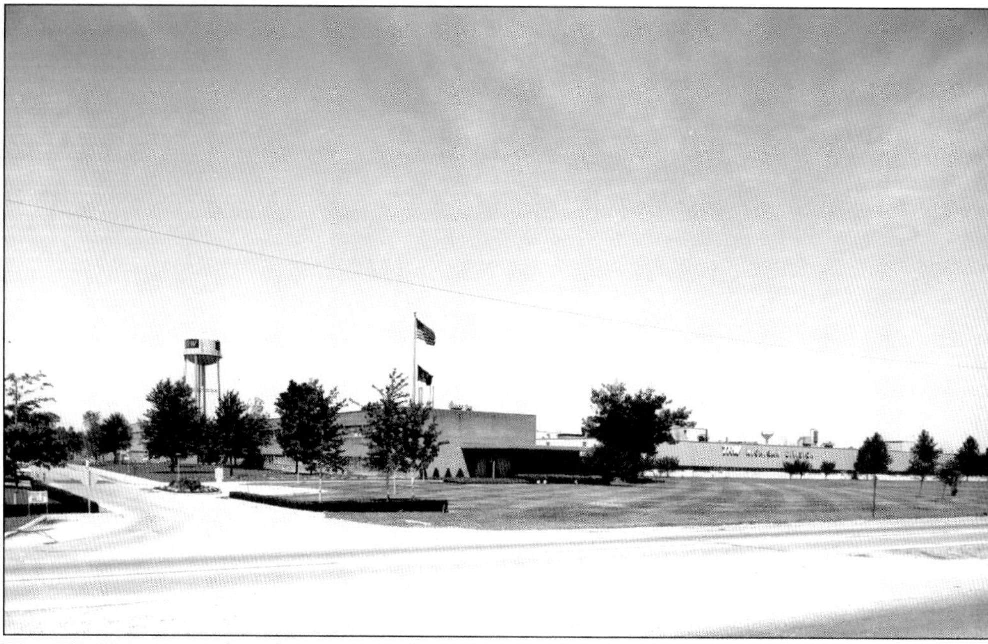

The TRW Plant. This plant, located on the west side of Van Dyke Avenue between 14 and 15 Mile Roads, opened in 1956 under the name Thompson Products. A corporate merger changed the name to TRW in 1958. The manufacturer of auto parts was one of the early factories in the township. Prior to the coming of TRW, the land had been the Weig farm for close to 75 years. This photograph may have been taken in the late 1960s.

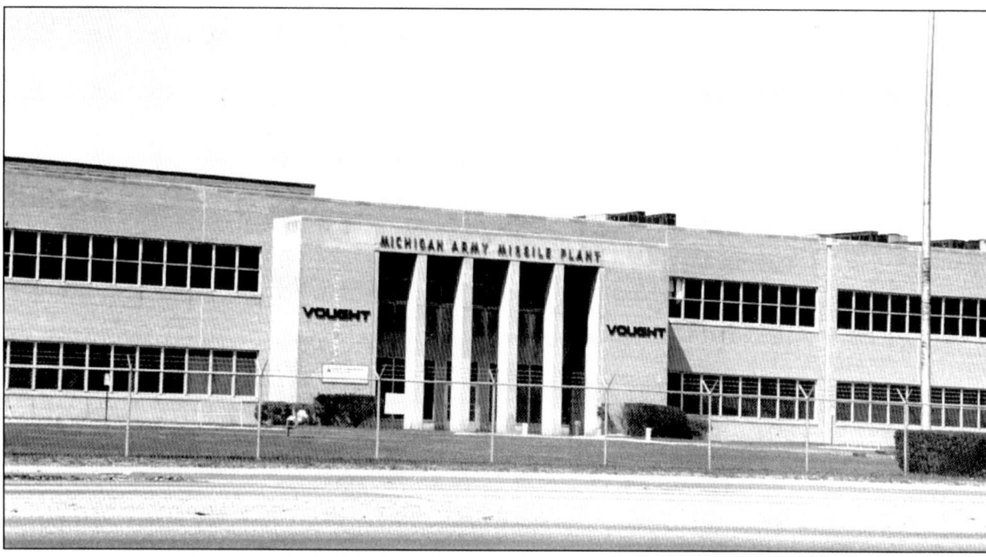

Vought Missile Plant. In 1954, the Chrysler Corporation Ballistic Missile Division opened this new plant, located on the west side of Van Dyke between 16 and 17 Mile Roads, where they built Jupiter missiles for the army. Water lines were extended north from Detroit for this facility, enabling the beginning of industrial expansion in Sterling Township. The plant built missiles until it closed in 1980 due to lack of contracts. Volkswagen of America then bought the plant to build Rabbits, though it never opened for production. Daimler Chrysler again operates the facility as an auto plant. This view is from the 1970s.

Six

GOVERNMENT

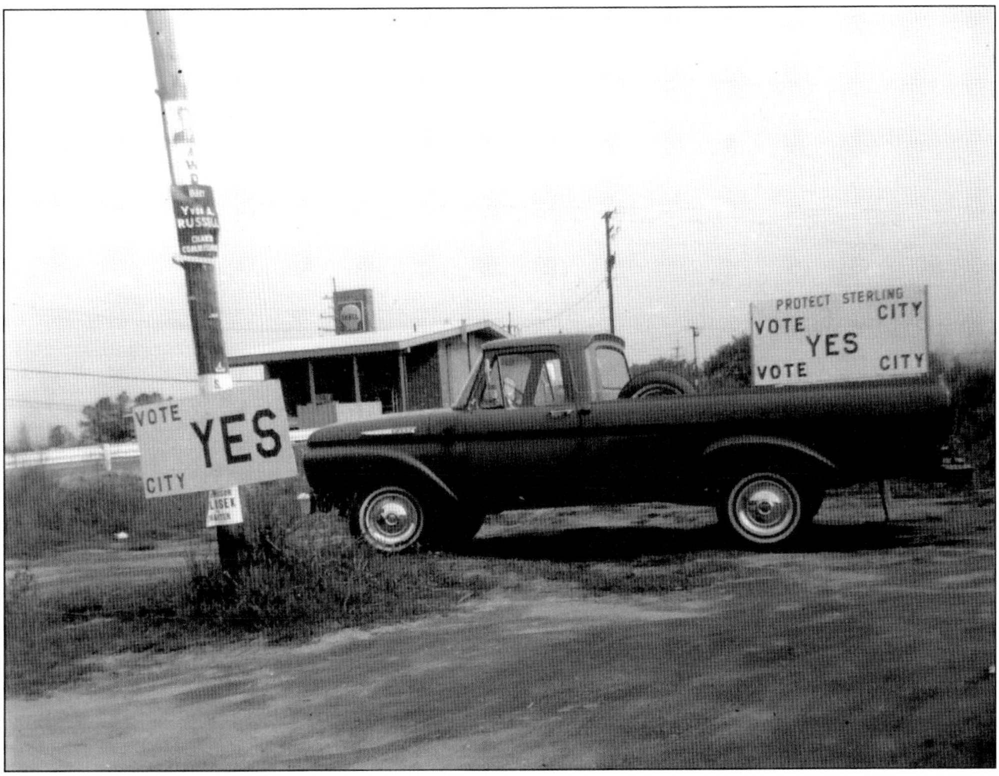

VOTE YES. The issue of the township becoming a city was a hot topic during the 1960s. In this photograph from June 1966, Barney Calka's truck is being used as a billboard. The truck is parked across from the old fire station on Van Dyke Avenue at Plumbrook Road, where Calka worked as a firefighter. "Protect Sterling" refers to the possible annexation of the township, or parts of it, by the cities of Warren and Utica. Incorporation would prevent this annexation. Plumbrook Shell, still standing, is in the background.

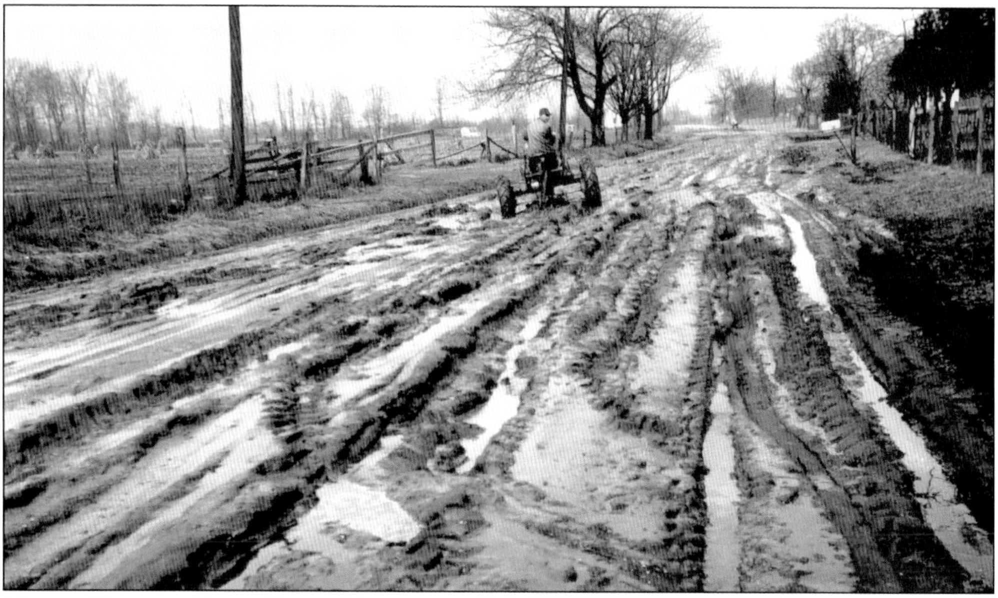

MUDDY CLINTON RIVER ROAD. This unpaved road was very typical of roads in the township in 1950. Otto Ahrens, who lived along Clinton River Road, navigates his way through the muck on a tractor. Van Dyke Avenue, through Sterling Township, was just paved around 1940. Utica Road was paved earlier, as it was a main road between existing communities, but other roads such as the River Road, as it was called, and the mile roads were much later to be improved. Living with the mess was a part of life during parts of the year for many farmers, who had to park their cars a ways from their homes and regularly needed horses to pull stuck vehicles out. (Photograph courtesy of Eleanor Ahrens.)

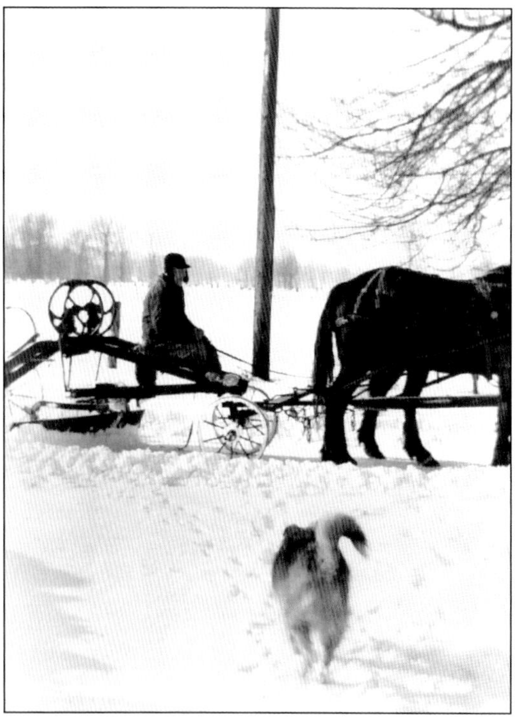

PLOWING THE SNOW. Fred Quandt, whose farm was on Clinton River Road near Stadler Road, is seen plowing the River Road with a team of horses in 1924 as a dog comes over to investigate. Before the days of city snowplows and county road commission trucks, farmers all pitched in to keep the roads near their property clear. (Photograph courtesy of Eleanor Ahrens.)

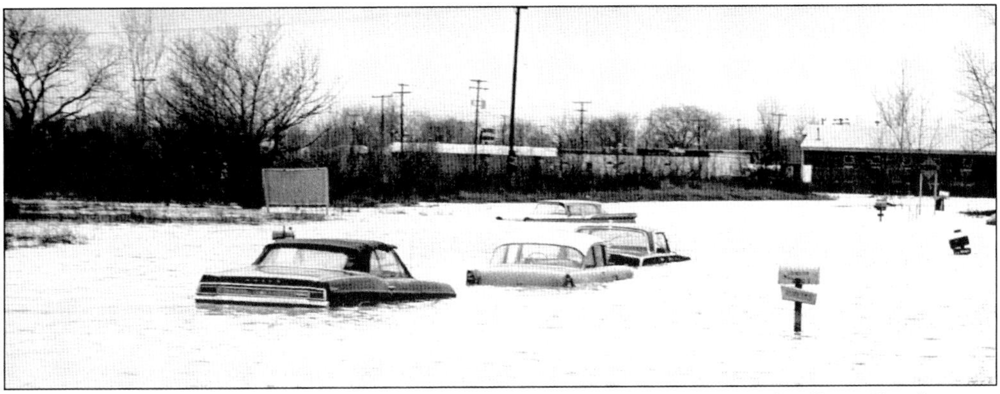

FLOODED 15 MILE ROAD. The southwest corner of the township periodically suffered severe flooding due to low elevation, poor natural drainage, and problems with poorly planned sewer and storm drains. Pictured is 15 Mile Road, looking west toward Dequindre Road, after severely heavy rains around 1966. Abandoned cars litter the roadway. When the new city management administration was elected in 1968, they immediately instituted new master planning, installed new sewers and sump pumps, and established building regulations. The church at the far right of the scene is still standing. (Photograph courtesy of the Utica Sentinel.)

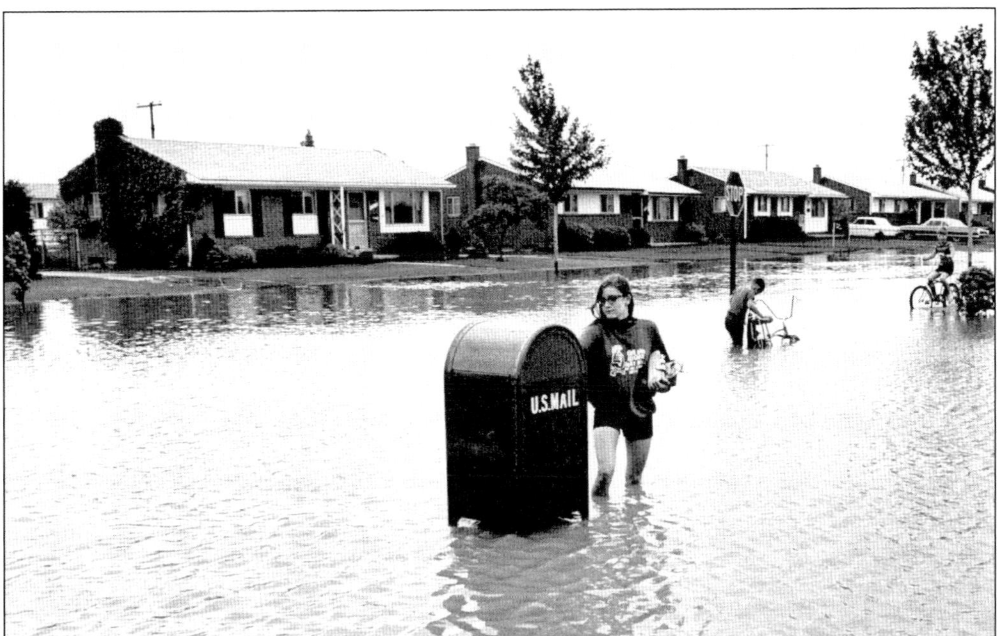

TARRYTON FLOOD. Some subdivisions that were allowed to be constructed by the township board experienced drainage and sewer problems. The Tarryton neighborhood, known as the Cigarette Sub for its street names, endured many floodings of streets and basements during the 1960s. This flood, at the corner of Camel and Parliament Streets, was in June 1968. Such problems were a hot topic at the time. When the new city management administration took over on July 1, immediate action was taken to remedy the problem. The neighborhood is east of Dequindre Road and north of 14 Mile Road. (Photograph courtesy of the Utica Sentinel.)

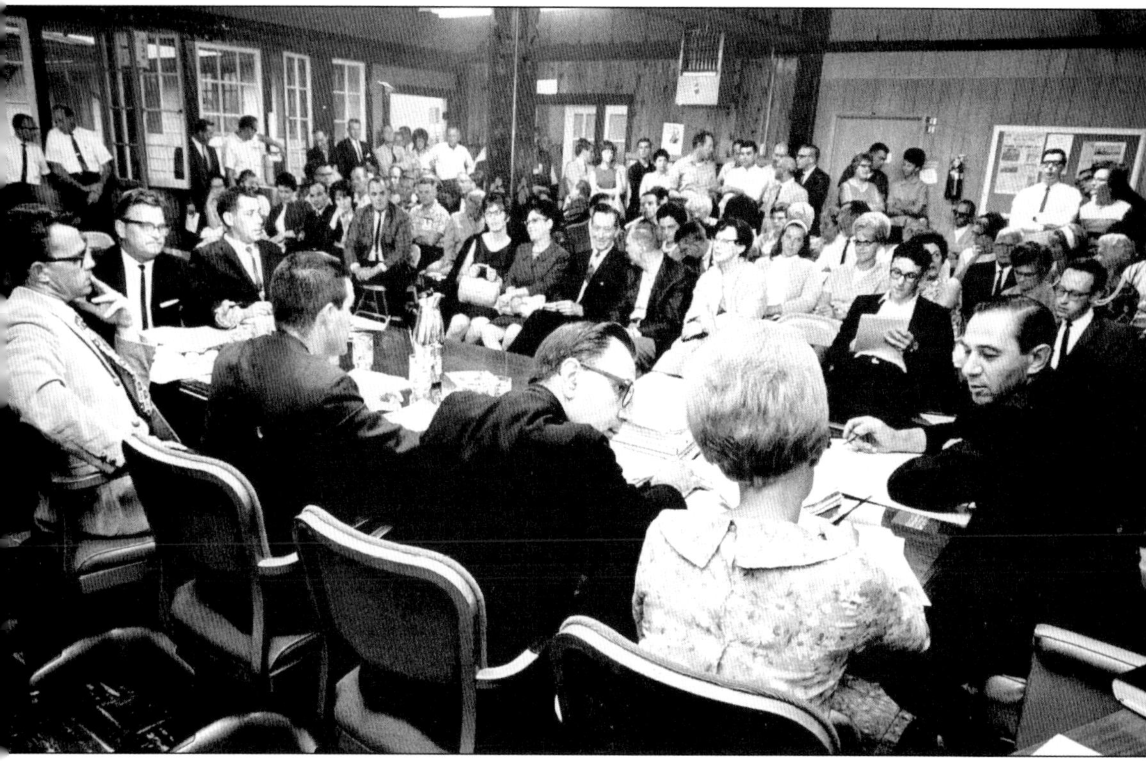

TOWNSHIP BOARD MEETING. The Sterling Township Board of Trustees is shown at a meeting held in the Annex in July 1967. The building, located on Utica Road, was the former clubhouse of the renowned Clinton Valley Country Club golf course, and after the acreage was sold off and subdivided during the 1940s, the building was operated as the Clinton Valley Inn by Michael and Lillian Sowinski. In 1966, it was sold to the township and used for meetings and offices until 1968, when it became the first Sterling Heights City Hall and headquarters for the police department. The pictured meeting focused on sewer problems. Supervisor William Valusek is seated at the head of the table on the far right. (Photograph courtesy of the Utica Sentinel.)

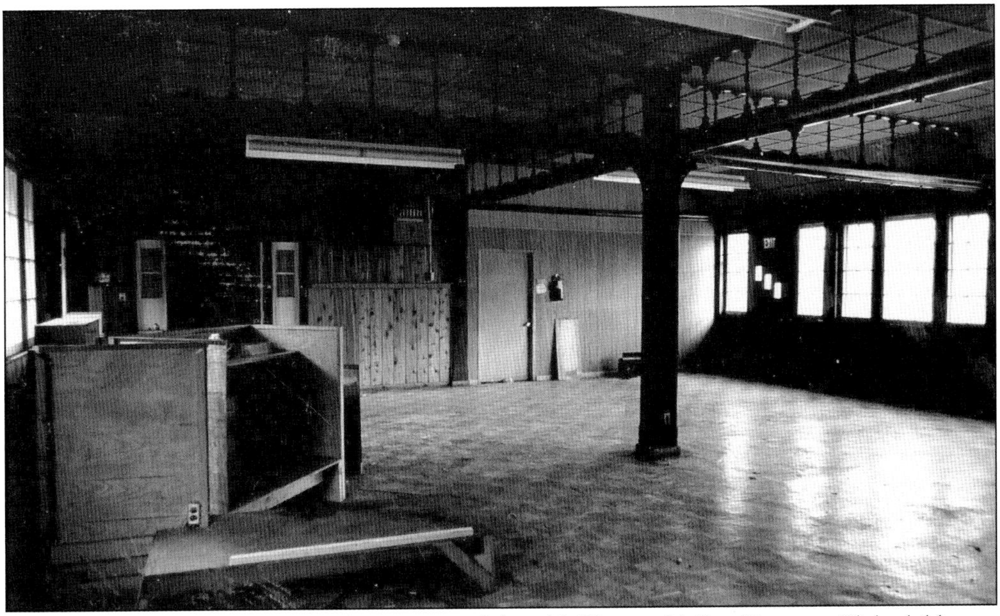

STERLING ANNEX. Pictured is the interior of the old Clinton Valley Country Club clubhouse as seen in 1966, just before the township moved their offices in. The Annex, housed township and, later, city administration from the time they moved from the small town hall building on Van Dyke and Plumbrook Roads until the new municipal building was completed in 1969. The police department then used it as their headquarters until the late 1970s, when their new station was completed. The building was located on Utica Road south of 19 Mile Road on the current site of the Sterling Heights Nature Center.

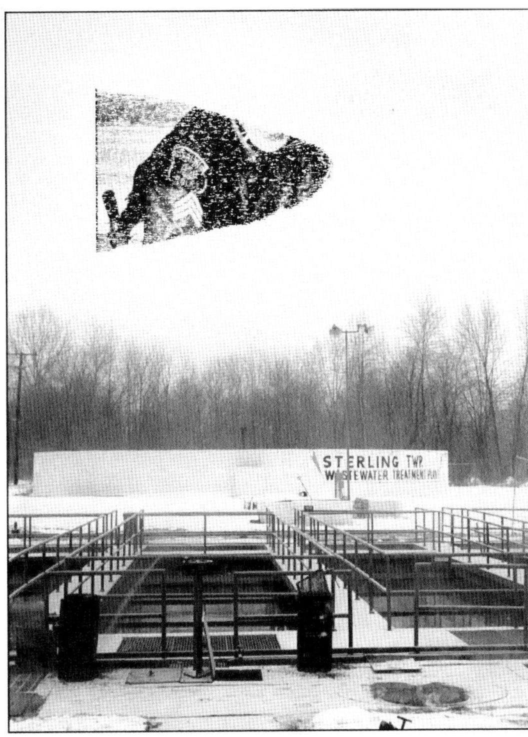

WASTEWATER TREATMENT PLANT. Township residents depended on this treatment facility located on Clinton River Road, south of the M53 freeway. Upon the city's connection to the Detroit Interceptor in 1971, this facility was closed down. During the area's rapid growth during the late 1960s, this facility, which was originally built to service the Dresden Village subdivision, strained to keep up with development. Problems arose with major pollution of the Clinton River.

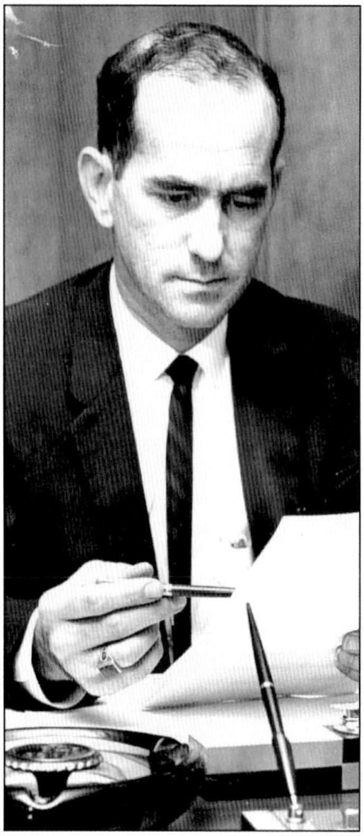

CHIEF MAURICE FOLTZ. Born in Romeo, the highly respected Maurice Foltz (pictured in 1967) worked in public safety in a number of Detroit area communities before he was hired by township supervisor William Valusek to establish the first police force in Sterling Township. Headquartered in the old town hall building on Van Dyke Avenue, the new department had 12 officers to service the community of 22,000. Foltz later remembered that the area was growing so fast they had to draw their own maps. He retired in 1981 from a department of 220 employees, returned to Romeo, and began operating Frontier Town, a collection of old-time shops.

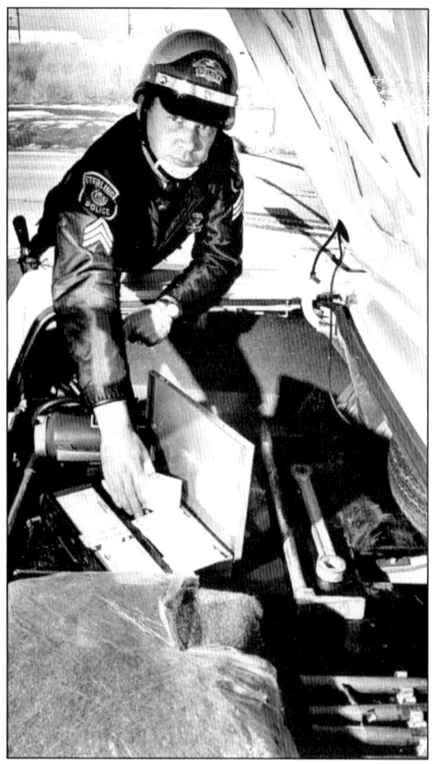

CHECKING THE EQUIPMENT. In this 1968 photograph, Lt. Richard Stokes checks supplies in the trunk of his patrol car. The first police force for the township was formed in 1966 with 12 officers working out of the old town hall building on Van Dyke Avenue at Plumbrook Road. The officers wore helmets as part of their uniform at the time. Prior to the Sterling Police, residents depended on the occasional drive through of Macomb County sheriff vehicles and the Michigan State Police.

JOSEPH DELIA. Sports leagues, summer playground programs, Easter egg hunts, and more were all brought for the first time to Sterling Township residents by Joseph Delia Jr. Pictured in 1966, he started the township parks and recreation department in that same year. After his death from cancer at the age of 51 in 1980, the City of Sterling Heights honored him by naming a major city park after him. Joseph J. Delia Jr. Park is located on 18 Mile Road west of Ryan Road and serves as a major athletic complex for city programs.

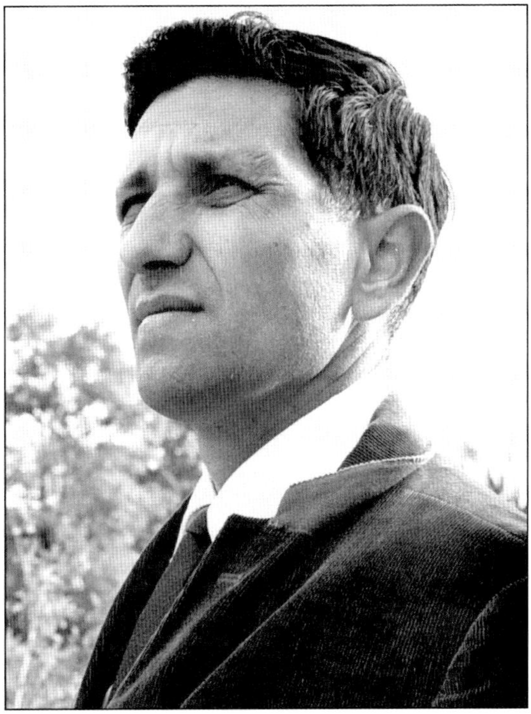

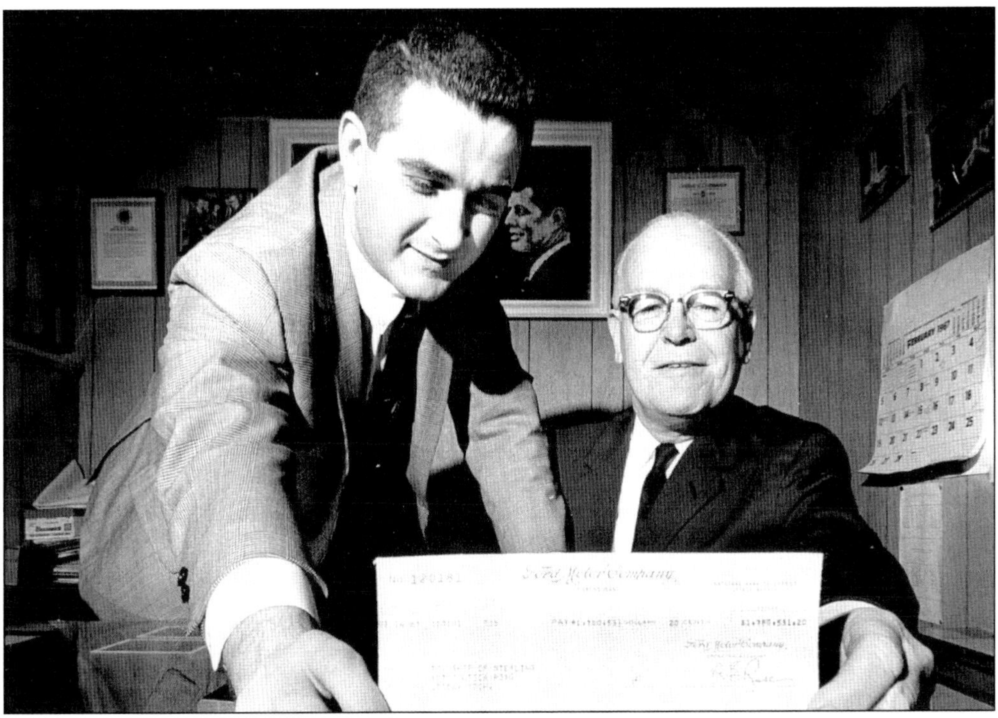

TAX PAYMENT. Richard O. Brown (left), township treasurer, accepts a check for $1.7 million from a Ford Motor Company official for its property tax payment in 1967. The township never before had a taxpayer so substantial, forever changing the financial environment for the community and for the area schools.

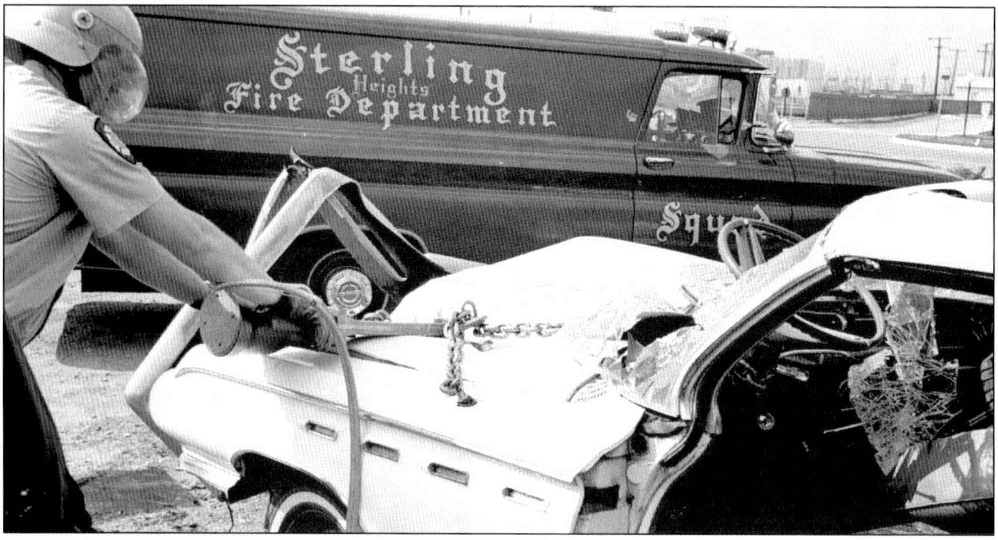

RESCUE DEMONSTRATION. A Sterling Heights firefighter demonstrates special equipment used to rescue accident victims around 1970. What is especially notable about this photograph is that the truck in the background shows how the word "Heights" was added to "Sterling Fire Department" lettering after the name change that came with becoming a city in 1968. (Photograph courtesy of the Sterling Heights Fire Department.)

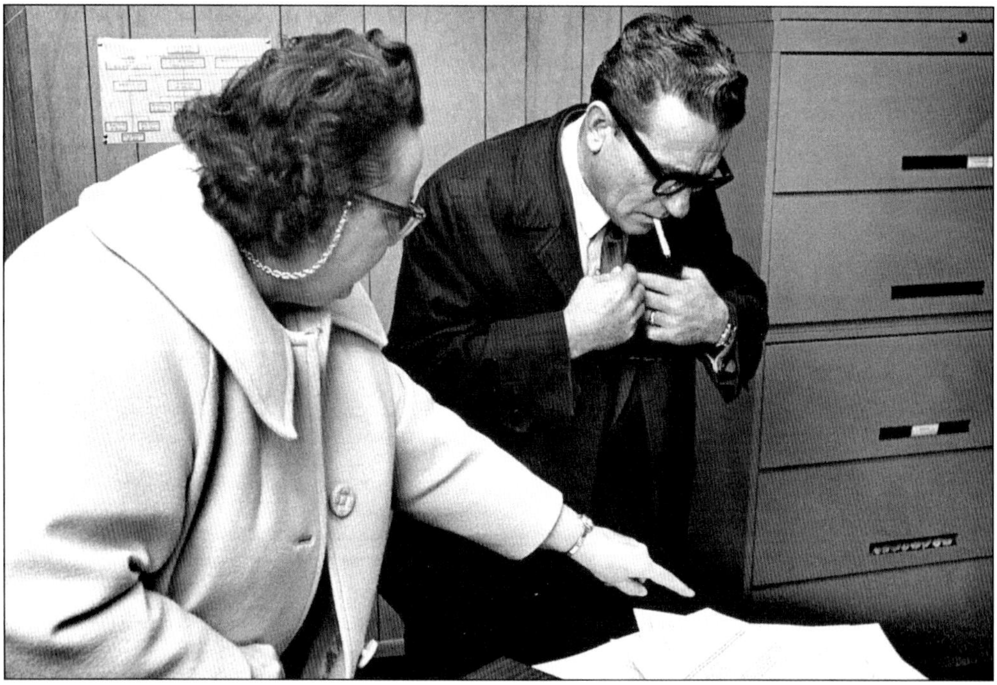

GENEVIEVE BUTELLA AND WILLIAM BROWN. In this 1967 view, civic watchdog Genevieve Butella and William Brown look over petitions. Brown was a de facto mayor, elected as mayor of the new city of Sterling Heights to accompany the strong mayor form of government charter, which ended up not passing, therefore not providing him a job. Genevieve Butella was very active in township and city politics for years. She attended meetings, was on commissions, and was very vocal about her views, becoming quite controversial at times. (Photograph courtesy of the Utica Sentinel.)

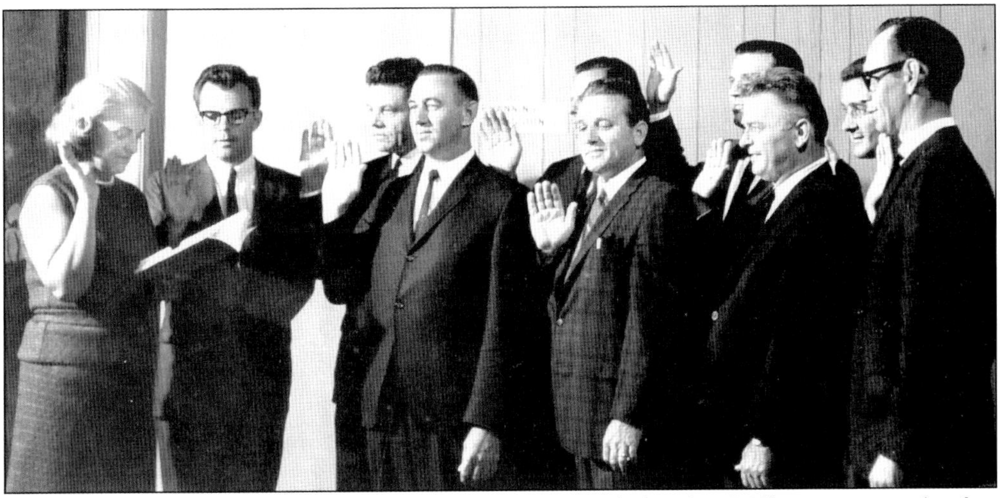

FIRST CITY CHARTER COMMISSION. Macomb County clerk Edna Miller swears in the first charter commission members in June 1966. From left to right are the following: (first row) William Valusek (township supervisor), William F. Brown (trustee), Harry Awdey (trustee), and James E. McCarthy (liquor enforcement administrator); (second row) Bruce G. McDonald (trustee), Anthony Dobry (former supervisor), William Kerner (former treasurer), John C. Morrison (clerk), and Richard O. Brown (treasurer). This group wrote a "strong mayor" charter, which was later voted down. (Photograph courtesy of the Utica Sentinel.)

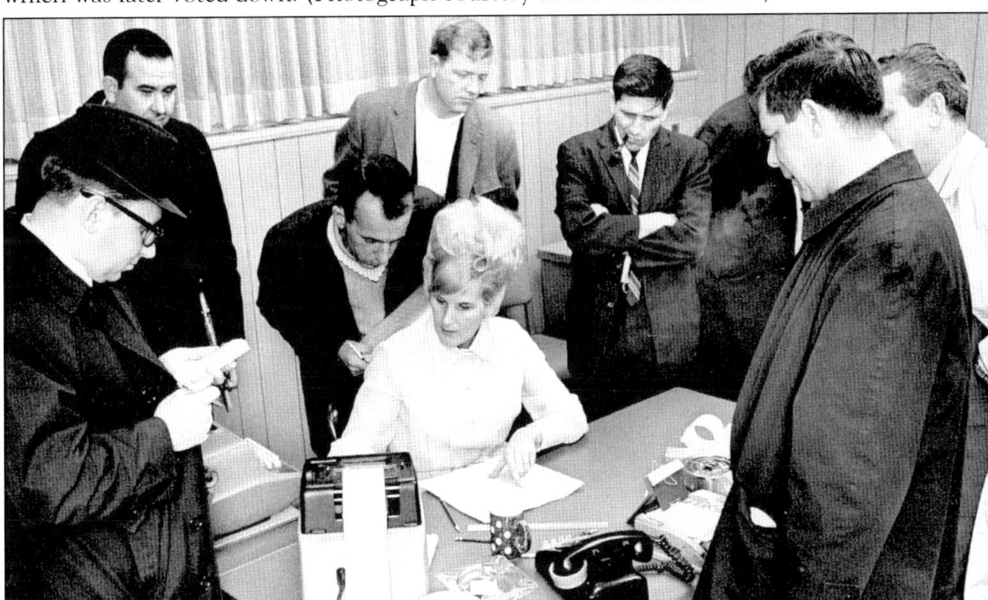

TALLYING ELECTION RESULTS. Mona Kreisch, secretary, and her adding machine are the center of attention on March 4, 1968. The anxious onlookers include Stanley Rainko, Lowell Summers, Joe Cisneros (newspaper reporter), Paul J. O'Reilly, Joseph Delia, and Victor Smith. The election was to choose charter commission members, and the winners were David E. Brown, Paul J. O'Reilly, David Barron, Lyle Robertson, Charles Cooper, Al Martin, Chester Rivard, Stanley Rainko, and Robert G. Evans. The majority of the slate elected supported a council and city manager form of government. This was the second charter commission elected. (Photograph courtesy of the Utica Sentinel.)

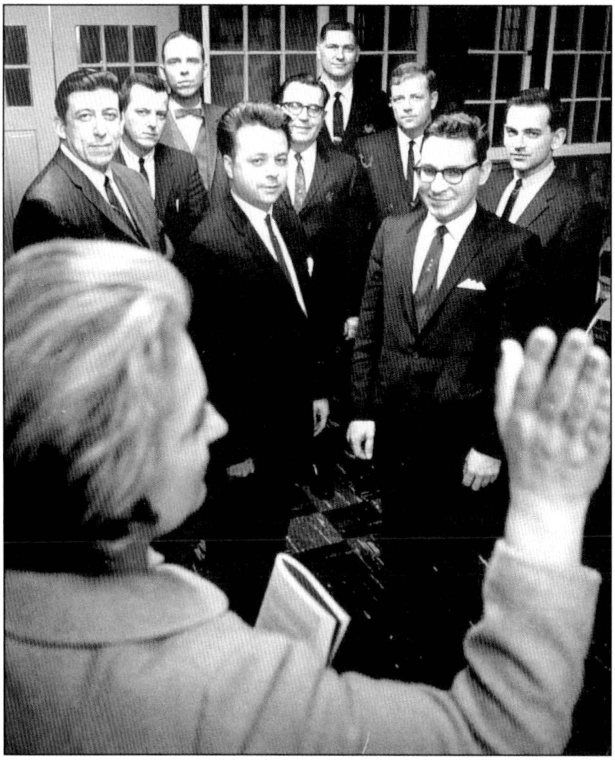

THE SECOND CHARTER COMMISSION. The citizens try again for cityhood in 1968 with the swearing in by Macomb County clerk Edna Miller of a different charter commission, this one supporting a city manager form of government. Commission members, pictured from left to right, are (first row) Al Martin, David Brown, and Stanley Rainko; (second row) Daniel Barron, Robert Evans, Paul O'Reilly, and Chester Rivard; (third row) Lyle Robertson and Charles Cooper. (Photograph courtesy of the Utica Sentinel.)

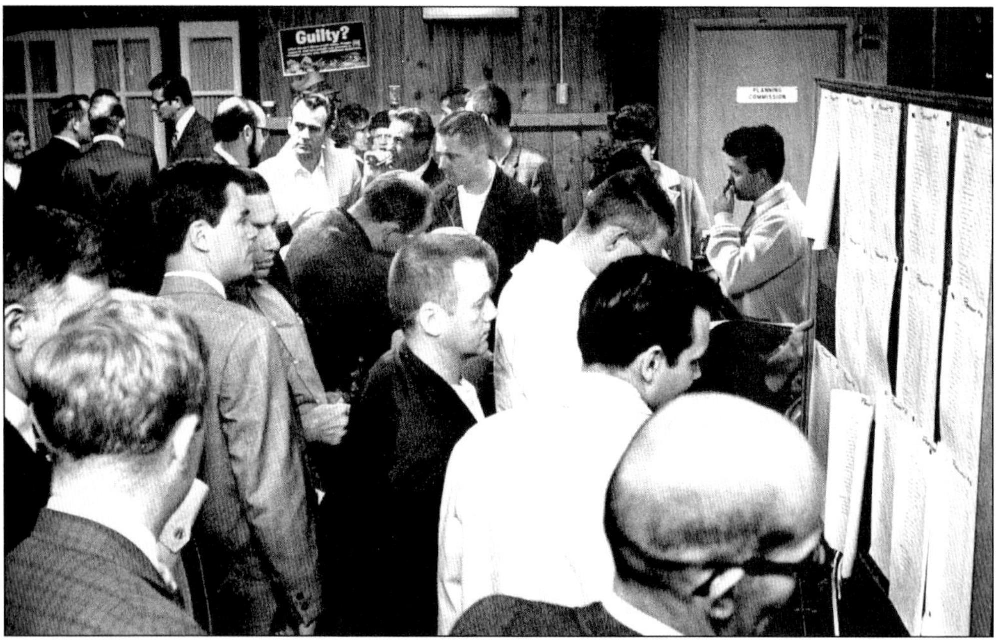

AWAITING ELECTION RESULTS. It is May 25, 1968, and residents are watching election results come in at the Sterling Township Annex, the site of government offices at that time, located in the old Clinton Valley Country Club building on Utica Road. Voters approved the charter creating the city of Sterling Heights with a council and city manager form of government by a margin of almost two to one. (Photograph courtesy of the Utica Sentinel.)

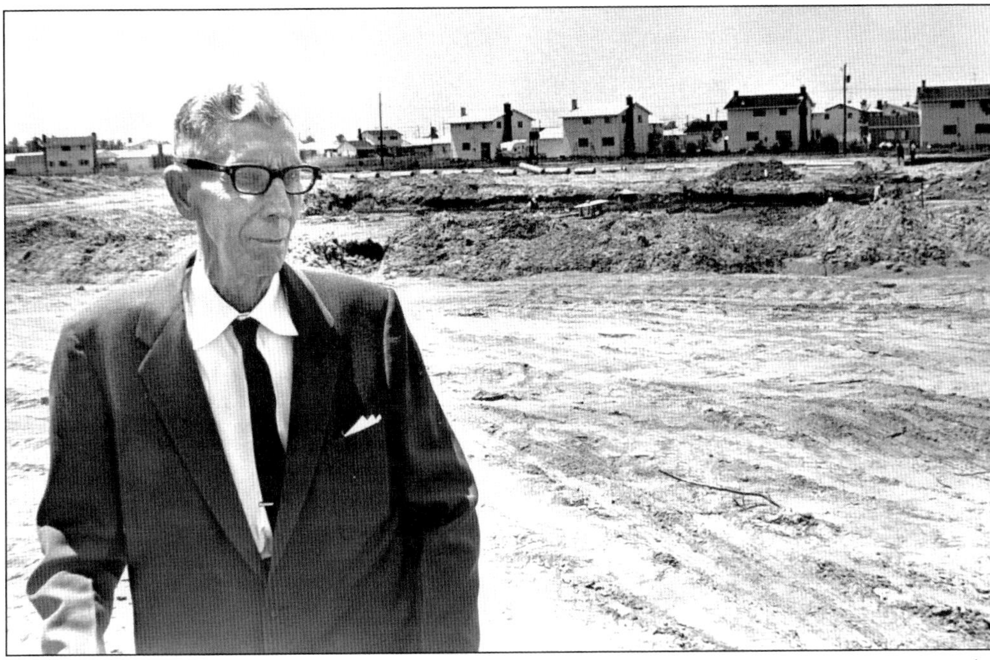

CHANGING OF THE GUARD. Arthur Priehs, former Sterling Township supervisor, gazes out at the future of the community. Priehs stands at the construction site of the new municipal building on Dodge Park Road around 1968. He was supervisor from 1941 to 1961, during a time when farmers ran the government. That changed in the early 1960s, when subdivision homeowners came in and took the reigns. (Photograph courtesy of the Utica Sentinel.)

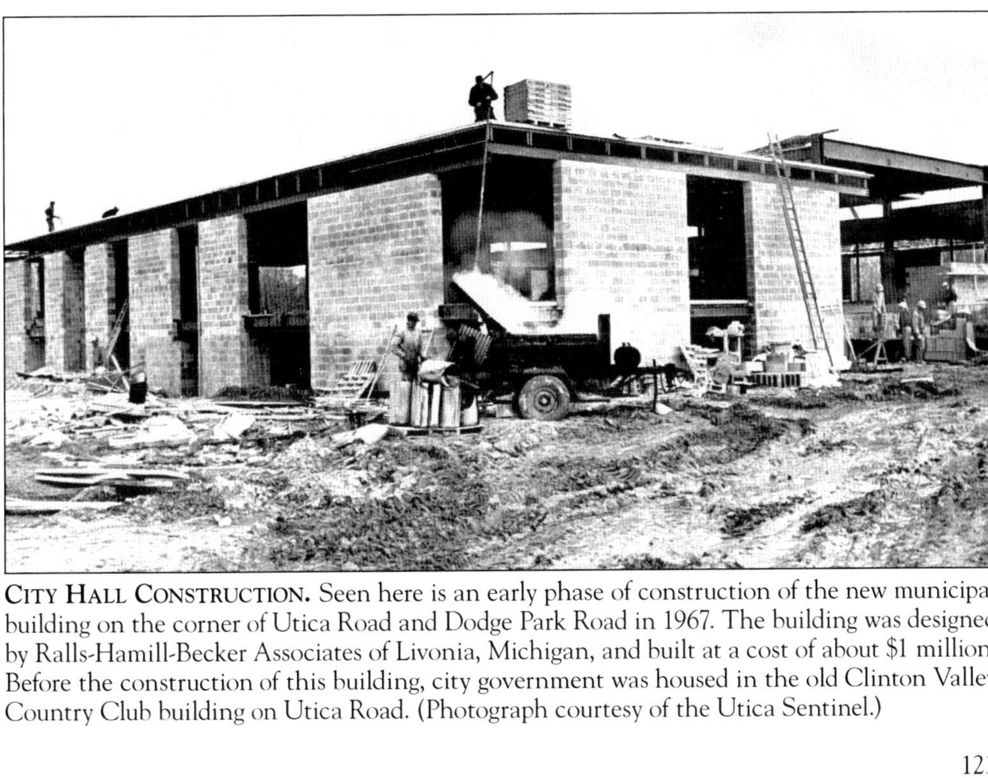

CITY HALL CONSTRUCTION. Seen here is an early phase of construction of the new municipal building on the corner of Utica Road and Dodge Park Road in 1967. The building was designed by Ralls-Hamill-Becker Associates of Livonia, Michigan, and built at a cost of about $1 million. Before the construction of this building, city government was housed in the old Clinton Valley Country Club building on Utica Road. (Photograph courtesy of the Utica Sentinel.)

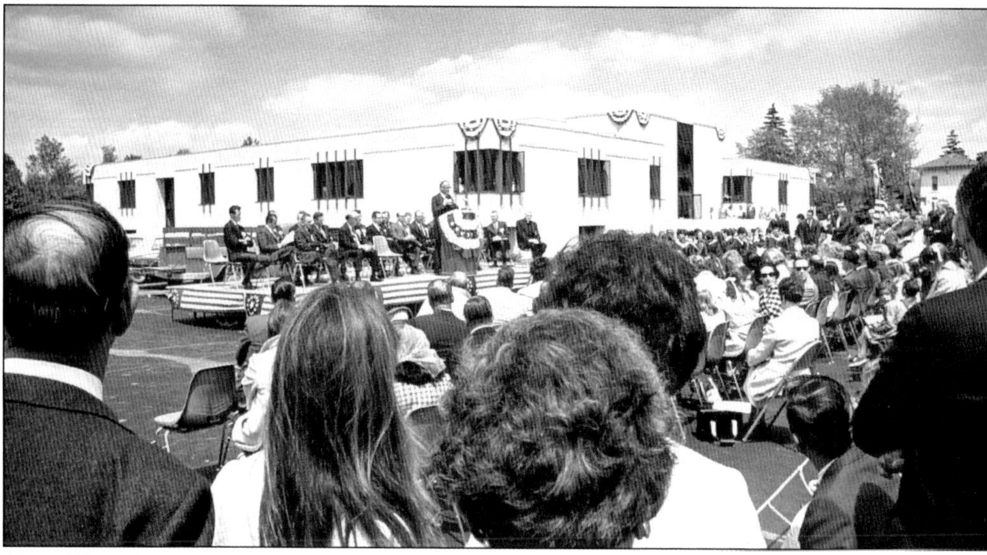

CITY HALL DEDICATION. Congressman James G. O'Hara delivers the main address to more than 500 people at the dedication of the new municipal building on May 25, 1969. The building, located at 40555 Utica Road at Dodge Park Road, sits on land that had been part of the William Upton farm. It was originally designed to carry five additional floors to accommodate offices of the elected officials in the strong mayor form of government. The towering expansion was abandoned as the result of citizens approving the city manager government instead. Offices were no longer needed for the mayor and council members.

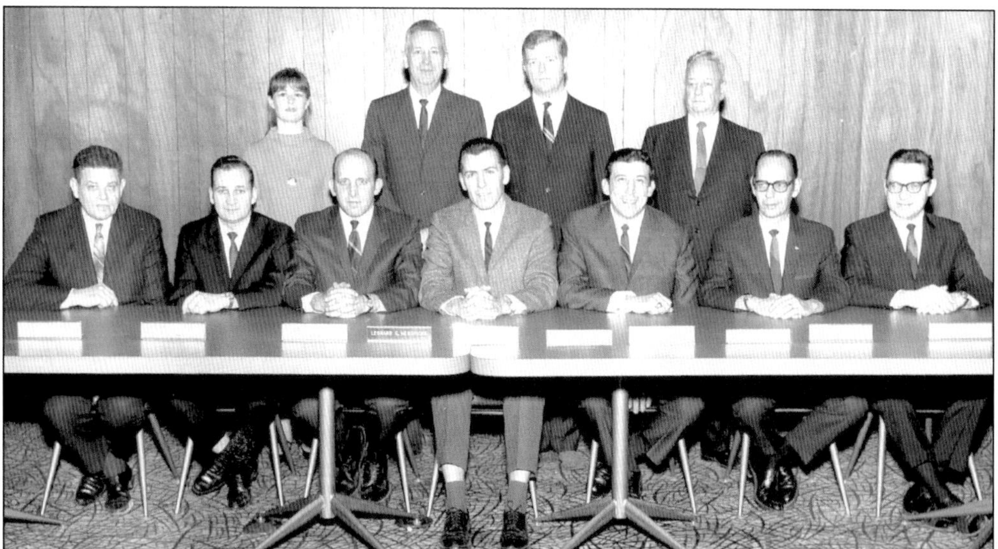

FIRST CITY COUNCIL. Pictured here in 1968 is the very first city council with other officials elected by the residents of the brand-new city of Sterling Heights. From left to right are (first row) Anthony Dobry, F. James Dunlop (mayor pro tem), Richard D. George, Gerald Donovan (mayor), Al Martin, James E. McCarthy, and Stanley Rainko; (second row) Barbara Yager (recording secretary), Leonard Hendricks (city manager), Paul O'Reilly (city attorney), and George Bunker (city clerk). This group represented a changing of the guard in the local government. It is said that by 1962, the reins of township government had passed from the farmers to area homeowners associations.

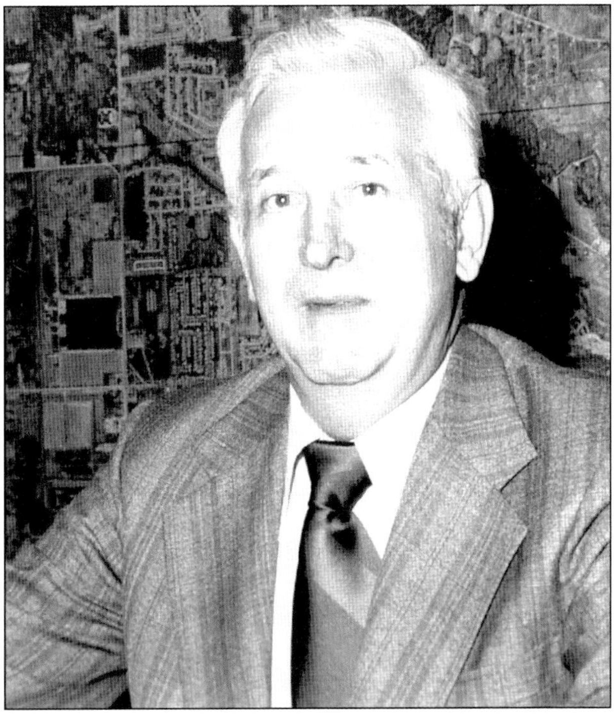

LEONARD HENDRICKS. Born in Mississippi and educated in the Detroit area, the soft-spoken former city manager of Clawson, Michigan, has received glowing reviews from most of his contemporaries as being a "selfless public servant." Hendricks got the job as the first city manager of Sterling Heights in 1968 and guided the young city until 1982, except for an 18-month period beginning in 1974.

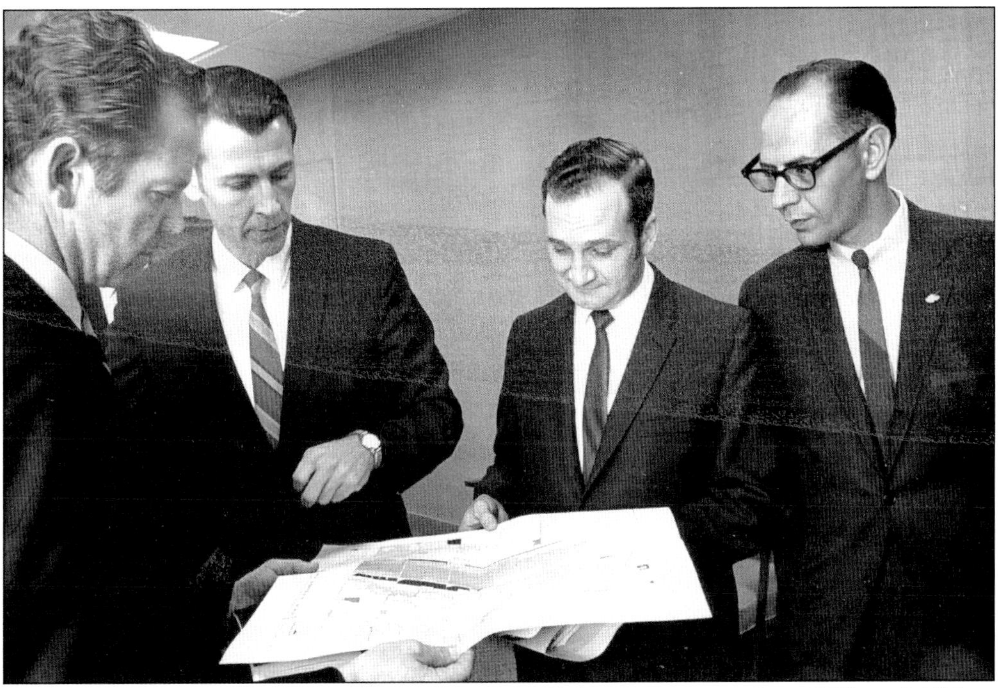

GOVERNOR MILLIKEN GETS A TOUR. Showing off the new city to Gov. William Milliken (far left) are, from left to right, Mayor Gerald Donovan, Mayor Pro Tem F. James Dunlop, and councilman James McCarthy. The June 1969 meeting included lunch at Mr. F's. Before the lunch, Dunlop accompanied the governor on a private tour to see the many attributes of the city. (Photograph courtesy of the Utica Sentinel.)

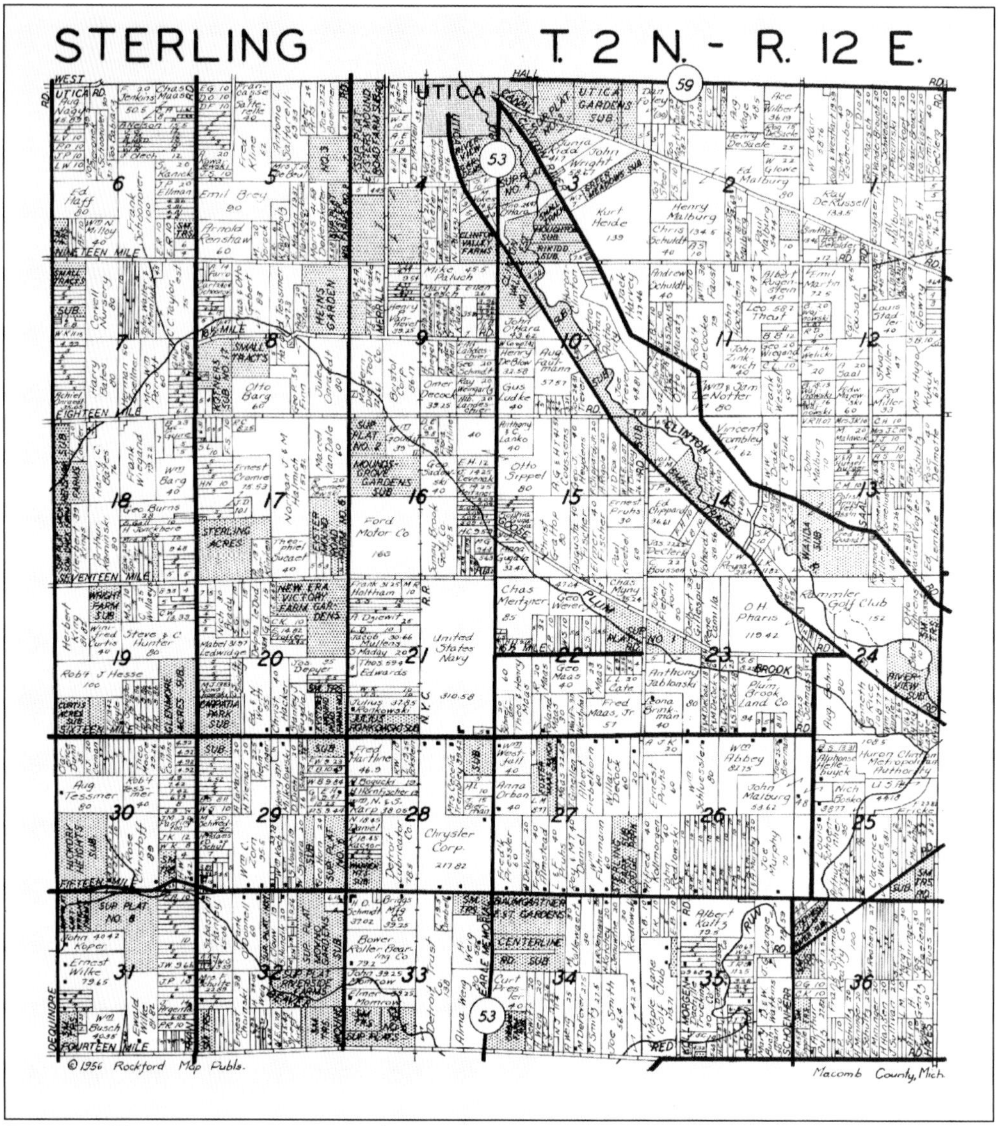

STERLING TOWNSHIP MAP, 1956. Almost 10 years before achieving cityhood, farms were smaller than ever, and some had been sold and platted as subdivisions by real estate speculators, even though no streets or houses had been built yet. The "Golden Corridor," the north–south strip between Mound and Van Dyke Roads that was planned for industrial use, can be seen, bisected by the Michigan Central Railroad tracks, which had been there since before 1875.

INDEX